Get **more** out of libraries

Please return or renew this item by the last date shown.
You can renew online at www.hants.gov.uk/library
Or by phoning Hampshire Libraries
Tel: 0300 555 1387

 Hampshire
County Council

THE BEAST, THE EMPEROR AND THE MILKMAN

THE BEAST,
THE EMPEROR AND
THE MILKMAN

A bone-shaking tour through cycling's
Flemish heartlands

HARRY PEARSON

BLOOMSBURY SPORT

LONDON · OXFORD · NEW YORK · NEW DELHI · SYDNEY

BLOOMSBURY SPORT
Bloomsbury Publishing Plc
50 Bedford Square, London, WC1B 3DP, UK

BLOOMSBURY, BLOOMSBURY SPORT and the Diana logo are
trademarks of Bloomsbury Publishing Plc

First published in Great Britain 2019

A catalogue record for this book is available from the British Library

Library of Congress Cataloguing-in-Publication data has been applied for.

ISBN: HB: 978-1-4729-4504-4; PB: 978-1-4729-4506-8;
eBook: 978-1-4729-4503-7

2 4 6 8 10 9 7 5 3 1

Typeset in Adobe Garamond Pro by Deanta Global Publishing Services, Chennai, India
Printed and bound in Great Britain by CPI Group (UK) Ltd, Croydon CR0 4YY

To find out more about our authors and books visit www.bloomsbury.com
and sign up for our newsletters

For Steve, Jimmy and
Albert – kings of the roadside.

CONTENTS

Some notes
about language

Belgium is a country with three official languages: Flemish (known to linguists as Belgian Dutch), French, and German (spoken in a small area to the north-east of Liège). This means that towns, cities and geographical features tend to have at least two names. In this book I have generally used the name by which the place is known to the majority of the local inhabitants (Kortrijk rather than Courtrai, Liège rather than Luik, Ronse rather than Renaix and so forth). The exceptions to this are when a city has an accepted and well-known anglicised form (for example, Antwerp for Antwerpen, Brussels for Bruxelles/Brussel) or, in the case of the Flemish cities of Brugge and Ieper, when the French names Bruges and Ypres are so well known to British readers that to alter them would be needlessly confusing.

I have also tried to give Flemish riders the names by which they are known at home rather than the French versions they are commonly given in Britain – Odiel Defraeye rather than Odile Defraye, Sylveer rather than Sylvère Maes, and so forth. This may seem a little wilful, but I can't help wondering how it would play in Wales if a cyclist from Swansea called Ieuan Hywel had won the Tour de France and found himself referred to in all the history books as John Hewill.

Language pronunciation is a complicated business. I will confine myself to three pointers on Flemish that may help a little with some of the more common names in the coming pages: 'ij' is pronounced to rhyme with 'hay'; 'ie' is sounded as in the English word 'grief'; and 'ae' like the 'ar' in 'smart'.

N
North Sea
THE NETHERLANDS
ANTWERP
SINT-NIKLAAS
HERENTALS
BRUGES
LOKEREN
FLANDERS
GHENT
WETTEREN
OSTEND
Kuipke
Aalst
ROESELARE
ZOTTEGEM
WAREGEM
DE PANNE
OUDENAARDE
BRUSSELS
GERAARDSBERGEN
YPRES
KORTRIJK
ROUBAIX
WALLONIA
FRANCE

PROLOGUE
Brick chimneys and iron men

'The smell of a freshly opened bottle of beer is the smell of my country,' the great Liège-born writer Georges Simenon said. If the scent of Belgium is that of good ale, then the defining sound of the nation is the swish of bicycle tyres on wet roads, the whistling of wind through spokes, the juddering thrum of steel frames on cobblestones.

Bike racing is madly popular all over Belgium, but in the northern, Dutch-speaking half of the country it goes far beyond that. It is part of the national identity, beloved by young and old, male and female. In terms of the number of fans football may be more popular, but when it comes to the consciousness of Flanders there's little doubt that bikes are the thing. In small Flemish towns middle-aged ladies who lunch unfurl Lotto–Soudal brollies, toddlers wear beanie hats proclaiming their affection for Tom Boonen and teenage girls fashion capes from flags covered in photos of cyclocross genius Sven Nys, 'the Cannibal from Baal'. Compared to this a few K.A.A. Gent scarves and the odd Club Brugge bumper sticker are nothing.

You can no more imagine Flanders without bicycles than you can France without garlic, Germany without sausages. Even those rare Flemings who profess no interest in the sport will, when pushed, trip off the names of the heroic riders of the past – Buysse, Maes, Van Steenbergen, Schotte, Van Looy, Van Springel, De Vlaeminck, Godefroot, Maertens,

Van Impe, Museeuw – with the ease of a Jesuit priest reciting the catechism. Cycling is in the psyche and in the blood. It is as unavoidable as the weather.

There are only around five million Flemings spread across the northern Belgian provinces of East and West Flanders, Antwerp, Limburg and Flemish Brabant, yet their bike riders have been a dominant force in a global sport for well over a century, hoovering up one-day Classics and Grand Tours at a rate that would do credit to a nation ten or fifteen times the size. Flemish riders have won the three major stage races 18 times, Paris–Roubaix 46 times (no British or North American rider has ever won it), Milan–San Remo 11 times (French riders have won it only twice more, the Spanish six fewer), the Men's Elite Road Race at the UCI World Championships on 20 occasions (one more than Italy, 12 more than France). With the exception of New Zealand in rugby union, it's hard to think of anything comparable.

That it came to be this way is down to the personality of the Flemish. Flemings are northerners. They like ale and chips and complaining (I'm a Yorkshireman, so don't bother writing in). They live indoors, hidden behind net curtains, nurturing strange passions for cacti and chicory and songbirds and pigeons. Like all northerners they nurse a sense of grievance against the south, which may stem from an ingrained, though never acknowledged, sense of inferiority. In his wonderful documentary *Magnetic North* the English writer and broadcaster Jonathan Meades observes that northerners have the superiority of the warm south fed to them in the womb. The Mediterranean lifestyle, the art, architecture, food, sex is all so much tastier and more beautiful than anything we can manage. And so northerners come to love the north with the same fierce defensiveness that a mother loves an ugly child. As the great Jacques Brel (from Schaarbeek, a suburb of Brussels) sang in his hymn to northernness, 'La Bière': '*It's full of horizons/that drive you mad/But alcohol is blond/The Devil is ours/And hopeless people/Need both of them.*' In Flanders they needed cycling too, but perhaps even Jacques Brel couldn't find a rhyme for that.

Every nation uses sport to reveal the character traits it most admires. Cycling is a brutal test of endurance. It is about suffering, pain and hardship. Like farming – which for centuries was the cornerstone of the Flemish economy – it is shaped by the landscape, prey to the vagaries of the climate. It is no use whining at the gnashing wind, the spit-thick rain, the sucking, bitter soil, the icy air that makes your joints swell, cobbles that jar your body until your nose bleeds – you just get out and get on with it. The Flemish like toughness, obduracy and fortitude; guts, nuts and phlegm. Their biggest bike races – Omloop Het Nieuwsblad, Dwars door Vlaanderen, E3 Harelbeke, Ghent–Wevelgem, Ronde van Vlaanderen (the Tour of Flanders) and Scheldeprijs – are held between the end of February and the beginning of April. They could have organised them in the late summer when, historically, the great Tours were over, the weather is warm and balmy, the cobbles dry and almost benign and there are no great puddles concealing potholes deep enough to trap a wild pig in. But what would be the fun in that?

The relationship between the Flemish and bike racing is a grand romance, but like all great love affairs this one had to begin with an introduction.

Karel Van Wijnendaele was born Carolus Steyaert in 1882 in a village between Torhout and Lichtervelde in West Flanders. The name of his birthplace was Bakvoorde, which was almost a pun on popular preconceptions about Flemish life among Francophones. The fifth of 15 children, Van Wijnendaele never knew his birth father, a flax worker who died when Carolus was 18 months old. His mother quickly remarried, to a local farmer named Richard Defreyne, and she moved with her five children to his house in Torhout. Nearby stood the castle of Wijnendaele, from which Carolus would eventually take his pen name.

These days Torhout is a typically sleepy Flemish small town, the sort of place where the old ladies place cushions on the ledges of upstairs windows and lean out over the street, watching the comings and goings of their neighbours, every once in a while earnestly adjusting their bosoms. Torhout has its own special, fiery mustard – the Flemish like hot mustard – and the walk from the station to the centre of town takes you past the Smoking Cue Billiard Hall, the Zwarte Leeuw Café (advertising itself as the local of Torhout 1992 football club supporters) and the Criterium Bar, which has windows decorated with cartoons of Peter Van Petegem, 'the Zwarte van Brakel' (loosely 'the Black-haired one from Brakel'), double winner of the Ronde van Vlaanderen. The plaque commemorating the town's association with the man who invented that race is on a nondescript apartment block next to a chemist's with a window display of constipation medicine.

In a nearby café, where the radio played a Dutch-language version of the country and western hit 'Blanket on the Ground', I ordered a coffee with cream. The waiter was in his early twenties, wearing a black Motörhead t-shirt. I mentioned to him that I was British and interested in bike racing. 'Well,' he said, 'there was a guy from round here who won that crazy course you used to have over there.' It turned out he meant Eddy Vanhaerens, who in 1978 became the only non-British rider ever to win London to Holyhead – at 427 kilometres the longest unpaced one-day race on earth. The waiter said he wasn't really interested in cycling. It was just he had this uncle that was always going on about it. 'I'd prefer to talk about rock 'n' roll, you know, but here it's as if Tom Boonen is lead singer in the Foo Fighters, or something,' he said. It was true that Boonen was a dominant figure in the Flemish cultural and sporting landscape. His popularity was so great I sometimes thought the only way it could ever be matched in England was if Olly Murs scored the winning goal in the World Cup Final and dedicated it to the memory of Princess Diana while saving a kitten from drowning. I asked the waiter if he thought Boonen could win the Ronde van Vlaanderen again this year, an unprecedented fourth victory. It was a question everyone in Flanders asked, as normal as enquiring of an Englishman if he thinks it will rain later. The waiter who wasn't interested in cycling shrugged. 'I don't think so,' he said. 'To win the Ronde you need a kind of . . .' he banged his right fist into the palm of his left hand three or four times. 'You know, like a big piston. But he is too old for that these days. Maybe Paris–Roubaix, though.'

Van Wijnendaele left school in Torhout at 14 (relatively old for Flanders, where most boys were working from the age of 12) and after a brief period on the farm found work as an errand boy at a chemist's shop, as a baker's delivery boy, a washer-up, a programme seller and finally as a lawyer's clerk. It was a visit to the Ostend cycle track in 1897 that changed his life. Seeing the world champion Robert Protin – who came from the southern, French-speaking half of Belgium, Wallonia – in action inspired him to become a pro rider himself. He bought a bike, adopted the racing name of Marc Bolle and spent the next three years trying and failing to win races. If he couldn't ride in professional bike races, Marc Bolle at least found that he could write about them. He'd begun earning extra cash by filing stories for various regional Flemish newspapers and soon was reporting on cycling for them too, as Karel Van Wijnendaele.

At that point cycling was something of a fringe sport in Flanders, lagging far behind football in popularity. All that was changed by the Tour de France. The great race had first been run in 1903 and the Flemish had been there – Julien Lootens from Wevelgem and Marcel Kerff from the Voeren in the far east of Limburg both completing the 2,428-kilometre course. For a few years the most successful Belgian rider was Aloïs Catteau, a French-speaker from just north of Roubaix, and it wasn't until 1909 that the Flemish really began to show themselves. In that year's race the first stage was from Paris to Roubaix across the cobbles of northern France. The Flemish contingent attacked throughout the day, despite or possibly inspired by the appallingly bumpy roads, and claimed their first stage win through Cyrille Van Hauwaert. A native of Moorslede in West Flanders, whose finely curled moustache and immaculately arched eyebrows suggested that he might have ridden in spats, Van Hauwaert had already won Paris–Bordeaux, Milan–San Remo and Paris–Roubaix and would finish fourth in the 1910 Tour, giving him a strong claim to being the first of the great Flemish riders.

However, it was the arrival on the scene of Odiel Defraeye in 1912 that produced the first sparks in the Flemish love affair with bike racing. Defraeye came from Rumbeke on the edge of Roeselare. He worked in a brush factory delivering messages and parcels by bike, sometimes covering 200 kilometres a day. As an amateur he hoovered up prizes in a manner that might later have been described as Merckxian. After his military service Defraeye went south and joined the prestigious French Alcyon team, who rode in jerseys of the kingfisher blue that gave the firm's bikes their name. Defraeye had a hard time of it at first. Like many Flemings he barely spoke French, and Alcyon did not regard Belgium as an important market and therefore saw little benefit in selecting him for the Grand Tours. Nor was he a model professional – after winning Milan–San Remo he gambled away all his prize money the following night. One thing was certain, though: Defraeye could ride a bike.

The Flemish dominated the 1912 Tour. Weather conditions were appalling, in the Alps the roads were more like mountain streams, but Defraeye, whom Alcyon had called up only at the last minute, hammered along them at record speeds, crushing his rivals like beetles. He arrived in Paris in heavy rain well ahead of his nearest rival, Eugène Christophe, and was greeted by hundreds of jubilant Belgian fans who put down their umbrellas and waved the national flag in his honour. Other Flemish riders also impressed. Marcel Buysse was fourth, emerging talent Philippe Thys was sixth and Jules Masselis, an amateur from Ledegem, won the stage into Dunkirk.

When Defraeye returned to Roeselare, 10,000 people lined the streets to greet him. For the first time in the modern era a Fleming had shown that he could take on the French and beat them. With his winnings he built a house and a café with a bike racing track attached to it. The brush-factory delivery boy was aged just 20. His victory and the riches it brought him would make cycling popular in Flanders, as a means to escape poverty and an expression of national identity.

For the budding cycling journalist and committed Flemish patriot Karel Van Wijnendaele, Odiel Defraeye's triumph could not have been better timed. Cycling boomed in Belgium, the number of licensed riders rising from a few hundred to 4,000. Tracks sprang up all over the country. Observing this, a publisher from Brussels, August De Maeght, decided there was sufficient market for a specialist newspaper on sport for Dutch speakers. He called it *Sportwereld* and one of the writers he hired to work on his new venture was Karel Van Wijnendaele, who had proved far better at writing about bikes than he had at riding them.

Sportwereld was an immediate success and quickly went from being a twice-weekly to a daily publication. Within four months the indefatigable and energetic Van Wijnendaele had risen to the position of editor. Right from the start the newspaper was about more than just sport. In its first editorial it promised to bring 'a world of thought' to the readership and to educate and inform them. The paper was written in more colloquial Flemish than most of its rivals, its reports – often pompous in the style of the time – peppered with West Flemish dialect. In those days practically every public institution in Belgium carried out its business primarily or even exclusively in French. The same applied to Belgium's national cycling federation. *Sportwereld* set out to change that once and for all. It was quite a battle, but after a ten-year campaign the authorities in Brussels finally caved in and the national cycling federation became bilingual. Not content with that, Van Wijnendaele and *Sportwereld* also campaigned for classes at Ghent University to be taught in Dutch rather than French, and introduced a literature page to discuss and promote the latest Flemish novels, poetry and plays – hardly the usual domain of a sports paper, where gear ratios and knee injuries tend to take precedence over neo-romantic verse.

But then Van Wijnendaele didn't see sport as simply a game, but as a means of effecting political change. Language was the key. George Bernard Shaw famously said that every time an Englishman opens his mouth he makes another Englishman despise him. Similarly, any commentary on the subject of Flemish will excite opposition from one corner or another. So when I say that the people of Flanders speak Vlaams, a dialectic form of Dutch descended from Frankish, I know that it will make some Flemings annoyed. 'We speak Dutch,' they will say angrily. 'They only say it is a dialect to make us feel smaller.' 'They' are the French speakers.

This may sound a little paranoid, but the Flemish have plenty of reason to feel persecuted. Belgium became an independent nation only in 1831, following a rebellion in Brussels against the Dutch. (Despite sharing a common language the relationship between Flanders and the Netherlands is not an easy one. Flanders is devoutly Catholic and conservative, the Netherlands liberal and Protestant/agnostic. The Dutch traditionally regard the Flemish as vulgar dimwits while the Flemings look on their northern neighbours as buttoned-up, smug tightwads.) The Dutch had – somewhat against their will – been handed Flanders and Wallonia as part of the readjustment of national boundaries following the end of the Napoleonic Wars during which France had annexed them from Austria, who had taken them over from the Spanish . . . At first the Flemish refused to take orders from the new government in Brussels but eventually they were forced to do so with the help of the French army. The new country ('created by the British to annoy the French' as Charles de Gaulle summarised it) consisted of two linguistic groups: the Flemish and the Walloons. (After World War One a third linguistic group, the German speakers of the area around Eupen in the far north-east, would be added to the mix, but they don't seem to be much interested in bicycles.) It's a common misconception that the Walloons spoke French. In fact around 70 per cent of them spoke their own language, Walloon, which was grounded in the Latin-based *Lingua Romana* of the Holy Roman Empire. In order to resolve the problem posed by a country made up of two sets of people whose speech was incomprehensible to each other, the new Belgian government and the king, Leopold (who, to confuse things even further, was German), decided to make all of them speak a third language, French. French, with its roots in the warm Mediterranean, was still viewed across most of Europe as the language of culture. Most educated Belgians already spoke it and, since they made up the ruling class, it seemed an obvious choice, to them at least. French became the official tongue of the nation. It was the language of the government, the civil service, the local authorities, the armed forces and all secondary and higher education.

Wallonia was the industrial heartland of Belgium. Hundreds of thousands of immigrants from Italy, Portugal and eastern and central Europe came to work in its coalmines, steel furnaces and factories. Perhaps because of that, or because Walloon came from the same linguistic family as French, successive Belgian governments' strenuous efforts to get rid of Walloon – which actually intensified in the 1950s – were largely successful. Today only about 300,000 people actively speak it – and some of them are in Wisconsin.

Vlaams proved altogether harder to dislodge. In Flanders, French became the language of the middle class. Nineteenth-century Flemish writers such as Emile Verhaeren (from Sint-Amands) and Maurice Maeterlinck (from Ghent) wrote in French. Flemish was considered backward and uncouth, the language of the peasantry and the workers. The Flemish speakers might have given the world Antoon Van Dyck, Jan Van Eyck and the Breughels, but to the ruling class in Brussels they were pig-ignorant bumpkins whose main function in life was to harvest turnips. West Flanders was viewed as some outlandish dead zone of mud, despair and mangelwurzels, while Limburg was a province of fruit and fathomless stupidity.

In the 1920s, when it was proposed that some lectures at Ghent University might be given in Flemish, an MP rose in the Belgian parliament and said that to replace French culture with Flemish culture was like substituting a candle for a lighthouse. When Antwerper Hendrik Conscience's first novel was published in 1837 his father was so incensed that his son had chosen to write in Flemish he hoofed him out of the house.

Conscience, whose romantic style and choice of historical subjects seemed partly inspired by Sir Walter Scott, would go on to become a key figure in the rebirth of Flemish nationalism, his novel *The Lion of Flanders* sparking a new mood of cultural self-confidence. It would inspire Hippoliet Van Peene to write the song 'De Vlaamse Leeuw' ('The Flemish Lion'), the unofficial anthem of Flemish nationalists and subsequently the official anthem of Flanders.

The Belgian state was 50 years old before the first speech in Flemish was heard in the national parliament in Brussels. Orders in the army were barked out in French. In 1873 there had been an infamous murder trial in which two Flemings had been wrongfully convicted and hanged largely because the court proceedings were carried out exclusively in a language they did not comprehend. It was only after this tragic affair that Flemish was made available within the justice system. Later that decade the Belgian government allowed classes in secondary schools to be taught in Dutch, but it wasn't until 1930 that the first exclusively Flemish-speaking university was opened, and French would remain the sole official language of Belgium until 1967.

If the Flemish sometimes appeared a little too eager to tell you, 'We Flemings were an oppressed people,' there is no doubting the fact that they had grounds to feel aggrieved. In much the same way nations within the British Empire saw international cricket as a means of proving their readiness for self-determination, Karel Van Wijnendaele saw cycling as a means of achieving social justice. The popularity of Odiel Defraeye in the wake of his Tour de France triumph prompted Van Wijnendaele to make another decision he felt would boost the standing of his beloved Flanders while also helping to promote his newspaper. Belgium already had one major cycle race, Liège–Bastogne–Liège (nicknamed 'La Doyenne' and first run in 1892), but that was in Wallonia. In Flanders there was nothing except the Scheldeprijs, a low-key affair that confined itself to the roads around Antwerp. Van Wijnendaele decided to rectify the situation by creating the Ronde van Vlaanderen, a race that would be, *Sportwereld* proclaimed, a product of 'the Flemish people and the Flemish soil'. Henri Desgrange and his newspaper *L'Auto* had done the same thing with the Tour de France, and the Giro d'Italia had been the invention of *La Gazzetta dello Sport*. It was a model that clearly worked.

The first Ronde was in May 1913. Thirty-seven riders entered a race that began in the Ghent Korenmarkt, wound its way through Sint-Niklaas, Aalst, Oudenaarde, Ypres, Kortrijk, Veurne, Ostend, Roeselare and Bruges and back to Ghent where it finished in the velodrome at Mariakerke. Van Wijnendaele later said the race was 370 kilometres, but that seems to have been an exaggeration and it was likely nearer to 320 kilometres. What was certain was that it covered most of the major towns of East and West Flanders on roads – the term was used loosely – that varied from poor to execrable; from cobbles as gappy as a village idiot's grin and cinder paths barely wide enough for a wheelbarrow, to tracks churned up by the daily procession of dairy cattle to the milking parlour. So horribly dangerous was the route, in fact, that the French teams forbade their Belgian riders from competing.

The winner was Paul Deman. A bicycle salesman from Rekkem near Menen in West Flanders, Deman had entered local folklore when he rode the 1911 Tour de France on a bike put together from parts gifted to him by fellow traders (though he had to supply his own tyres).

Deman didn't have to knock together his bike for the Ronde but it still took him over 12 bone-shaking hours to complete the course. It was worth the effort. The first prize was substantial, the equivalent of more than a year's wages for most Flemings. Unfortunately, it was rather more than *Sportwereld* could afford – Van Wijnendaele had miscalculated. The new race didn't deliver the big boost in sales he'd anticipated and the uptake of tickets to watch the climax in the velodrome was poor. At the roadside the Ronde had drawn tens of thousands of spectators, but watching the race for free and paying to see it were two different things. Daunted but undeterred, Van Wijnendaele pressed on, moving the finish for the following year's Ronde to the velodrome at Evergem. Sadly, despite the presence in the field of superstar Marcel Buysse from nearby Wontergem, ticket sales were again poor and only a couple of hundred people saw Buysse cross the finish line first. *Sportwereld*'s investors were vexed by this state of affairs. Some called for the Ronde to be scrapped. Van Wijnendaele might have faced a real fight to keep his race alive, but in August 1914 Kaiser Wilhelm intervened. Germany invaded neutral Belgium, sweeping across the country's north-eastern border.

The Belgian army resisted the invading German forces gallantly but were rapidly pressed back. All the major cities were overrun and within months only a tiny corner of their small country remained in Belgian hands – a triangle of West Flanders with a border that ran from the ridgeline south-east of Ypres to the fishing port of Nieuwpoort at the mouth of the river Ijzer. The Belgian king, Albert I (or Albert, King of the Belgians, as he preferred to style himself) took up residence in a large house in the seaside town of De Panne. The remains of the Belgian army, which, since Wallonia and Brussels had been conquered, was now predominantly Flemish, occupied the trenches that protected him. Albert had appealed to the Flemings' patriotism in a famous speech in which he called on them to 'remember the Battle of the Golden Spurs' (a victory that is to the Flemish what Bannockburn is to the Scots) and they had responded. In the next four years over 30,000 of them would die fighting to keep at least a sliver of their homeland free.

In the rest of Europe King Albert is regarded as a heroic figure, known as Albert the Brave. He's one of the few Belgians who have streets named after them in France. In Biarritz I stayed in a hotel that had a large bust of him in the lobby. To the Flemish, however, he is not a hero but a villain and a traitor. In order to ensure that the Flemish kept on fighting he promised them all kinds of linguistic and social reforms, only to forget them once the war had been won and Belgium liberated. The ultimate insult was to find the graves of the Flemish fallen inscribed with the words 'Mort pour la patrie'. Even in death they weren't paid tribute in their own tongue. The monarch seems to have been oblivious to the offence he'd caused. When Albert died in 1936, in that most singular of events – a Belgian rock-climbing accident – there were many who saw a conspiracy in it. 'They say that maybe he was killed by angry Flemish nationalists,' people in Flanders will tell you. It's plain they don't believe it, but you sense that a small part of them wishes it were true.

The events of World War One helped crystallise a political movement based around the rejection of French culture and renewed pride in Flanders and Flemish life and art. Cycling, the most Flemish of all sports, became an integral part of that renaissance.

Sportwereld shut down during the war. When it re-emerged in 1919 it was more popular than ever, with circulation rising to 200,000. Hailed as 'the troubadour of Flemish muscle', Van Wijnendaele became almost as big a celebrity as those who rode in the race he'd invented.

Between the first Ronde and the start of World War One, Flemish riders had continued to batter their rivals in the Tour de France. The year 1913 saw 140 competitors lining up in the Place de la Concorde for the start. The road between Paris and Tours had nails dropped on it strategically by local fans. The result was a mass wave of punctures, which lead to 29 abandonments, but if the idea was to disrupt the Belgians, it had little effect. Jules Masselis finished the day in equal first place with three of his fellow countrymen – Defraeye, Marcel Buysse and Alfons Lauwers. The following day the rider from West Flanders took the race lead by winning the sprint into Cherbourg. Defraeye took over from him on the stage into Brest. Marcel Buysse won the next day's marathon stage to La Rochelle, but Defraeye held on to the lead by coming second. The heat had been intense during the early stages and by the time the race arrived at Bayonne only 52 riders were left. The next day, as the peloton wound its way into the foothills of the Pyrenees, Defraeye surprisingly decided he was in no shape to continue and abandoned the race. Frenchman Eugène Christophe took the overall lead, but after riding heroically up the Tourmalet he was slapped with a time penalty when it emerged that a small boy had operated the bellows in the forge in which he was repairing a broken fork on his bike frame – assistance was frowned upon. As a consequence Philippe Thys took the overall lead with his compatriot Buysse in second. Buysse overhauled Thys on the stage to Perpignan, but was then caught hitching a ride in a car following a crash and demoted to fifth. On a monster stage to Grenoble, Thys consolidated his lead. Buysse won a spectacular run to Geneva that included climbs of the Col du Lautaret and Grand Galibier and then on the stage into Belfort won again, earning his nickname 'the Locomotive' by belting away over the Ballon d'Alsace like an express train. The distinctly un-railway-engine-like car ride had cost him dear though, and despite his brilliance he was still only in fourth place. Buysse would win another two stages, but Thys still took the main prize eight minutes and 37 seconds ahead of Gustave Garrigou. Buysse finished third.

The tall, thin Philippe Thys came from Anderlecht, on the edge of Brussels. In France sports journalists nicknamed him 'the Basset Hound' because he leaned forwards over his handlebars when riding, like a dog on a scent. Like a basset Thys was not explosive, but he was remorseless, unperturbed by hardship or outside distractions. The moniker hinted too at a certain jowly glumness, a heaviness of manner, which the French tend to see in the Flemish, whether it is present or not.

The 1914 Tour began on the same day that Archduke Franz Ferdinand was shot in Sarajevo. The race began with a midnight parade of riders down a gaslit Champs-Élysées, watched by tens of thousands of cheering spectators. It was a fiercely contested race eventually won by Thys. The decisive stage came in the Pyrenees where 'the Basset Hound' doggedly pursued leader Firmin Lambot, a Walloon from Florennes near Namur, up to the top of the Col d'Aspin and then descended at such ferocious speed he overtook the lead cars. He held grimly on through the Alps despite constant attacks by Lambot and the French riders Jean Alavoine and Henri Pélissier who, perhaps mindful of the way the Flemish riders had supported one another in previous races, seemed to have formed a Francophone confederacy against him. By the final stage into Paris, Pélissier was just three minutes behind the Belgian. The Frenchman's attempt to claw back the lead was gallant, but his popularity with the local public proved his undoing as his breakaway was constantly held up by fans eager to pat him on the back, so blocking his route. Thys won by just under two minutes. Five days later German troops crossed the border into Belgium.

Paul Deman had not been involved in the excitement of this great Tour, but the winner of the first Ronde emerged from the war as a bona fide hero. Living in occupied Belgium, Deman had helped the Belgian resistance by carrying messages to and from neutral Holland hidden in the frame of his bicycle. Eventually the Germans cottoned on. In 1918 he was arrested and jailed in Leuven. Sentenced to face a firing squad, Deman escaped death when the Armistice was signed on the day his execution was scheduled. In recognition of his gallantry the French awarded him the Croix de Guerre, a medal for acts of heroism, created in 1915. Deman continued to ride after the war and won Paris–Roubaix in 1920 and Paris–Tours in 1923. When he retired from cycling he took a job at a bike shop at the foot of the Kluisberg, one of the most famous climbs of the Ronde.

The first edition of the Ronde van Vlaanderen after the end of the Great War was one of the most extraordinary in the race's history and helped finally establish the race as a notable international event. Henri Van Lerberghe, better known throughout Flanders by the diminutive Ritten or Ritte, had fought on the front line with the Belgian army. He came to the Ronde directly from his barracks, borrowing a bike from the brother-in-law of a fellow competitor, Jules Masselis, the man who had briefly led the 1913 Tour de France. In the quiet moments before the race got under way Van Lerberghe shouted to a field that included Marcel Buysse that he was going to 'ride you all into the dirt'. This caused a good deal of amusement, and looking at photos of Van Lerberghe you can see why. He was a small, slight man with the moustache and cockeyed expression of a slapstick comedian. He looked more likely to accidentally knock a policeman's helmet off with a ladder than to pedal to victory in a one-day Classic. The Flemish champion Jules Van Hevel certainly found the outburst funny and began chuckling loudly. The two men nearly came to blows. 'I'll ride you off my wheel right in front of your own house,' Van Lerberghe yelled. He was true to his threat, belting away from the field in Ichtegem – Van Hevel's home town – with 120 kilometres to go and ploughing on alone into a headwind. Van Lerberghe was tough but the chasing pack were still more entertained by his antics than unnerved by them. Before the war Van Lerberghe had shown a passion for attacking with no regard to the consequences, taking a vast lead only to blow out exhausted long before the finish. The newspapers had even taken to calling him 'the Death Rider of Lichtervelde' because of his suicidal approach. Sure enough, Van Lerberghe began to falter. Weak with hunger he stole a bag of food intended for Marcel Buysse and with that in his stomach his pace picked up again. Still the field might have caught him had a train not pulled directly across the course. Van

Lerberghe picked up his bike and, according to legend, clambered in one door of a carriage and out through the other, remounted and carried on racing. The train did not move for a long time. When the pursuing pack arrived, none of them showed the same initiative; instead they waited for the track to clear. By the time it did Van Lerberghe was so far ahead of the field that when he arrived at the velodrome in Gentbrugge where the race finished he had time to go into a café and order a beer. The first one tasted so good, he had another. When the director of the track heard what was going on he sent a *soigneur* to fetch him. By now Van Lerberghe was several more beers to the good and was so wobbly on his pins he had to be led onto the track by a marshal. Tired and emotional, he slowly completed his lap of honour shouting at the crowd to go home 'and come back tomorrow. I've half a day's lead on the rest of them.' That was an exaggeration, but even with the pause for drinks Van Lerberghe still won by nearly a quarter of an hour, the biggest winning margin in the history of the Ronde. Many historians have cast doubt on the final part of the story, but Van Wijnendaele approved of it and gave it currency. He knew that, in an era before television, sport, particularly cycling, thrived on myth. Journalists were not there to debunk legends but to create them, to bring drama to the daily lives of their readers. Moreover, *Sportwereld* had a mission to inspire and rouse the population of Flanders, to fill them with confidence, to write stories that were, in Van Wijnendaele's phrase, 'carved out of the granite of the Flemish folk'. The tale of the Death Rider of Lichtervelde's tipsy victory on a borrowed bike was everything *Sportwereld* stood for. So what if it wasn't true?

Van Lerberghe never won another race. It hardly mattered. There's a plaque to him in his home town, mounted on the wall of a butcher's shop in the long main street, just down from another marking the birthplace of Charles Joseph Van Depoele, the electric tram pioneer, and a café with a window display of cartoons of Roger De Vlaeminck, four times winner of Paris–Roubaix. The Death Rider of Lichtervelde is often referred to as 'the First of the Flandriens'. In Flemish cycling 'Flandrien' is a very specific term, referring only to riders who epitomise those characteristics the Flemish hold most dear, the ones Van Wijnendaele sought to mythologise and celebrate.

In 1914, when the men of the Northumberland Fusiliers marched up to the muddy killing ground of the Ypres Salient, the one-storey stone houses that characterised rural West Flanders reminded them of Tyneside. For two decades I lived in a Northumbrian cottage that might have inspired such homesickness. The cottage had once been three – families of eight people living in one room each with its own range for heating and cooking, a communal washhouse adjoining the outside privies and coal sheds. Before we bought the house the surveyor came. He listed off the endless faults – the woodworm in the roof beams, the rotten floor joists, the crumbling pointing, and the potentially explosive septic tank. 'What about the chimneys?' I asked. The surveyor laughed. 'No need to worry about them,' he said. 'I tell you, if an atom bomb ever lands on Northumberland everything will be flattened except those bloody chimneys.' Photographs of the Ypres Salient during World War One suggest the chimneys of West Flanders were equally resilient.

As far as I can tell there is no precise English translation of the French word '*flahute*', but whenever I hear it something about the sound brings to mind the image of a Tynedale chimney. *Flahute* was the name the French gave the typical Flemish pro cyclist. The two things share many characteristics: both are squarely built, sharp-edged and functional to the point of grimness, devoid of any pretention to prettiness.

The *flahutes* did not entrance spectators with their elegance, their good looks or their grace. While riders such as Fausto Coppi, Louison Bobet or Luis Ocaña appeared to sail effortlessly along the road, the *flahutes* chugged forwards like tugboats. Their efforts were sweatily palpable, their burly thighs pumped, their scabby elbows waggled, their knotty heads bobbed. You could almost hear the clanking of their joints, the steam whistling from their ears. The hills of Flanders were short, sharp and predominantly cobbled. Riding up them required special skills. Great climbers such as Charly Gaul, Federico Bahamontes and Julio Jiménez danced lightly on the pedals, ascending fleet-footed as mountain goats. That didn't work in Flanders. In Flanders you had to club and hammer at the pedals. Climbing here was less of a waltz, more of a clog dance. Even when it was sunny and dry the *flahutes* finished caked in mud. Every pedal stroke looked like agony, but on the *flahutes* went, remorseless and filthy as the winter rain. When all the world had descended into the mud and the chaos, the *flahutes* remained upright. 'When I was suffering, then I was happy, because if I was suffering I knew everybody else was dead,' said 'Iron' Briek Schotte, who was born in a village a few miles outside Kortrijk in West Flanders in 1919. Schotte was the greatest of all the *flahutes*, and only great *flahutes* were Flandriens.

One summer day in 2016 I took the bus from Kortrijk to Desselgem. Dropped off near a petrol station, I proceeded to get hopelessly lost in what appeared to be an endless modern housing estate. It was blazingly hot and people seemed entirely absent. I wondered if I'd missed a news bulletin telling everyone in West Flanders to stay indoors because there was a homicidal maniac on the loose. I started to feel that at any minute I'd hear someone shout, 'That must be him!' followed by a gunshot and a searing pain in my chest. Not that I'm melodramatic or anything.

Eventually, dripping with sweat, I found a woman in a blue smock who was busily sorting out the pavement in front of her house. The Flemish are not just house proud, they are pavement proud. It wasn't uncommon to see people weeding the paving slabs, or brushing the kerb outside their homes. The lady in the blue smock was taking a brass hand-fork to some grass that had had the temerity to pop up and make things look untidy.

I asked her about the Briek Schotte memorial. 'Oh yes,' the lady said, getting up and mopping her brow. She pointed and swerved her hands to indicate the route. 'Not more than one kilometre,' she said. Then she smiled and said, 'He was the best.' Everyone in Flanders admired Briek Schotte, he was to Flemish bike racing what Bill Shankly was to British football, or Vince Lombardi to US gridiron – small, tough and filled with powerful wisdom.

I found the square named in honour of Alberic Schotte (Briek is a diminutive form). There was a bronze bust, an iron sculpture depicting Schotte on his bike and, on the gable end of a house, a massive black-and-white photographic portrait of the elderly Schotte by Stephan Vanfleteren. In the photo he is dark-eyed, pallid skin creased against the hard bones of his face. His expression is keen as an eagle's and as fierce. It made me think of my old history teacher, a Welshman from the Valleys, who'd been the regular stand-off for Cardiff in the 1950s. 'You go to play in France,' he'd say, 'Toulouse, Toulon, the heartland of French rugby football. It's not an experience you'll forget. Big men, they were, huge. Oh, I tell you, it lives with you ever after: the brutality, the ferocity and . . . the smell.' Briek Schotte had the Welsh schoolmaster's intensity. You certainly wouldn't have wanted him catching you sticking chewing gum under your desk.

When Briek Schotte was made, the mould was broken, likely by Briek himself with a powerful stamp. He wasn't good looking, had none of an athlete's grace or poise, but he had the charisma that often comes with hardness, a brutal panache. Whether it was true or not, people would tell you that Schotte had brown ale in his *bidon* and a feedbag filled with beef stew and *stoemp* – the Flemish potato and vegetable mash.

Schotte grew up on a farm on the outskirts of Desselgem. He claimed that he took his first Roman Catholic communion aged ten and was then hustled out of the church to watch the Ronde pass by. 'Cycling is religion,' he'd say later. It was easy to see how he came by that opinion.

Briek (or Brik, ideas on how to spell his name vary) was one of six children. The local school was half a dozen miles away and the young Briek was expected to ferry two of his younger siblings to school mounted on the handlebars and crossbar of his bike. Pedalling with his passengers developed his powerful legs, and before setting off and after returning home he was expected to help out on the farm.

The result was the typical *flahute* physique: barrel chest, thick midriff, mighty, tubular legs. Schotte had a face weatherbeaten and tough as alder bark. On a bike he had a certain anti-style, rolling from side to side as he pressed down furiously on the pedals looking – like his contemporary, the Czech distance runner Emil Zátopek – in perpetual torment. Perhaps there was some kidology in it, for he'd later say, 'My position on the saddle made it look like I was suffering more than I actually was.'

Briek has a legendary quality to the Flemish. He was the ungainly, raw and untutored farm boy who rose up from the squelchy Flemish mud and took on the Italians and the French in the 1940s and 50s, men like the elegant Fausto Coppi with his spiffy sunglasses and seraphic smile and Louison Bobet, whose photographic image seems to give off a whiff of cologne and pomade. In comparison there was no glamour in the Flemish scene. The Flemish teams were underfunded – the riders were paid on average a third as much as their Italian and French counterparts received. Their bikes were often inferior and their kit spartan. The situation persisted for decades. When Dirk De Wolf joined the Italian Gatorade team in 1992 he was given 22 pairs of shorts for the season. 'In Belgium I wouldn't see that many in five years!' he exclaimed.

It was David against Goliath.

In truth many great cyclists were from similar backgrounds to Schotte – Coppi was the son of a peasant farmer (when he gave his mother a fridge he'd won in a race, she used it to store firewood), Jacques Anquetil's parents grew strawberries. The difference is that Coppi and Anquetil didn't look like farmers. Schotte did. It's easy to picture him hefting a hay bale, or driving geese to market.

Schotte rode in his first race aged 15, a local *kermis* – a race associated with a fair or carnival – for which, or so it seems, many of the riders had

21

warmed up with liquid luncheons. He first came to wider attention aged 19 when he finished second in the Grote Prijs van Kortrijk behind Albert 'Bertan' Sercu from Bornem, a future winner of Het Volk. That same year Schotte won his first major prize, the Tour de l'Ouest, a race cut short by the Nazi invasion of France.

The following year he entered the Ronde – a truncated version, run with the occupying Germans' permission and involving only Flemish riders – and finished second behind Achiel Buysse. By now he'd left school and was working on the farm. It is said the villagers of Desselgem were so concerned at the effect this was having on his ability to ride big races they clubbed together to hire a labourer to work in his place.

Schotte was world champion twice, endearing himself to the Flemish when he interrupted a radio interviewer after his 1948 win in the Dutch city of Valkenberg by yelping, 'Mother! Mother! Can you hear me? I have won and become world champion!' In 1950 he repeated the feat in Moorslede, 50 kilometres from his home.

Briek was a bright man with an interest in the wider world. During the war he carried on working on the family farm, making small packets of money from any races that were going; after it he taught himself to speak French, Italian and English using language courses that came on long-playing records – the peloton at major races was increasingly multinational and it paid to know what your rivals were saying. It's hard to imagine Briek in an armchair listening attentively as the teacher says, 'Now, repeat after me: the rain in Spain falls . . .' Much easier to imagine him in the 1948 Tour de France, a race of rare brutality run over the neglected road surfaces of post-war France in weather so bad it seemed to presage the End of Days. Of the 120 riders who started the race, a mere 44 made it back to Paris. Schotte came second to the great Italian Gino Bartali.

Schotte rode in the Ronde van Vlaanderen 20 times, finishing 16 of them and winning in 1942 and 1948. 'I was not the fastest rider, but I was strong and tough,' was his own typically modest summary of his abilities. He died aged 84, on 4 April 2004, a few hours before the start of that year's Ronde van Vlaanderen. It was a piece of timing even Karel Van Wijnendaele couldn't have made up.

After she had given me directions the lady in the blue smock paused a moment, collecting her English. 'There is another statue of Briek Schotte, you know, in Kanegem, where he was born,' she said. 'Before they went to build it they asked him if it would be OK. He told them, yes, but on two conditions: it must be no bigger than lifesize, and they must not put it on a pedestal.' She studied me for a moment to see if I'd understood, then nodded her head decisively and went back to pulling the weeds out of the pavement.

1
THE FINAL 200 KILOMETRES

Sluitingsprijse Oostmalle, 19 February

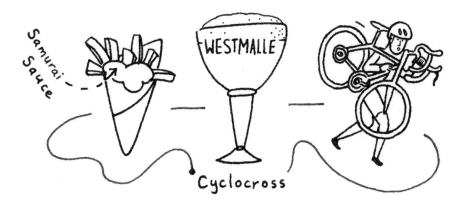

In mid-February 2017 I moved into an apartment near Ghent Dampoort station, not far from the site of the old Gentbrugge velodrome, scene of the Death Rider's ale-swigging antics in 1919, and a few hundred yards from a café that had once belonged to Vin Denson, a British rider who in the early 1960s had come over to what English people then called 'the Continent' to try his luck as a pro racer alongside compatriots such as Tommy Simpson and Alan Ramsbottom. Of the four bike racers who have been voted BBC Sports Personality of the Year, one of them, Tommy Simpson, lived in Ghent, while another, Sir Bradley Wiggins, was born there.

After I'd unpacked I had a chat with my new landlord, who told me he had no interest in cycling whatsoever but couldn't help thinking the races I was in Flanders to watch would be deadly boring because 'Peter Sagan is just too strong. He will win everything, like Eddy Merckx did.' Next I went off to the Trollkelder, a bar a Flemish hotelier once commented 'has never ceased to be unfashionable', for a glass of Westvleteren Abt. The ale from the Trappist Abbey of Westvleteren, down on the fringes of the Flemish hop-growing country near Ypres, is sometimes described as 'the greatest beer in the world'. I'm not sure I agree with that, but at 13 euros for a third of a litre it's surely one of the most expensive. When I came to pay, it dawned on me that I'd had my first Westvleteren here on the eve of Ghent–Wevelgem in 1995. The race was won by Dane Lars Michaelsen, but my abiding memory is of the close-up view I got of Djamolidine 'the Tashkent Express' Abdoujaparov's thighs, each of them wider than my chest.

'I've been coming here for 22 years,' I said to the barman when he handed me my change. He shrugged, 'No need to stop now, then.'

The following day I headed up to the final race of the Belgian cyclocross season, the Sluitingsprijs Oostmalle, which had been running on an old airbase north-east of Antwerp since 1995.

Though it's a fringe sport in most of the world, cyclocross is dear to the hearts of the Flemish. When I spoke to Johan Museeuw, three times winner of the Ronde and a rider sometimes called 'the Last of the Flandriens', he was driving his teenage son to a cyclocross race in West Flanders. When asked to name his boyhood heroes he said, 'Freddy Maertens, because his parents had a laundry near my home and we used to see him on training rides; Eddy Merckx because, well, he was Eddy Merkcx, of course; and Roger De Vlaeminck because he did cyclocross like me.'

Museeuw had been a junior cyclocross champion and only really started riding on the road to keep himself fit for the winter. Even when he was a pro at the top of his game with the Italian Mapei team, he'd still talk wistfully to journalists about the day when he could quit the warm roads of Tuscany and go back to humping a bike up through the dank wooded hills of wintry Flanders.

As an outsider it was hard to see what made Museeuw, who seemed a genuinely sensible man, so enthusiastic about the sport. Cyclocross is one of those things that at first glance appears a trifle nuts, but which on closer inspection is revealed to be totally insane. It is basically a cross country run, carrying a heavy and unwieldy load, with added opportunities to fall off a bicycle. The Flemish also really like motocross, so much so that Stefan Everts, a rider from Bree in Limburg, has been voted Belgian Sportsman of the Year five times, which is twice more than Tom Boonen. Eddy Merckx, naturally, has won it more times than anybody else.

All in all I think it might be interesting to see the 'cross' element applied to other sports. I'm sure gymnasts wouldn't look quite so perky if they had to carry the vaulting horse up a sodden hill and across a five-bar fence before they jumped over it. The fact it isn't perhaps tells us something about cyclists.

Cyclocross is a wet, cold and filthy sport that looks like a one-way ticket to misery, which is why, of course, the Flemish love it. And they really do love it. When the world championships were held in Koksijde in 2015, 70,000 people paid to watch.

I didn't suppose the event in Oostmalle would attract such numbers, but to be on the safe side I caught the train up to Antwerp just after the sun rose, not that you got much sign of its presence through the February clouds. The train rattled north through suburbs of red and yellow brick houses, the long gardens filled with livestock. I spotted rabbit hutches, pigeon lofts, pygmy goats, Jacob sheep and, in the back garden of a 1970s semi-detached in the middle of a housing estate, a couple of Shetland ponies. I was convinced that by the end of the trip I'd likely see an alpaca and possibly a brace of ostriches too, though in the end the only ostriches I saw were in a sewage farm near Aalst.

Out into the countryside of pollarded willow trees we went, the sunlight emerging from morning mist across the flat fields of corn stubble. There was nobody around save one man running along a path between ploughed fields who looked less like a jogger than somebody who'd just escaped from a chain gang.

In the low and marshy Waasland we passed neat village football grounds with floodlight pylons, flanked by narrow dikes. In the fields were ranks of polytunnels, phalanxes of greenhouses, long aluminium piggeries and clusters of new-build detached homes, some in the sort of odd shapes that have given rise to the popular website Ugly Belgian Houses. Not, I should say, that all the new houses were unsightly. Some were very sleek and stylish indeed. The great Irish rider Sean Kelly – who'd lived for most of his racing career in Vilvoorde – was so impressed with modern Belgian houses he'd driven round Flanders taking photos and making notes before building his own home in County Tipperary.

We passed through Bornem, along the banks of the Schelde, where there were clusters of holiday chalets each with a little jetty and a large pond surrounded by competition fishermen looking to hook fat carp, chubby rudd and ruddy chub. Just outside Niel a group of 40 cyclists crossed a steel-framed bridge over the Schelde. The group swung left in formation, fluid as a shoal of tropical fish. I thought of the opening scenes of the wonderful German documentary *The Greatest Show on Earth*, the peloton of the Giro d'Italia sweeping down the hairpin bends into Sorrento, a lovely piece of film that captured the beauty of sport as well as anything I'd seen.

To get to Oostmalle I had to get bus number 417 from Antwerp, direction Herentals. Herentals is a place of some significance in Flemish cycling. It was home to the great Rik Van Looy, the rider who had dominated the one-day Classics during the 1950s and 60s. The fans had nicknamed him 'the Emperor of Herentals'. He was born in the nearby village of Grobbendonk – which admittedly has a less regal ring to it.

As I waited for the bus I was aware that I had no idea what Oostmalle looked like or where I should get off when I arrived there. Luckily the bus was packed with people going to the cyclocross. I talked to two young blokes sitting opposite who lived in Antwerp but hailed originally from the countryside around Westmalle, home to another famous Trappist brewery. One of them asked if cyclocross was popular in the UK. I told him not really, that it isn't on terrestrial television – which for some old-fashioned reason I still take as the benchmark of all things. In the Lena Dunham film *Tiny Furniture*, when she asks of some celebrity she's just been told about, 'Is he *really* famous or just *internet* famous?', I applauded spontaneously. The Westmalle lads and I chatted about the TV coverage of cycling in Britain and Belgium. One said, 'Yes, I was in England once when the Tour de France was on and they only showed the final hour of the race. Here in Flanders it's different – we only show the final 200 kilometres.'

He said he was particularly looking forward to today's racing because he had heard they were selling Westmalle beer in the bars. I asked if that's why he was eating an apple. He laughed. 'Yes, I have this now and then beer – all the nutrients a man needs.'

The drinking at cyclocross is more or less legendary. My friend Jimmy went to the world championship in Koksijde and came back shaking his head. 'Man, I tell you, these Belgies can sink some ale,' he said, mimicking a man carrying a tray laden with pints. And when it comes to drinking beer it's not easy to impress a Geordie.

I'd arrived in Ghent without any notebooks. I found some in a store called Hema, which is kind of like Woolworths, offering an odd assortment of stuff from luggage to knickers via stationery and cotton buds. The notebooks came in a three pack and were very reasonably priced. It was only when I got the first one out of my bag on the shuttle bus to the cyclocross course that I realised it had the words 'Always be a Unicorn' on the cover in glittery silver letters. I was slightly embarrassed to be seen with it. Luckily nobody seemed to notice, possibly distracted by the pink glitter pen I was writing with.

As we paid our entrance fee of ten euros a teenage girl walked past with a wire-haired dachshund on a leash. She was wrapped in a flag proclaiming her devotion to Wout Van Aert. Born in Herentals, Van Aert was only 22 years old but was already a double world champion. He'd been Belgian champion twice too, won the UCI World Cup a couple of times and the Super Prestige once. In 2016 Van Aert had entered his first big road race as an adult and won the prologue time trial of the Tour of Belgium, finishing ahead of specialists like Tony Martin of Germany. He was young, hungry, powerful and quick. Already people were comparing him to Roger De Vlaeminck and Johan Museeuw. The Flemish fans told me they reckoned he'd do one more season in cyclocross then make the switch to road racing for 2018 (which he did, riding powerfully in the spring Classics and making the podium in the Strada Bianca, on a day of torrential rain in Tuscany). Riders like Roger De Vlaeminck used to road race in summer and do cyclocross in winter, but these days that's not possible. The road-race teams wouldn't let them. Why risk injury when they could be in a gym riding an exercise bike, or out in the Middle East promoting the brand in the sunshine on empty asphalt roads? Van Aert was so good expectation was building. 'He will be a great one for sure,' the apple-eater said, then, with a characteristic Flemish boldness-rollback, added, 'For sure . . . probably . . . maybe.'

I wandered off to watch the junior race, which had just about reached the midpoint. The course in the woods was not quite the mudbath I'd anticipated. It was sandy heathland, and though there were some sharp little climbs none of them lasted for more than five or six metres. The sand was deep, though, and there were springy roots sticking up everywhere – the sort you'd see if you were walking and think, 'Lucky I didn't catch a foot in that or I'd have measured my length.' They had the potential to send riders straight over their handlebars, or spinning to the ground with a snagged pedal.

I found a spot near the first wooded section. The physical strength of the competitors was impressive – on the steepest banks you could see how they used their arms and shoulders to thrust the bike over the final hump, building up the muscles that make a *flahute*. It was the bike-handling skills that caught the eye, though: the turns were tight, there was limited room for manoeuvre and multiple obstacles to be dodged, the switches from flat to slope and straight to bend came thick and fast. It was easy to see why so many of the best roadmen – including the apparently Merckx-like Slovakian Peter Sagan – cut their teeth in cyclocross.

After the race finished I went over to where the team and supporters buses were parked. Many spectators had come on their bikes. A couple of primary school kids in full Belgium international cycling kit were riding around among the pine trees and along the fringes of a stagnant-looking pond that gun dogs kept jumping in and out from. I dodged round a couple of damp Labradors and found the stalls selling scarves and shirts and flags devoted to riders and teams. Mathieu van der Poel, nicknamed 'the Sniper', had a whole stall to himself. World champion in 2015, Van der Poel was born nearby in Kapellen but rides for the Netherlands. His father, Adri, is Dutch. Adri was also world cyclocross champion. There's bike racing on both sides of the family. The Sniper's maternal grandfather is Raymond Poulidor, one of the best French riders of the 1960s.

I bought an immense bobble hat in the colours of the Belgian national team jersey, spending 30 euros on something I know I'll never actually have the courage to wear in public (though in bed while watching the football, who knows), then walked off to get something to eat and drink. Sadly the promised Westmalle seemed only to be available to people who had paid for the VIP area, a series of white marquees along the finishing straight. There was only fizzy lager or *genever* for the hoi polloi. There's some argument over who invented gin (*genever* is the Dutch word for juniper – from which the name gin is derived). It was either the Dutch or the Flemish. Few disagree, however, that the stuff distilled in Flanders is the best. I bought enough tokens to get a tot of *genever*, which was served warm and neat and tasted like it would cure any stomach complaint (and quite a few lung and throat problems too), and a big cone of *frites* with samurai sauce. Even here the chips were cooked to order – the oil in the fryers bubbling like a cauldron filled with eels. I have tried every one of the sauces served at Belgian chip shops over the years and have settled on samurai. It's a sort of bloody mayonnaise, which tastes vaguely like those barbecued sausages your dad accidentally squirted with lighter fuel because he'd had one too many cans of pale ale and was mad that the charcoal wouldn't burn properly.

As I was sloshing sauce all over my boots, Jelle Camps, the winner of the junior race, cycled past clutching a massive bouquet of flowers in his right hand. A 75cl bottle of Westmalle Tripel was tucked in the pouch at the back of his warm-up jacket. As he passed through the crowds several of the older blokes made a jokey move to steal it from him, to the gradually diminishing hilarity of the women around them.

With the possible exception of Wimbledon or 1970s British wrestling, I don't think I've ever been to a top-level sporting event that attracted so many women. If not quite a 50–50 split it's certainly around 60–40. The idea that the women have been towed here by husbands or boyfriends can be quickly discounted. There are lots of groups of half a dozen women without men attached – the sort of boisterous bands you'd see having a night on the town in any English city. There're all ages too, from primary school kids up to white-haired grannies. Cycling in Flanders is for everyone, not just blokes.

There are dozens of people dressed in special anoraks proclaiming them to be supporters of one rider or another. Homemade banners are much in evidence too. 'Sweeck – You Never Walk Alone' read one I noticed, mainly because the woman carrying it swung round and clonked me on the head with it. It wasn't her fault. She was just trying to monitor Laurens Sweeck's progress as he churned through an area that looked like a beach volleyball court. The second time she did it I decided it was time to move on.

In between races music pumped out remorselessly. It was the kind of gruesome thumping Europop you might think went out of fashion a decade ago, and probably did everywhere else in the world. It has to be said that there are many things to love about Flanders, but the music played in public places is not one of them. If you're one of those people who said you'd kill yourself if you ever heard 'The Ketchup Song' again, then don't visit Belgium without a shotgun is my advice. Even in hipster cafés you'll find yourself enduring Eric Clapton's 'Wonderful Tonight' as you eat a grilled seitan burger with sourdough bun and organic hand-gathered mizuna greens.

Clapton wouldn't get a look in at cyclocross, mind. Too trendy. The PA operators here are eager to remind people that Belgium is the land that gave us Patrick Hernandez's 'Born to Be Alive', a song of which the best I can say is that the Swedish version of it is worse.

Between the junior race and the women's race there was a chance for amateurs to have a go at riding the course. I suspected the main purpose of this was actually to churn the whole thing up and make it even more difficult for the elite riders. One thing it showed, though, was just how tough the ride was and how easy the pros made it look. Even blokes in Lycra with the build of whippets had to dismount and carry or push their bikes up hills the elite juniors just ploughed up, the better ones barely inconvenienced by the sort of steep, sandy banks that sucked all the energy out of lesser calves and thighs. One old boy in full kit, who had the face and body of late-period Les Dawson, pushed his bike round practically the entire course receiving rapturous applause and yells of encouragement from everyone he passed. The beer drinking lived up to the legend.

I have reached an age when I can no longer stand upright for quite as long as I once could. By the time the women's race was due I'd started to look rather enviously at the people carrying shooting sticks. I found my way into one of the wooded sections and eventually located a tree that didn't already have some other old codger leaning against it. It was well placed at the top of a narrow slope where the sand was deep enough to bury somebody in.

Two old men, whose pale skin and blue ski hats made them look like Smurfs in reverse, took up a strategic position on the outside of a tight corner midway up the climb. Every time a rider came off or was forced to a standstill by the difficulty of the incline, they reacted as if it was a personal triumph, clapping their hands and patting each other on the back. Sportswriters might get excited about effortless grace, these Flemish veterans liked to see riders struggling.

Sanne Cant from Antwerp has been Belgian and European champion multiple times, but she'd had to wait until this season to win the world title, her way to the rainbow jersey barred by the greatest female cyclocross rider of all time, Marianne Vos of the Netherlands. With Vos finally vanquished, the 26-year-old appeared unstoppable. She was so much quicker than all the rest of the competitors it was more of a victory procession than a race. She was trailed by fellow Fleming Laura Verdonschot and the Dutch rider Maud Kaptheijns, but they were far behind by halfway, and Cant rode throughout with a broad grin on her face, enjoying her own brilliance.

As soon as the flag went up in the elite men's race it was plain that it was going to be even less competitive than the women's event. It took Van Aert less than a lap to blast the field to smithereens. When he arrived on the tarmac section for the first time he was already 20 seconds ahead of the nearest pursuer; by the end of the second lap the gap had risen to 30.

I'd wandered away from the grim celebrants of misfortune by then and found myself standing next to the point where the riders left the woodland after negotiating two wooden slats set crossways over the track. They were a couple of feet high. Van Aert dismounted, picked up his bike and carried it over the fences with a smooth effortlessness that must have taken years of practice. His main rival, David van der Poel (the Sniper's younger brother), bunny-hopped over them, which looked cooler and drew admiring yelps from a cluster of teenagers, but actually seemed to slow him down.

I stood where the sand track met the tarmac, which gave me a good view into the final wooded section and along the finishing straight. As it happened I was also next to the steward tasked with giving the hook to those back markers who had missed the time cut. He was a burly elderly man in a Lotto baseball cap. He had a thick walrus moustache and the slow-moving benign aspect of a Saint Bernard. He had a clipboard and stopwatch and an assistant, a blonde woman in a thick warm-up coat. Once they worked out the times, the big man stepped out into the centre of the track and ushered those riders who were too far behind through a gap in the fence with a conciliatory smile that suggested his job was painful to him – like a vet telling you that, sadly, the kids' hamster isn't going to make it. The riders seemed to appreciate it, offering him a rueful grin and a shrug as if to say that they knew he was only doing his job.

When the first rider was sent through the fence, he pulled to a halt and was immediately assailed by a couple of small boys, brothers by the look of them, who started excitedly asking him something in Flemish. The rider was wiry and smiley with sandy hair. He stared at the boys, trying to understand what they wanted. It turned out he was English. 'They are wanting your racing numbers as a souvenir,' the boys' dad explained.

'Oh, OK,' the rider said, unpinning the numbers from his jersey and handing them out. 'Not sure if I'm exactly souvenir material, though.'

'Hey, you crashed early,' the dad said. 'Tough to recover from that.'

'Tough even without that,' the Englishman replied. 'You won't believe it but back in England I actually win races. But here . . .' he raised his eyebrows. It's the sort of self-deprecation the Flemish appreciate.

'But you have enjoyed it?' the dad asked.

'Sure, it was great fun,' the rider replied with genuine conviction. 'To tell the truth I'm Southern England champion. Mind you, being Southern Belgian champion would be a whole lot harder.'

The dad thanked him for his time and the numbers and the rider pedalled slowly away back in the direction of the car park and the van he'd likely changed in. When subsequent riders were pulled I watched as the younger ones were joined by girlfriends who appeared heartbroken on their behalf, the older ones by wives who listened patiently to their explanation for failure with the air of somebody who is actually thinking that they should really have changed the beds this morning. Mums were concerned and sometimes irate at other riders for upsetting their young lads; dads were sterner, offering sound advice: 'Now, what you ought to have done there . . . it's about hitting the corners . . .'

Van Aert, meanwhile, surged round the course like some unstoppable force. He was so much better than everyone else there was hardly anything for the crowd to get worked up about, though one supporter with a massive Flemish flag decided to make his own entertainment by deliberately lowering it so that it slapped the face of Van der Poel. 'Please do not wave banners over the course, thank you,' the announcer reproached them in Dutch, French and English. It could have been worse. In the 2016 world championships in Heusden-Zolder, Belgian fans had bombarded Dutchman Lars van der Haar with plastic beer glasses, some of which still had the beer in them.

Van Aert won by close to a lap, ahead of Tom Meeusen from Brasschaat, a notoriously wealthy little town not far from Antwerp. Van der Poel was third. I walked off back to the shuttle bus. In front of me a group of women in red anoraks pledging their allegiance to Toon Aerts began gyrating and mimicking sinking beer to the strains of 'Hands Up (Give Me Your Heart)' by Ottawan. A middle-aged man in a loden coat and leather cowboy hat staggered by them with the sly grin on his face of someone who is so mortally drunk they think nobody else can tell. Everyone had enjoyed themselves.

The origins of the sport of cyclocross are obscure, though most people seem to credit its invention to the Frenchman Daniel Gousseau. One of the things it is easy to forget about the bicycle is that until it came along the most popular form of transport was the horse. Horses are expensive to buy and to keep and were beyond the pocket of most ordinary people. The bicycle changed the situation. It was relatively cheap and inexpensive to maintain. You might say it was the working man's steed. Gousseau certainly seemed to think so. A private in the army, he took to following the cross country courses the officers tackled on horseback mounted on his bike. Soon several others had joined him in the pursuit. For the cycle manufacturers, the notion that what they were producing was an all-terrain vehicle was clearly a bonus. Gousseau organised the first formal cyclocross races and in 1902 launched the French national championships. Belgium was the next country to embrace the new sport and organised its own national championship for the first time in 1910. It was won by the Basset Hound, Philippe Thys. Second and third place were not recorded, perhaps giving rise to the infamous notion that in Flanders if you are not first in a bike race, then you are last.

The popularity of cyclocross gradually spread throughout Europe, helped by the fact that 1910 Tour de France winner Octave Lapize attributed his success to a winter spent plugging through the mud. The first international criterium – precursor to today's UCI World

Championship – was held on the outskirts of Paris in 1924. It was won by the Frenchman Gaston Degy. The Flemish riders Henri Moerenhout and Theo Van Eetvelde finished second and third. The following year Moerenhout went one better and took first prize – another Fleming, Jos Van Dam, grabbed silver.

Generally the French continued to dominate the race, though Belgian Georges Ronsse finished second in 1928 and 1930 and third in 1931. Ronsse had the sleepy eyes and large smooth nose of a Tove Jansson cartoon. He came from Antwerp and was Belgian cyclocross champion twice. He was also professional road race world champion in 1928 and 1929, won Paris–Roubaix twice, the marathon Bordeaux–Paris three times and, to top it off, also finished first in Liège–Bastogne–Liège, the Scheldeprijs and Paris–Brussels, fifth in the Tour de France and won three Belgian track titles. Ronsse rode for the powerful French Automoto team.

The great Sylveer Maes – a double Tour de France winner – was the next Flemish cyclocross rider to win the international criterium, roaring to victory in 1933. The following year Maurice Seynaeve from West Flanders took gold, with Maes second. Seynaeve – who was Belgian national cyclocross champion from 1934 to 1937 – won again in 1936. Unlike Ronsse and Maes he was no all-rounder and rarely bothered with road races, though he was good enough to come third in the Ronde van Vlaanderen in 1928. Photos of Seynaeve give an eccentric impression of the early days of the sport. In one he is training in a thick woollen jumper and plus fours, in another his more practical garb of shorts and a long-sleeved polo shirt is topped off with a helmet that looks like a leather bowler hat with added earflaps. At one prize-giving the champion is fending off the winter chill in what appears to be a lady's dressing gown, at another he sports elbow-length gauntlets.

After Seynaeve the French took control again. Even the doughty Jef Demuysere, Belgian national cyclocross champ in 1932, could not shake them. Robert Oubron, Roger Rondeaux and André Dufraisse dominated the racing scene from the late 1930s onwards into the 1950s.

In 1950 the first cyclocross world championship was held. It was won by Frenchman Jean Robic. The Flemish seemed to have lost their way entirely and while Italians, Swiss and West Germans won the race they recorded only one podium finish in the first 13 years of the championship – Firmin Van Kerrebroeck second in 1957. The drought came to an end in fine style in 1966 when Erik De Vlaeminck, brother of Roger, won gold. He'd go on to take the title five more times and, with his brother Roger and Berten Van Damme (aka 'the Lion of Laarne') also winning it, the Flemish would take almost total control of the event. Since the world championship began, Flemish riders have won 68 medals in the elite men's race, twice as many as any other nation. Flemings have been world champions 12 times this century, and Flemish riders occupied all three spaces on the podium in 2002, 2003, 2004, 2005 and 2012. Mario De Clercq from Oudenaarde (world champion in 1998, 1999, 2002), Erwin Vervecken from Herentals (2001, 2006, 2007) and Sven 'the Cannibal from Baal' Nys (2005, 2013) became national heroes, and there were few Flemings who didn't have a soft spot for poor Kevin Pauwels from Ekeren who managed to finish third five times between 2011 and 2017.

Perhaps the greatest cyclocross rider of them all, though, was Roland Liboton from Rillar just outside the great university city of Leuven in Flemish Brabant. Liboton was Belgian national champion from 1980 to 1989, won the world title four times and finished second once. It says something for his talent that despite those achievements most Flemish cycling fans smile wistfully at his name and mutter about disappointments and what-might-have-beens.

Liboton, you see, had been recognised as a genius from a young age. He'd been Belgian junior cyclocross champion in 1976, won the army world championship in 1977 and the under-21 title in 1978. Generally known by the diminutive Roel, Liboton cruised to three successive world titles, the first when he was just 22 years old. He was formidable when going uphill, unbeatable going down and uncatchable on the flat. He could sprint and he could clamber. His bike-handling skills were subtle and brilliant. He had courage and panache. During the 1983–84 season he entered 30 races and won 28 of them, including the world championships, a victory achieved despite the intervention of a Dutch fan who jumped onto the course and punched him in the stomach. No wonder people spoke of him as the Eddy Merckx of cyclocross.

Then suddenly it all went wrong. In 1985 at the world championships in Munich, an event he was such a runaway favourite to win it was a wonder any of the other riders bothered turning up, Liboton, riding fitfully and well below his best, struggled in tenth. In 1986 he was expected to regain his title and slap aside his adversaries on a muddy course in Lembeek that might have been designed for him – and likely was. Instead of hammering his foes in a Merckxian manner, Liboton rode as if anticipating disaster, abandoning on the second lap. In 1988 he failed even to make it to the starting line, pulling out of the race late claiming that he was sick. I'm not sure if there's a cycling equivalent of the yips or stage fright, but if there is, Liboton seems to have had it. Flemish cycling writers attributed the collapse to a paralysing fear of failure, though Liboton later dismissed the idea, commenting that his critics didn't give his opponents the respect they deserved.

Though he still dominated in Belgium, his days as an international champion were over. When he surrendered the Belgian title in 1990 he practically gave up racing altogether. Liboton may have won four world titles, but his was promise unfulfilled, at least in the eyes of the fans.

That didn't stop him sounding off about the younger generation, though, and in later life he became one of those retired sportspeople eager to dismiss those who come after them as a bunch of spineless, overprivileged fops. In 2015 the Belgian Cycling Union fired him from his coaching role after he lambasted the riders of the national team – including Van Aert and Nys – for allowing Mathieu van der Poel to win the title for the Dutch and then going out on the town afterwards. 'All failed and then they dance bare-chested like women around a pole, just disgusting,' he complained to the press. Later he'd suggest that the current crop of riders 'didn't have the balls' of his generation. Wout Van Aert might be the next great Flemish rider, but to Liboton's jaundiced eye he was no Flandrien.

2
A MOTOR FOR A HEART

Omloop Het Nieuwsblad, 25 February

Like boxing or sprinting, cycling is an adversarial sport. Many of the greatest eras and most memorable races have been built on bitter rivalries: Fausto Coppi against Gino Bartali, Jacques Anquetil versus Raymond Poulidor, Bernard Hinault battling Greg LeMond. Some of these clashes have been genuinely acrimonious, while others, such as the apparent feud between the great Italian Alfredo 'the Trumpeter of Cittiglio' Binda and Jean Aerts from Laken – who won 11 stages of the

Tour de France in the 1930s and was so nattily dressed *Sportwereld* dubbed him 'the Brummel of the Bicycle' – seem to have been entirely concocted by newspapers to generate sales. Whether real or imagined, the rivalries have all been exaggerated and at times exacerbated by the print media.

I'd been in Flanders a week and every day I'd bought a copy of the Flemish tabloid *Het Laatste Nieuws*. Most Flemings I met looked down on the paper, referring to it as 'the Lowest News' and mocking it in much the same way educated people in Britain once ridiculed the *News of the World*. Frankly, I had little interest in the newspaper's political stance or salacious mindset, and even less chance of comprehending it. I bought *Het Laatste Nieuws* because it had a cycling supplement that ran to over a dozen pages *six days a week* (the only reason it wasn't seven days a week was because *Het Laatste Nieuws* didn't have a Sunday edition). *Wielerkrant* (which, slightly unimaginatively, means *Cycling Newspaper*) was written in breezy tabloidese. As a small boy I had, belatedly, learned to read by studying the backs of the football cards that came with Barratt's bubblegum. This had left me with the vague feeling that I might master a foreign tongue simply by staring at *Gazzetta dello Sport* or *Marca*. This policy had worked, more or less, with *L'Équipe*, though it had skewed my vocabulary to such an extent that, while capable of a relatively fluent discourse on Paul Gascoigne's latest crisis, I couldn't buy a train ticket without pointing and making chuff-chuff noises.

Wielerkrant proved a good deal less penetrable than *L'Équipe*. This was because it is written in Dutch, a language that seems to include far more vowels than are strictly necessary. In fact, looking at it some days, I became convinced that the Flemish publishers had bought up a job lot of As, Es and Us and told the printers they weren't getting any more consonants until they'd used them all.

Luckily for me *Wielerkrant* is filled with photos, infographics and lists, which, if I concentrated, I could just about make myself believe I understood, though in truth my Dutch is limited to a few tourist phrases, generally pronounced so ineptly as to be incomprehensible.

In the build-up to the first major road race of the 2017 cycling season *Wielerkrant* was pushing the idea of a mighty head-to-head between Peter Sagan and the latest Flemish hero, Greg Van Avermaet, who'd taken the gold in the Olympic road race in Rio de Janeiro the previous summer. Van Avermaet was the first Flemish rider to win the Olympic road race since André Noyelle in Helsinki in 1952. Noyelle came from Ypres and turned pro shortly after the Olympics, joining the French team Alcyon–Dunlop. He won many minor races after his Olympic success, but nothing big. Van Avermaet was 31 years old, a tall, fair man with the sort of blandly handsome face that might belong to an ex-boyfriend in a Sandra Bullock romcom. His pro career was more impressive than that of Noyelle – he'd won three stages of the Tour de France – but it didn't suggest he'd be much of a rival to the mighty, hairy Slovak. Sagan had won the green points jersey in the Tour de France five times in succession and was reigning world champion (a title he'd also won in 2015). He'd won the one-day Classics Ghent–Wevelgem in 2013 and 2016, E3 Harelbeke in 2014 and the Ronde van Vlaanderen in 2016. Oh yes, and he'd also got four stages of the Vuelta to his name, held the European title and been junior world mountain bike champion. All this, and the man they called 'the Tourminator' was still only 27. As head-to-heads went it looked like a 2CV taking on a monster truck. Even Van Avermaet seemed in awe of Sagan, deflating all talk of the pair becoming locked in some sort of cobbled Classics shootout by telling any journalist who'd listen that he believed the Slovak would dominate one-day racing throughout the year.

After a week of mounting excitement, the day to finally see just how great Sagan's season was going to be had arrived. On the streets that ran towards Ghent's main railway station, clusters of people in thick coats and myriad cycling caps accelerated with anticipation as they sighted the trees of Citadel Park. There was a tingle in the air, a spring in every stride. It was the final Saturday in February, the first race of the European Classics season, and we were heading towards the start of the historic and comprehensively voweled Omloop Het Nieuwsblad. Nobody wanted to be late.

The teams were being presented in Ghent's famous velodrome De Kuipke ('the Little Tub'). The venerable old place had been built by the Apostel-Mampaey family. Louis Apostel came from Boom, south of Antwerp. He built his first velodrome in his home town in 1907. The steeply banked cycle track was made of concrete. Unfortunately Louis took the decision to build his velodrome on a foundation of sharp sand. Soon builders were turning up from all around the area and stealing wheelbarrowloads. The velodrome was slowly undermined and started to collapse. By 1927 it had been abandoned and the local authorities ordered that it be pulled down in the interests of public safety. Now all that remains of it is a street name.

Louis was soon joined in the business by his son Jos and son-in-law René Mampaey (later a grandson, Benny Apostel, would be added to the firm). They became the most famous velodrome builders in Europe. As well as De Kuipke they designed and completed velodromes in Nice and Marseille, two in Ostend, the Sportpaleis in Antwerp (still the largest indoor arena in Europe), the famous velodrome of Gentbrugge – scene of Ritten Van Lerberghe's legendary antics – and others in Oudenaarde, Wilrijk and Brussels. All these were built in a 39-year period. In the years after World War Two the popularity of track cycling gradually dwindled and there was little demand for velodrome builders. The Apostel-Mampaey family moved into selling bicycles, and Louis Apostel's descendants still have a couple of shops on the outskirts of Antwerp.

The velodrome in Citadel Park in Ghent was built on the site of an old greenhouse, and opened in 1927. Originally it too was called the Sportpaleis, but the short track and steep banking eventually earned it the nickname that became official. The Little Tub was gutted by fire in

1965 and was rebuilt, though it seemed to me that bits round the edges of the velodrome had simply been abandoned. The track is most famous for hosting the annual Six Days of Ghent, a festival of racing featuring professional riders in multiple events that runs in late November.

De Kuipke has a rich history. It also has a powerful smell. This was because the organisers had placed half a dozen portable urinals right next to the entrance. Walking in, the first thing that struck the visitor – almost literally – was an overpowering odour of urine, the next was the booming sound of the Lotto PA system blasting out a Dutch version of the Proclaimers' '500 Miles'. It was hard to tell which of the two was more likely to make you gag.

After escaping from the eye-watering ammonia stench and fighting my way through the vast group of cycling fans who seem to love nothing more than to gaze in awestruck wonder at the team buses, I found myself standing at the point from which the riders were entering the velodrome. Twenty or so yards over to the left I watched people walking in through an entrance with a printed sign reading 'VIPs Only' over the door. They didn't look like VIPs, there were no laminates on lanyards in evidence. So I approached one of the security guards and asked if I could go in.

He looked puzzled. 'For sure, why not?'

I pointed to the sign. The security guard looked at it. 'Oh shit,' he said. 'That shouldn't be there.' And he reached up and tore it down.

After submitting to a perfunctory search of my bag I went into the velodrome through a doorway covered with those heavy strips of opaque plastic they use to seal off cold-storage areas. The elderly man in front of me, who was tall, bald and had the general look of Arnolfini in the Van Eyck painting, briefly became tangled up in it and flailed his arms about blindly like he was battling a giant squid.

Inside the velodrome the riders were being presented to the assembled fans. These occasions always follow a similar pattern: the riders come out to booming hip-hop and assemble on a stage where they are asked a series of increasingly stilted questions in an admittedly impressive variety of languages by a man who sounds a bit like a childless uncle attempting to make conversation with his 14-year-old nephews. When the Bora–Hansgrohe team of Peter Sagan assembled, the MC went over to English to ask Flanders-born Irish rider Sam Bennett, whose father had been a pro footballer in the Belgian league, if living in Ireland was better than living in Belgium. 'It's about the same,' he replied.

'Is the weather nicer?' the interviewer asked. 'It's about the same,' Bennett replied again, after which enlightenment the Bora–Hansgrohe team rode off to the sound of a US rapper bellowing that everybody could suck his dick.

TV camera crews were passing through the seats filming the craziest of the supporters. In front of me, members of the fan club of the promising 24-year-old Flemish rider Jasper Stuyven were unfurling umbrellas celebrating their hero and blocking the iPhone cameras of dozens of people who were filming events on the track, presumably so they could download it onto a laptop and entertain their neighbours with it later.

'Do you like your new team jersey?' the interviewer asked the next group of riders. 'Yes,' one of them replied. 'There's quite a lot of red in it, isn't there?' 'Yes, and a bit of orange too.'

A couple of middle-aged women in matching anoraks celebrated this exchange by waving a Lotto–Soudal flag above their heads. A family of six walked past in brand new Tom Boonen supporters' scarves and blue-and-white *Het Nieuwsblad* cycling caps, bearing the legend '*de koers is van ons*' ('the course is ours').

The arrival of Jasper Stuyven's Trek team sent his fan club and most of the arena into a frenzy. The people around me uttered a collective whooshing noise that seemed to encompass both surprise and delight and then proceeded to laugh so merrily at every reply he gave it suggested a post-racing career as a stand-up comic. As Blur's 'Song 2' blared out two lads unrolled a giant banner dedicated to Stuyven's teammate, Ghent-born Edward Theuns, and a man dressed in what may have been a Napoleonic admiral's uniform stalked by in the company of a chap in electric blue training shoes and a waistcoat with the words 'Kristoff F*an Wervik' on the back and began waving a Norwegian flag, presumably in celebration of Alexander Kristoff, the Oslo-born rider who'd won the 2015 edition of the Ronde. It seemed like a signal, so I grabbed a free programme and team list and headed off to Ghent Sint-Pieters railway station to catch the train to what I hoped would be a strategic point in the coming race.

The field contained a lot of familiar Flemish cycling names. There was a Steels, a Capiot and, inevitably, a couple of Planckaerts. If you throw a stick at the peloton of any Flemish bike race the chances are you'll hit a Planckaert. It seems unlikely they are all related to one another, but somehow it feels as if they are.

The first Planckaert I encountered was Eddy. By then he'd been retired a few years. He'd put on weight and left his chin unshaven. With his characteristic ringlets of hair and his leather jacket he looked less like a superstar cyclist than the sort of bloke who'd turn up on *Rock Family Trees* talking about playing with Dire Straits ten years before they had a hit. Perhaps that wasn't coincidental. Eddy had some aspirations as a drummer. He'd even cut a few records with his best mate, the Flemish folk musician Ivan Heylen. One of them was called 'We Got to Win'.

When I first saw Eddy he was on stage at the start of the Ronde van Vlaanderen in the windswept square at Sint-Niklaas, a city midway between Ghent and Antwerp, being questioned by an interviewer who'd been talking about bike racing with people for so long he'd given up trying to find anything interesting to ask them. In Eddy's case that was probably just as well. A radio journalist I knew who worked on Flemish national station VRT's early morning show told me she'd once made the mistake of asking Eddy what his worst experience as a cyclist had been. She then had to listen to a graphic description of racing while suffering from gastroenteritis. 'The shit was running down my thighs like a waterfall, that sort of stuff.' She recalled, 'It's as well it wasn't going out live, or nobody in Flanders would have finished their breakfast.'

She said all this with a smile. No matter what he did, people liked Eddy. They spoke of him with an amused, indulgent look, like somebody recalling the time a long-departed and loyal dog had snaffled a pack of sausages.

Eddy had been a Flemish cycling legend from his teenage years back in the mid-1970s. He'd won the junior Belgian national road title three times, cranked out an average of 50 race wins a year and picked up bundles of cash by winning every prime sprint that was available. Hundreds of supporters followed him to every race. Even as an adolescent he was being paid the equivalent of £100 appearance money.

Eddy was the younger brother of Willy, Tour de France points classification winner in 1966, and Walter, who won the Ronde and E3 in 1976. The Planckaert boys lived in Nevele, East Flanders, with their mother, Augusta, and their sisters in a two-bedroom farmhouse. The brothers shared a bed. Their father had been killed in a car crash when Eddy was a child, Augusta so badly injured in the accident she was never able to work again. Times had been tough for the Planckaerts until Willy's success in the Tour de France. When he'd come home in the green jersey the offers to appear in the little summer *kermis* races that were a feature of August in Flanders came flooding in. He rode in every one that he could – two, sometimes three a day – pocketing an appearance fee for each one. At the start of September he returned to the farm with a suitcase stuffed with cash. That summer saved the Planckaerts financially but it did for Willy's career. Exhausted, his immune system shot, he contracted hepatitis soon afterwards and – though he'd go on racing as a pro for another ten years – was never the same rider again. It was the kind of brutal self-sacrifice that Flemish cycling revelled in. 'Planckaert is a hard name,' Walter would say. The family lived up to it.

Every day the young Eddy trained with Walter, a big man whose heavy face had a hint of doom about it. They got up at dawn and did the same 100-kilometre undulating circuit, never changing out of a big gear no matter what. 'It was a matter of pride,' recalled Eddy, 'the Little One'. 'Just ride on and on in the 14 or 15 sprocket. If there's a hill or a headwind you just press harder on the pedals. That was the way it was. It made me strong, and strength is everything in Belgian racing.'

The Planckaerts' farm had no bathroom. After training, the brothers washed in a bucket of cold water in the yard. In the afternoon Eddy worked for a gardening firm cutting lawns. He didn't need the money – he was making enough from racing – but his brothers, both born in the 1940s, insisted on it. They wanted Eddy to see what things were like for the ordinary Flemish fans, to appreciate the life of a pro that was his destiny, to keep him humble. He went to bed at nine o'clock each evening. Even by the standards of rural Flanders in the 1970s it was not a glamorous life.

Eddy turned pro with the Flemish Mini–Flat team in 1980. He was 21. He had class, panache and a ferocious will to win. He and his brothers were afraid of flying and drove to races even if the start was 500 miles away. In 1981 he won a stage of the Tour de France that finished in Belgium at Zolder. In 1982 he won four stages of the Vuelta a España back to back. In 1988 he emulated his brother Willy by winning the green jersey. In 1991 he won Paris–Roubaix by a few millimetres from Canada's Steve Bauer. Eddy's greatest and most astounding victory, however, came in the Ronde van Vlaanderen in 1988.

Eddy had almost won the race in 1982. Now he was leading a Flanders-based ADR team that included Dirk Demol, Fons De Wolf and the neophyte Johan Museeuw. Weather conditions were perfect – that is to say it was cold, wet and windy. Riders froze, fell and walked away caked in mud, shaking their heads and cursing. Only the hardest survived. Sean Kelly attacked on Oude Kwaremont and took a bunch of riders with him, including Planckaert. With 14 kilometres left Australian Phil Anderson put the hammer down. Only the Dutchman Adri van der Poel and Eddy could keep up. On the ascent of the Bosberg they shook off Van der Poel. After that things turned a little surreal. As Eddy told his friend and biographer Ivan Heylen:

> From that moment on Phil Anderson tried everything. He accelerated. He made me several offers. He would have given his life if I had let him win. He really couldn't understand why I didn't accept. But I said to my ex-teammate from Panasonic that we should go for it. He understood.
>
> The finale was incredible. He kept on accelerating. One time I thought he was gone and that was the only time in my life that I passed the limits. When you're completely worn out, thinking you might drop dead from fatigue, you reach another dimension.
>
> Suddenly it seemed I was floating over the road. It's a bit embarrassing to say it, but I ejaculated, and not just a little bit. A hundred metres later I was at Phil's wheel again and I knew I would beat him. I had reached a divine state.

Anyone who thinks Eddy had made up that last bit should take a look at the photo of him crossing the finish line in Ninove. Though I'd advise you against doing so if your mouth's full.

Eddy retired from racing in 1991. He wasn't by any means the last of the Planckaerts. Willy's son, Jo, won Kuurne–Brussels–Kuurne in 1999 and Eddy's boy, Francesco, had also ridden as a pro, though with limited success. Other Planckaerts unrelated to Eddy's clan would also emerge. Two Planckaert brothers, Baptiste and Edward, would be joined in the peloton by Stijn and Brecht Planckaert. Nor was Willy the first Planckaert to make an impact on the Tour de France. Jef Planckaert had finished fifth in 1960. Jef came from Poperinge in West Flanders and was part of Rik Van Looy's famous Flandria team. He seems to have been no relation of the East Flanders Planckaerts, or any of the others.

'Eddy's a sweet man,' the Antwerp radio journalist who'd had to listen to his runny-tummy story said with the characteristic fond smile, 'but a total hillbilly. Or at least he would be if he lived near any hills.'

There was certainly a comedy redneck element to Eddy's post-retirement life. Back in 1974 his mate Ivan Heylen had had a massive hit with a rustic singalong tune 'De Wilde Boerndochtere' ('The Wild Farmer's Daughter'). Sung in West Flanders dialect in a voice so loud and rasping it knocked crows out of trees, the song tells the story of an encounter between an innocent country boy and the beautiful daughter of a local farmer. Heylen, who actually came from East Flanders, is generally regarded by Belgian music writers as a massive embarrassment to the land of Jacques Brel and Plastic Bertrand. But Heylen's records were just as popular in Flanders as those of the Wurzels – a comparable act from around the same time who sang about the joys of cider and tractors – were in Britain. Despite the sneering, 'The Wild Farmer's Daughter' sold 250,000 copies and was top of the charts for several weeks. In the interests of research I have tried to listen to it several times and never got beyond the 90-second mark. To be fair to Heylen, I should say that is far longer than I have managed with anything Sting has recorded since leaving the Police.

Like the Wurzels', Heylen's success was short-lived and he ended up as a journalist, a shoddy fate for anybody. Along the way, the singer became good friends with Eddy and helped him write a book, *Het Geslacht Planckaert*, which Google helpfully translates as *The Sex Planckaert*, though I believe *The Planckaert Breed* is perhaps more what the authors were aiming for. Though then again . . .

In 1998 Heylen decided to make a film based on his 24-year-old hit record. As writer, director and producer he cast Flemish singer, actress and pin-up, the aptly named Wendy Van Wanten, as the eponymous heroine. Van Wanten had previously hosted gameshows and played a strict yet saucy headmistress in the Belgian TV sitcom *Meester*. For the part of the innocent young country lad Heylen mysteriously opted for

Eddy Planckaert. Eddy had limited acting experience and was 40 years old, but since Van Wanten was 38 perhaps it made sense. The resulting film is said to contain the longest sex scene in Flemish film history (and no, I don't have any idea what the second longest is, though Jan Bucquoy's masterful *The Sexual Life of the Belgians, 1950 to 1978* might be a starting point for those of you who are eager to find out. Bucquoy, I feel compelled to add, once ran the Museum of Underpants in Brussels). Fortunately nobody ever got to see it. Just after the film was completed Heylen became embroiled in a legal dispute with his leading lady. She got a court order blocking the movie's distribution. Furthermore the judge also banned Heylen from discussing it in public. Eddy's tilt at erotic movie stardom was therefore nipped in the bud. Later he'd appear on the Belgian edition of *Celebrity Big Brother* and *De Planckaerts*, a Flemish cycling answer to MTV's *The Osbournes*, in which an increasingly dishevelled Eddy, apparently bankrupt after losing all his money in a Ukrainian timber deal gone wrong (or something like that), arses about in a log cabin in the Ardennes. The series proved such a hit in Belgium it became a cartoon strip. Which in some ways summarises the trajectory of Eddy Planckaert's career.

Eddy Planckaert had won the Omloop twice (back in his time it had still been called by its original name, Omloop Het Volk). The history of the traditional curtain-raiser to the cycling season was rooted in one of the murkier aspects of Flemish lore. It was in many ways the anti-Ronde. To understand how it came to be on the cycling calendar we have to return to Karel Van Wijnendaele. In the years following World War Two the race that he'd invented grew bigger and bigger. Despite the atrocious roads, increasing numbers of riders from around Europe began to enter, bringing with them dash and glamour. For the Flemish the opportunity to see their own lads upholding the honour of Flanders by beating seven shades of snot out of swaggering Frenchies like Henri 'the Iron Wire' Pélissier (not so handsome as his brother, but nevertheless a legendary womaniser who would die after being gunned down by one of his mistresses) proved irresistible. By the 1930s police estimated that 500,000 fans were watching at the roadside. The Flemish riders saw off Pélissier, but their dominance couldn't last for ever. The first foreigner to win the race was Swiss champion Heinrich Suter in 1923. Suter – who'd take Paris–Roubaix that same spring – adopted a scientific approach to racing. A calm and measured competitor, the Swiss was one of the first athletes to understand the benefits of interval training, building up his speed and stamina on indoor tracks with short intense bursts. His approach didn't sit well with the cycling purists of the day, however. They liked to see riders preparing by going on gruelling 200-kilometre rides in the wind and rain. Cyclists were supposed to suffer – the public demanded it and the organisers of races did everything to ensure it (Henri Desgrange, the man who ran the Tour de France, even introduced a rule that made it illegal for riders to finish a stage wearing fewer clothes than they'd started it in). Cycling fans today who grumble that computers, heart monitors and the like are robbing the sport of its romance – and, yes, that includes me – are part of a historic tradition.

The number of entrants for the Ronde increased every year until, in 1933, there were 164 hopefuls at the start line in Ghent. The prize money had risen too. In 1930 first prize was 2,000 Belgian Francs, in 1935 2,500. Bear in mind that at that time most workers earned less than four francs an hour. On top of that there were prizes for every rider who finished inside the top 20, and a whole range of spot prizes offered by shopkeepers, manufacturers, councils and the like, usually based on intermediate sprints, or being the first past a specific point in the race – perhaps a factory gate, a café or village sign. Some of these were cash, most were goods, a few were livestock. A rider might finish the Ronde and find himself better off to the tune of a couple of hundred francs, a crate of beer, a carton of cigarettes and a brace of pigeons. The Ronde van Vlaanderen enabled the households of many Flemish cyclists to acquire their first wireless sets, washing machines and fridges. The prizes were a nice bonus, and if the money wasn't life-changing it was a whole lot more than you could earn harrowing potatoes or trimming the dags off sheep's backsides.

By 1931 Van Wijnendaele was sole owner of *Sportwereld*. Unfortunately his business acumen never quite matched his journalistic skills. Despite its high circulation, his newspaper lost money. He was forced to sell to the Standaard publishing group, who would eventually merge the title with its daily newspaper *Het Nieuwsblad*, and which therefore took over the organisation of the Ronde. Despite the sale, Van Wijnendaele stayed on as editor.

When the Nazis conquered Belgium in May 1940 they did what they had done in many of the countries they had invaded – gave a vestige of power and autonomy to a previously oppressed group. The Flemish were suddenly allowed to speak their own language freely and run, up to a point, their own affairs. The occupation is a murky time in Belgian history. As Georges Simenon, who lived in occupied Liège during World War One and occupied France during World War Two, observed, during such times people tend to do what they need to do to survive and then, after liberation, to hide their shame, point an accusatory finger at others. The ambiguities and complexities of trying to carry on with normal life when your country has been taken over by a totalitarian regime are sensitively explored in Flemish Nobel laureate Hugo Claus's courageous novel *The Sorrow of Belgium,* in which the central character's father, the owner of a small printworks, is offered the contract to produce posters for the occupiers. Does he turn it down and risk their wrath and potential bankruptcy, or accept and risk being accused of aiding the enemy? That was the sort of choice that the Flemish faced. Having been fortunate enough never to live through a war, never mind a Nazi occupation, it's not for me to cast judgement on people who have. What I will say is that there is a very fine line between getting on with normal life and collaborating – and walking it must have been very, very difficult.

Het Nieuwsblad changed its name to *Het Algemeen Nieuws– Sportwereld* (the *General News–Sports World*) and became – to some eyes – a little too close to the Nazi regime. Whether that is true or not, what is inarguable is that the newspaper continued to organise and stage the Ronde, which became the only cycling Classic to be run in German-occupied territory. It did so not only with permission of the Nazis but also with their support and help. When Belgium was liberated *Het Nieuwsblad* and *De Standaard* were both suspended from publication because of the role some felt they had taken during the occupation. Van Wijnendaele himself was investigated for collaboration, found guilty – despite his protestations of innocence – and banned from journalism for life. The ban was lifted in 1948, apparently in light of an episode in which he had helped to hide an RAF pilot whose plane had been shot down over Belgium, then aided his escape back to Britain.

Other cycling people did not fare so well. Lucien Storme had won Paris–Roubaix in 1938 despite suffering a broken chain. His life would end tragically in 1945. Arrested for smuggling in Armentières, he attempted to escape from jail in Lille, was recaptured and deported to a Nazi work camp near Siegburg in Germany. The camp was liberated by the Allies but in the confusion that followed Storme was shot in the neck by an American soldier and died a couple of hours later. He was 29. The man who had finished second to Storme in Paris–Roubaix was Lode Hardiquest. Hardiquest had won the Ronde in 1936. After the liberation he was tried for collaborating with the Nazis and sentenced to eight years in jail – some say mistakenly (he had relatives who'd joined the Gestapo and that seems to have counted against him). After his release Hardiquest became a recluse. He killed himself in 1991.

Perhaps the confusion of the occupation can best be summed up by looking at what happened to King Albert's successor, his son Leopold, who acceded to the Belgian throne in 1934. Leopold III was handsome and dashing. Married to the beautiful Princess Astrid of Sweden, he was popular on both sides of the linguistic divide. When his wife died in a car crash in 1935 there was a heartfelt outpouring of grief across Belgium.

The king soon began to lose public goodwill, however. In the years leading up to World War Two he became increasingly autocratic, arguing publicly with Belgium's democratically elected government over policy. Then the Germans invaded. The Belgians fought bravely, but, like pretty much everyone else in Europe, they were quickly overwhelmed by the Nazi blitzkrieg. When it became obvious that Belgium was doomed, the French and the British governments, as well as his own prime minister Hubert Pierlot, entreated Leopold to leave the country while he still had a chance and form a government in exile in London. He ignored them and instead stayed in Brussels. Leopold's explanation was that, as commander-in-chief of the armed forces, to have deserted his men while they were still engaged with the enemy would have been an act of cowardice. Unfortunately he was not simply an army officer, he was also the head of state – a position he would continue to hold throughout the Nazi occupation, a time he spent under a rather relaxed house arrest in the royal palace at Laken.

Had Leopold's decision to stay in Belgium been an act of principle? Or was he hoping that when Britain fell – as it most surely would – and the war was over the Nazis would allow him to rule his country again, perhaps with the total power Belgium's constitution had previously denied him? Had he remained behind because he genuinely thought that was the best way he could help his people, or because it appeared his surest way back to the throne?

In the years that followed the liberation, Leopold's, actions became the dominant issue in Belgian politics. It was a time of uncertainty and upheaval. Governments were elected and dismissed with alarming rapidity, the office of prime minister changed hands seven times in five years. No one was able to resolve the question of whether Leopold – now living in exile in Switzerland – should be allowed to remain as king. Finally, in 1950, a referendum was held. It was agreed that a 55 per cent vote in his favour would see Leopold return. Less than that and either a republic would be declared, or a successor appointed.

The result was just about the worst possible for all concerned. Leopold got 57.68 per cent support. The king took this as a mandate, but not everyone felt the same. In Flanders the pro-vote was 72 per cent, but in Wallonia 58 per cent had voted for him to go, and in Brussels 53 per cent had made the same judgement. You might wonder why the Flemish, who had been so furious about the actions of King Albert, should be so supportive of his son. The answer was that the Roman Catholic Church backed Leopold, and Flanders did what the Pope asked.

Undeterred by dire warnings of what the consequences might be, Leopold announced he was coming back to Brussels. Wallonia rebelled. In the Pays Noir miners went on strike; 80,000 Wallonian workers marched on the palace and fought with royalists and police. Leopold returned anyway. Four days later, half a million Walloons walked out of their workplaces. Four days after that, police opened fire on a demonstration in Liège, killing three people. With trades unions promising a massive response and the country close to civil war, Leopold finally agreed to abdicate in favour of his son Baudouin. The crisis was averted.

The whole row had been about whether Leopold was a collaborator or not. In the end, despite five years of sifting through the evidence, Belgium could not decide one way or the other, and so it was easier just to make a clean break, start again and forget all about it. And that, perhaps, was the attitude that would come to prevail about the Nazi occupation.

But despite Van Wijnendaele's exoneration, the Ronde's reputation was, in some eyes, tarnished. In 1945 *Het Volk* (the *People*), a Ghent-based newspaper that had kept its distance from the Nazis despite having been founded to combat the spread of Marxism, decided to organise a new and untainted Flemish Classic. The race was originally called Omloop van Vlaanderen, but Van Wijnendaele took legal action, claiming it was too close to the name of his own race. The courts found in his favour. So Omloop van Vlaanderen became Omloop Het Volk. It ran under that name for the first 63 editions.

The years passed. By the late 1990s newspaper sales had begun to nosedive. In 1994 *Het Volk* was taken over by the same Brussels publisher that produced *De Standaard* and *Het Nieuwsblad*. In 2008, after decades of struggle, it folded for good. The race that it had started in opposition to the one organised by *Het Nieuwsblad* was taken over by . . . *Het Nieuwsblad*. Karel Van Wijnendaele might have allowed himself a smile at the irony, but he had died in 1961.

* * *

After leaving De Kuipke I took the train to Zottegem where I was planning to hop on another to Munkzwalm and from there walk to the course's cobbled section called the Westhoek.

Over its 198 kilometres the Omloop followed much the same route as the Ronde van Vlaanderen, taking in the *hellingen* ('little hills') of the Flemish Ardennes. These are clustered in the countryside south of Ghent between Ronse and Geraardsbergen – a little bony spine that separates Flanders from Wallonia. The chain includes Bosberg, Berendries, Oude Kwaremont, Kluisberg, Kapelmuur, Eikenmolen and the Koppenberg – the latter a hill so famous it has its own website. The names of the *hellingen* resonate with Flemish cycling fans as those of Henry V's faithful lieutenants in the Crispin's Day speech do with Englishmen.

In the past few decades there has, to my mind, been a problem in Flemish bike racing – too many races fighting over the same small area. Where the spring courses once explored every corner of Flanders – passing the hop fields of the south-west, braving the choppy winds of the coastal plain and weaving through the blossoming orchards of Limburg – they now ignore most of it and fixate instead on the famous hills and cobbles. Today's race, Dwars door Vlaanderen, E3 Harelbeke and the Ronde are all centred around pretty much the same narrow belt of land. While everybody loves the cobbled climbs of the Paterberg, Kluisberg, Oude Kwaremont and the rest, there seems to me to be a danger that over-familiarity will deaden the mystique and kill public enthusiasm. Though, to be honest, there was little sign of that yet.

Unfortunately my train from Ghent was delayed, possibly by the sheer volume of boy scouts and girl guides who insist on travelling around Belgium on the railways at weekends, and I missed my connection. Outside Zottegem station I encountered a young French couple who were looking for a bus to take them out to watch the race on the Molenberg. The Molenberg is one of the *hellingen.*

Using an assortment of books, maps and phone apps the French couple and I managed to establish which bus would take us to the Molenberg and found it waiting at its stand. The driver, a kindly ruddy-cheeked woman who looked like a northern dinner lady, spoke neither English nor French, but when I mentioned that we were looking for a stop near a restaurant called *Mechelse Koekoek* – a name that has stuck in my mind because it means Mechelen Cuckoo, which confusingly is actually a breed of chicken that originated in the Flemish city of Mechelen – she nodded, took our money and off we set.

The bus bumped and jerked through the countryside. Occasionally we passed knots of fans walking to or from some spot on the course, or saw them in the distance across the flat fields of dark earth. Every so often we'd hear the bass clatter of TV helicopter blades, the surest sign that the peloton is somewhere nearby. Eventually the driver pulled into a stop and yelled that we had arrived. We got off the bus and looked around. There was not much to see. The Mechelen Cuckoo was shut for the winter. Down the road a mile or so in the distance was a farm shop. That was about it. I looked at my watch: 12.15. I looked at the Omloop Het Nieuwsblad race timetable. I looked back at my watch, then back at the timetable in the hope I'd misread it the first time. There was no dodging it – I had three hours until the race arrived at the Molenberg.

I was not too worried, though. I imagined that this time would be spent watching the race on TV in a pleasant bar with a glass of Trappist beer and possibly a plate of *witloofrolletjes* (chicory and ham in cheese sauce). Everywhere I have ever been in Flanders there has been a nice café at the top of the hill, so, while the French couple messed about with their backpacks in what I assume was a polite way of telling me they didn't really want to spend their afternoon in the company of a man older than their fathers, I walked off up the Molenberg to find it.

The Molenberg is only 56 metres high and 463 metres long, but since its introduction into the Ronde in 1983 it's built a savage reputation for chewing up racing cyclists. Part of this is because of its steepness – 14 per cent or thereabouts at the nastiest points – and the severity of the camber, which is so pronounced the hill might have been moulded from an upturned boat, but mainly it's because of the cobbles, which are big, lumpy and rough. The French call them *pavé*, the Flemish 'children's heads', though if you've a son or daughter with a head as misshapen as the ones on the Molenberg I'd advise you to take them to the hospital right away.

The surface is what the crowds come for and, as I walked up the hill, I passed dozens of people photographing it and posting the images on Instagram in what I'd later come to think of as *pavé* porn. Cobbles were one of the defining things about Flemish bike racing, but the survival of the fillings-dislodging surfaces that had so inspired Karel Van Wijnendaele had been put in jeopardy in the 1950s by the widespread use of asphalt to resurface Belgian roads. Asphalt had actually been invented by a Belgian, Edward De Smedt, back in the 1870s. A century later it threatened irrevocably to alter the nature of cycling in Flanders, making it safer, easier, faster and, well, much more boring. Race organisers were increasingly forced to scour the Flemish countryside to find their beloved cobbles. Often these were on narrow forgotten rural lanes like the one up the Molenberg. Eventually, thanks to pressure from the Flemish cycling community, the Belgian government took action to preserve the cobbles, and many of the most famous sections are now listed as historic monuments and kept safe from modernisers.

At the top of the hill I found a farm and a paddock containing 14 donkeys. There was no café. I walked on along the road convinced there was a café somewhere just round the next corner, but there were only beet fields and Flemish cycling stewards.

The Flemish cycling steward is a singular beast, generally swaddled in a mass of clothing until he (or she) is as bulky and slow moving as a sea elephant. Their skin is weatherbeaten to the colour of Georgian brickwork. Their hair – generally white or brindle – sprouts in wiry tufts from beneath some ancient cycling cap bearing the name of a long ago disbanded local team, sponsored by a maker of rupture appliances or wooden legs. All of them wear Belgian tricolour armbands, luminous bibs and appear to communicate solely using coloured flags, paddles and whistles. You might think the whistle has a limited range of expression. Not a bit of it. In the hands of a Flemish cycling steward the whistle can communicate everything from didactic rage, via sympathetic concern, to plangent melancholy at the ageless foibles of mankind. As it was springtime it was hard to avoid forming the impression that some of the whistling had nothing to do with the races at all and was simply a trilling call for love and companionship. Certainly there's little wonder that the world's greatest ever harmonica player, Toots Thielemans, was Belgian.

Thwarted by the absence of any café, I walked in a circuit around the village of Sint-Blasius-Boekel. It was pleasant countryside, rural and rolling with snowdrops in the hedgerows and the first lambs of spring jinking about in the daisy-speckled meadows. The weather was bright and clear too, though the Omloop has a reputation for ferocious conditions – in 1971 the race was postponed for three weeks due to snow, and cancelled altogether in 1986 and 2004.

The farm shop I eventually found proved to be a rather smart place specialising in meals to reheat at home, but I managed to furnish myself with a picnic consisting of a bottle of chocolate milk, a pack of Pim's biscuits (Flanders' answer to the jaffa cake) and a bag of pickle-flavoured crisps. The elderly lady behind the counter kept looking at me out of the corner of her eye as if she expected me to snatch a brace of oven-ready quail and make a dash for the door. I'd put this down to parochial suspicion of foreigners, but then as I left I caught sight of my reflection in a fridge door. I'd put on my cyclocross bobble hat. It made me look like the sort of person you wouldn't trust around metal cutlery.

Back on the summit of the Molenberg I sat on the grass by the donkey field and ate my picnic. The races passed close by several times – you could tell by the TV helicopter – but though the Molenberg has commanding views in practically every direction you could never see the riders, who seemed always to be shielded by trees.

The Omloop might not have the prestige of the Ronde, but its position at the start of the season has always attracted foreign entrants. Fausto Coppi won the race in 1948, but was subsequently disqualified for an illegal wheel change, which gave victory to Sylvain Grysolle from Wichelen in East Flanders. It was Grysolle's only big win.

Predictably the Flemish have dominated the race: great riders such as Herman Van Springel, Raymond Impanis, Roger De Vlaeminck, Frans Verbeeck, Freddy Maertens and Johan Museeuw have all won it. A trio of Flemings have won the race three times: Peter Van Petegem, Joseph Bruyère (born in Maastricht but brought up in Belgium) and Ernest Sterckx, who'd had a football stadium in his native Westerlo named in his honour after the third victory in 1956 (it's since been pulled down).

As the race got closer a crowd rapidly assembled on the Molenberg, people arriving by bike, motorbike and on foot. The amateur cyclists who pedalled up the hill to find a good spot were generally met with applause and cries of encouragement, not all of it ironic. When one man was beaten by the incline and dismounted he was roundly booed and responded by bending down and fiddling with his gears in the manner of a footballer who's just missed a penalty walking away faking a limp. As he tinkered with his derailleur, he was overtaken by an old man in a mac, cavalry twill trousers and stout brogues, riding a very old-fashioned-looking sit-up-and-beg bike of the sort that, in the North Yorkshire of the 1960s, would have been greeted with yells of 'Get off and milk it!' The bloke standing next to me who'd recently arrived on a motorbike laughed and shook his head when the old man crossed the summit without once rising from his saddle. 'I have seen him come up the Kluisberg and the Berendries,' he said. 'And now the Molenberg. Amazing.'

'Maybe his bike has a motor in it,' I suggested.

The man shook his head. 'No,' he said seriously. 'His motor is in here,' and he thumped his fist against his chest.

The race arrived. The cobbles were a mess and the steep ascent comes after a sharp right-angle turn that slows the field practically to a halt, but it was dry and the riders appeared relatively unfazed by the obstacle, though you could see their elbows juddering from the impact of the *pavé* as they came up the slope. They were gone in a few minutes. The spectators folded up their chairs, the stewards pocketed their flags and whistles. I headed off down the slope and caught the bus back to Zottegem. In the bar opposite the station I caught the last few kilometres of the race. When Van Avermaet upset all predictions by outsprinting Sagan to win, there were throaty Flemish cheers, glasses raised and dark, foamy ale was sloshed over the heads and shoulders of everybody in the place.

3

DONKEYS AND CANNIBALS

Kuurne-Brussels-Kuurne, 26 February

The Sunday after Omloop Het Nieuwsblad loomed grey and cold. I was slightly curling around the edges. Saturday was my birthday and I'd celebrated by drinking a bottle of sparkling Flemish wine. I'd bought it from a rather grand wine merchants' in the centre of Ghent. 'Is it good?' I asked the sales assistant, who had a Bengal-striped shirt and red braces. 'Oh yes,' he replied. 'It is made at a vineyard in West Flanders and has won many prizes.' That was good enough for me so

I said I'd take a bottle. As he was wrapping it I said, 'So what prizes has it won, then?'

The sales assistant finished covering the bottle in tissue paper and handed it to me. 'Well,' he said, 'it has, for example, been voted best sparkling white wine made in Belgium two years in a row.'

I took the train south from Ghent to Kortrijk – a 40-minute trip that crossed the boundary between East and West Flanders – and then hopped on a bus to Kuurne. There were other cycling fans on it too, easily recognisable by their caps and thick clothing, and we all nodded and smiled at one another shyly like members of some secret fraternity.

The start of Kuurne–Brussels–Kuurne is at the town sports fields, behind an impressive main stand of the football ground that's home to Eendracht Kuurne. The race-team presentation was in the car park on a temporary stage made from scaffolding. It was a far lower-key affair than the start of the Omloop and to my relief there was no music. I wandered around among the fans as the riders were asked the usual senseless questions about what breed of cat they liked best and whether they preferred waffles to macaroni cheese. After perusing the stalls selling team shirts and scarves, I came across the Jasper Stuyven fan club motorhome. There was a sign in the window in English inviting people in for a chat whether they were fans of Jasper's or not. Stuyven comes from Leuven and rides for Trek–Segafredo. He won the junior world road race title in 2009, but since turning pro his major achievements had been winning Kuurne–Brussels–Kuurne in 2016 and taking a stage of the Vuelta the year before that. He was 24 and talented, but I had been surprised by his obvious popularity in Flanders, so I thought I'd go inside and ask whoever was there about why everyone liked him so much. Sadly the door was locked.

As Kuurne–Brussels–Kuurne's name suggests, when the race was first held in 1946 it went from the Kortrijk suburb to the Belgian capital and back. In the 1960s taking a bike race into Brussels became problematic because of the traffic, and Kuurne–Brussels–Kuurne was rerouted to wiggle about the Flemish Ardennes and turn around near Galmaarden, close by Ninove – for many years the finish line of the Ronde van Vlaanderen. At that time it was briefly renamed 'the Circuit of Both Flanders' (i.e., East and West) but in 1979 it went back to its original name, even though it no longer actually went to Brussels.

Brussels is a bit of a puzzle. Capital city of Belgium, and historically it is part of Flanders, a point the Flemish emphasise by holding the annual *Gordel*, a – what else? – mass bike ride round the city boundaries organised by the Flemish sports agency, Sport Vlaanderen. The *Gordel* (which means 'belt') attracts around 75,000 participants. However, the vast majority of Brussels' inhabitants speak French, even though the city is officially bilingual. In modern Belgium, Brussels is its own region. So while both the Flemish and the Walloons might have legitimate claim to it, the capital belongs to neither (indeed the presence of the European parliament often gives it the feeling of a place that belongs to nobody, like a rented flat). In recent times the impossibility of resolving ownership of Brussels has often seemed like one of the few things holding Belgium together. So, like an unhappily married couple who cannot split up simply because they can't decide which of them would have the dog, the Flemish and Walloons continue to live and bicker together under the same political roof. That, at least, is my take on it. The radio journalist who'd interviewed Eddy Planckaert put it another way: 'We can't separate – who would get custody of the Royal family?'

In cycling terms Brussels is undoubtedly part of our story, or at least one of its most famous inhabitants is. The Belgian capital has not produced many top riders, but a couple of those it has have been outstanding. One was our old friend the Basset Hound, Philippe Thys. Thys was strong and self-confident – he predicted his 1913 Tour de France victory to the press before the race began and was heard to remark, 'When I want to win no one passes.' Thys won the Tour three times (a record that was not matched until 1955 when Louison Bobet completed his hat-trick). His victories came in 1913, 1914 and 1920, and Henri Desgrange, the race's originator, organiser and patron, believed that had it not been for the interruption of World War One the Basset Hound would have added two or probably three more victories to his tally.

The other great rider from Brussels was Eddy Merckx. In the Belgian New Year Honours List of 1997 King Albert II made Merckx a baron, possibly on the grounds that a country with what the British patronisingly call a 'bicycling monarchy' needed a bicycling aristocracy to accompany it. By then Merckx was sleek and rotund. Keeping trim is a problem for the retired pro cyclist: eating 3,500 calories for breakfast is a hard habit to break. Once they slip off the saddle for the final time many riders balloon up as if somebody just pulled the ripcord on a life jacket they're wearing under their shirt.

The last time I'd seen Merckx he was standing on a podium at the start of the Ronde van Vlaanderen in 1994, looking like a killer whale in a camel-hair coat. He was easily recognisable, of course, largely due to his eyelashes. They are the longest and most luxuriant in the history of sport. Even Betty Boop envies Eddy's eyelashes.

Merckx dominated cycling in the same way Don Bradman did cricket, Wayne Gretzky ice hockey. He did so through a combination of talent and iron determination mixed with a dash of the sort of cunning that would have brought a grin to the face of Niccolò Machiavelli. Baron, with its connotations of swagger and power brutally exercised, is the perfect prefix for Eddy Merckx.

Jørgen Leth's film *Stars and Watercarriers* covers the 1973 Giro d'Italia. During the race the Spanish climber José Manuel Fuente repeatedly attempts to break Merckx's grip on the leader's pink jersey. One afternoon the little Spaniard attacks in the mountains, jumping away from the pack and building a substantial lead. The rest of the peloton refuses to give chase so eventually Merckx sets off in lone pursuit. He catches Fuente on a steep, pine-fringed incline and cycles past him without so much as a second glance. Fuente tries to respond but, like a man trapped in one of those nightmares about missing a vital appointment, no matter how hard he pedals his goal just gets further and further away. As Merckx disappears over the hill the narrator announces in stentorian tones, 'This is how Merckx deals with those who challenge him!'

There is a myth in Flemish cycling about riders from poor backgrounds, men whose bellies were never full. Merckx, in fact, came from a comfortable background. His parents owned a shop. He was born into what the French call the *petite bourgeoisie*, the same background as Georges Simenon or Hergé. Yet Merckx's hunger for victory was as great as that of any peasant farmer's child. A US football coach famously taunted a less successful rival team with the words, 'The trouble with you guys is, you've all got your own teeth.' By this index of competitiveness Merckx would have won nothing, his enamel was so glowing he might have been a missing member of the Osmonds. Yet Merckx gobbled up his rivals with such relish the press nicknamed him 'the Cannibal'.

Nor was cycling in Merckx's blood. Unlike most cycling stars Eddy had no relatives, no uncles or cousins, who raced. Having devoted his early adolescence to basketball, he came to the sport relatively late, inspired by Stan Ockers' 1955 world championship victory.

One of Merckx's greatest rivals in the 1960s and 70s was Roger De Vlaeminck from East Flanders. De Vlaeminck had dark, sunken eyes and the knot-jointed legs of some rangy marsh bird. He was nicknamed 'the Beast of Eeklo'. De Vlaeminck was fiercely Flemish. He spoke Italian, a bit of Spanish and a smattering of English, but if any journalist questioned him in French he treated them as if they did not exist. To De Vlaeminck, French was the language of the enemy. People have said De Vlaeminck's reputation for hostility was undeserved, but in my opinion it is never wise to underestimate anyone who is known as 'the Beast'.

De Vlaeminck and his brother, Erik, raced for the same Flemish team. They set out to defeat Merckx and, like many of the best Flemish riders of that era, became obsessed with this objective, sitting on the Cannibal's wheel even when he was not part of the decisive breakaway. Eventually Roger saw sense, eased off on Merckx and started to win races. Erik went back to cyclocross and, some claimed, spent time seeing a psychiatrist.

There is little doubt that Merckx was the best rider of all time. During his career he won 525 races, just under a third of all the events he entered (at his peak it was over 40 per cent). He won every one of the Monuments – Milan–San Remo, the Ronde van Vlaanderen, Paris–Roubaix, Liège–Bastogne–Liège and the Tour of Lombardy – at least twice, finishing with 19 wins in the greatest one-day Classics, eight more than his nearest rival, Roger De Vlaeminck. He was accused of being boring, of killing the sport with his remorselessness. 'What am I supposed to do?' he asked. 'Maybe I would be smarter to hold back and give the races more suspense, but I'd be less honest.'

Part of the problem was Merckx's personality – he seemed not to have one. He was polite, withdrawn, enigmatic. Unlike other great champions he was not arrogant or aloof, but simply unknowable. He appeared to have no need for friendship. The Flemish rider Johan De Muynck called him 'the stranger in the peloton'.

Perhaps there was a reason for his reticence. Merckx's upbringing was comfortable but there was darkness in his family's past. In 1944 in the village of Meensel-Kiezegem a member of the local fascist Zwarte Brigade (Black Brigade) was walking to the parish fair when he got in an argument. In the ensuing fracas the man was stabbed to death. His mother called on the authorities to take action. The following day a force of 300 men drawn from the Vlaamse Wacht (the Flemish Guard, a paramilitary police force set up by the Nazis – Wallonia had its own equivalents, including the Rexist militia, infamous for their part in the Courcelles Massacre of August 1944), the German SS and the Gestapo entered the village. Three suspected members of the resistance were shot, houses were burned and 76 villagers shipped off to concentration camps. Only five of them returned. The man whose slaying had provoked this grisly massacre was Gaston Merckx. He was Eddy's uncle.

Merckx rode for Molteni. It was an Italian team, sponsored by a Lombard salami-maker, but its heart was Belgian. Eddy was aided by Flemings Jozef Spruyt from Viersel, Jos Huysmans from Beerzel and Joseph Bruyère, the Dutch-speaking Belgian cyclist born in Maastricht. After the Cannibal arrived, the Italian *directeur sportif*, Giorgio Albani, was fired and Lomme Driessens, who hailed from Flemish Brabant, brought in. Driessens had a reputation as a cycling huckster, a flim-flam man with a gift for concocting entertaining stories. Driessens got into team management by claiming to have been Fausto Coppi's *soigneur* and personal manager. In truth he seems to have done nothing more for *Il Campionissimo* than manage his travel arrangements on the rare occasions the Italian raced in Flanders. Whatever, Driessens parlayed this fib into one job after another and would become one of the most influential, and infamous, team directors of the 1960s, 70s and 80s. Those who didn't like Driessens, and there were plenty among the big names of Flemish cycling, called him 'Lomme the Liar'. Journalists, who will forgive just about anything for an attention-grabbing quote, loved Driessens – he was good copy. So much so that some sportswriters suggested that his chief purpose at Molteni was to try to make Merckx appear less machine-like, more lovable. It didn't work. Merckx – who as far as anyone could tell didn't much care for Driessens – carried methodically on, burying opponents and burning out his teammates (looking after Merckx on the road was hard work – his *domestiques* rarely lasted more than two or three seasons). Among cycling fans he was admired and respected, but never loved.

In *Stars and Watercarriers* an Italian rider briefly takes over the filmmaker's microphone during a dull stage and begins interviewing his fellow racers. Riding up to Merckx he asks, 'Eddy, isn't it possible for you to ease up and let somebody else win every once in a while?'

Merckx, smiling, replies in immaculate Italian, 'I hear what your complaint is, but I am indifferent to it,' and pedals away. With such hauteur it was clear Eddy Merckx was a baron long before the Belgian king recognised the fact.

* * *

Up by the start line of Kuurne–Brussels–Kuurne there was the usual semi-organised chaos as pro riders warming up for the race found themselves tangled up with amateur riders in full kit who'd come to watch, spectators who fancied a photo, and old ladies from the adjoining housing estates who were out walking their dogs and were not going to let an international sporting event interrupt them. It seems amazing that professional sportsmen will put up with it when they are supposed to be preparing to race. But then the start is more or less symbolic; the actual racing begins later – a notion that was conclusively proved when the starter's gun was fired and most of the riders carried on chatting and adjusting their kit for 30 seconds before bothering to set off, which seemed a bit rude.

I wasn't really concentrating myself, though, as I'd been distracted by a small Slovak boy dressed in full Peter Sagan gear, including a Bora–Hansgrohe team jersey so big it trailed along the ground. With his dark hair and jug ears he put me in mind of Mickey Mouse in *The Sorcerer's Apprentice*. I'd see the little lad and his parents – the father brandishing a Slovak flag – at every race Sagan took part in thereafter.

After the peloton had finally decided to go I looked around for an old man in a cycling cap to follow. In the past locating one had proved useful for following a race, because they generally know all the short cuts to get you to the next point on the course the peloton passes in the quickest possible time. Of course it doesn't always work. Once at Paris–Roubaix my mate Steve and I followed an old bloke in a Saint Raphaël cap into what turned out to be his back garden. Since his wife had plainly invited the extended family round for a barbecue this proved more embarrassing than it might have been. Though as Steve said, it could have been worse, they might have been nudists.

This time I fixed my sights on an old boy with bandy legs, a beige golf jacket and a faded Mapei–GB cap who seemed intent on getting somewhere in a hurry. I walked along 20 yards behind him looking for signs that he was eager to watch the next bit of a bike race rather than just find the nearest urinal. We weaved through side roads past terraced houses with window displays of nodding dogs, waving lucky cats and plastic mother-in-law's tongues, and down bin-lined back alleys, and finally arrived at a wide main street with a bakery and a chocolatier's on it, at which point the old man halted, took his team sheet from one pocket and a pencil from the other and looked at his watch.

I did the same. Like the Omloop, Kuurne–Brussels–Kuurne has often been badly affected by the weather. It's been cancelled three times – in 1986, 1993 and 2013. The 2010 edition of the race was one of the most brutal bike rides in Flemish history, thanks to the intervention of Cyclone Xynthia, the tail end of which whacked into northern Belgium bringing gale-force winds and thrashing rain. Of the 195 starters that day only 26 finished the race, which was shortened by 20 kilometres because of fallen trees blocking the route on the Knokteberg (aka Côte de Trieu) climb. It would be nice to report that a rugged Flemish rider won the race, but it was Dutchman Bobbie Traksel. In fact the Flemish acquitted themselves pretty poorly, only Davy Commeyne from Roeselare finishing in the top ten.

The old man and I had been standing on the pavement for less than five minutes when a cluster of stewards appeared, followed, coincidentally, by a dozen men on vintage mopeds who buzzed down a side street to Kuurne's main square, where they parked up and disappeared into a café.

The peloton soon passed us, the riders still chatting to one another as if they were out on a club run. When the car with the flag marking the back of the race went by, the old boy in the Mapei cap put his pen and his team sheet away and sauntered off up the street. I took this as a sign that the race had left Kuurne until later in the day and went off to find the bus. On the way I passed a luxury gin bar named Donky Shot, a big statue of a donkey, and several shops with pictures of donkeys in their windows.

Practically every small town in Flanders has an abusive nickname that's been given to them by another nearby town. The people of Poperinge are known as something that loosely translates as 'the Numbskulls' because they'd insisted on producing linen long after the market for it had collapsed. The people from Wilrijk near Antwerp are called 'the Goatheads' because of alleged failure to detect fraud in a local council election. The citizens of Leuven are called 'the Cow-Shooters' in honour of an incident in 1619 when nervous sentries mistook a herd of cattle for an invading French army, while those from Mechelen are dubbed 'the Moon-Extinguishers' in honour of an incident in the seventeenth century in which a combination of mist and moonlight convinced the locals that the tower of St Rumbold's Cathedral was on fire. People from Kuurne are called 'the Donkeys'. The name dates back to the days when the citizens of the little town grew vegetables and delivered them to Kortrijk early in the morning. The sound of their clogs on the cobbles woke up the townsfolk and they apparently shouted, 'Oh God, it's those asses from Kuurne.' What started out as an insult has now been embraced perhaps a little too warmly by the people of Kuurne and there's barely a business in the place that doesn't have some imagery of Ambroos the Donkey (named after a poem by Hugo Claus) on its signage. Donkeys, I should add, are very popular all across Flanders. Tom Boonen even has one as a pet. Her name's Kamiel.

Eventually I found a bus stop and was soon back in Kortrijk again.

During the Middle Ages Kortrijk had grown wealthy as a cloth manufacturing hub and a centre of the Flemish flax trade. It was famous for tapestries and rugs and, even today, if you're standing on a top-quality wool carpet anywhere in Europe there's a fair chance it came from

Kortrijk. Though it isn't as pretty as Bruges, as fashionable as Antwerp or as generally groovy as Ghent, I have a lot of affection for Kortrijk. In 1998 I'd come to the city for some rest and recuperation after four weeks covering the World Cup in France. 'Leaving France to holiday in Flanders?' my journalistic colleagues sneered. 'Are you crackers?' But Kortrijk fully justified my decision. It was delightfully strange. I came across a poster promoting an ice lolly with the arresting English name 'Big Nuts'; my tourist map carried an advert for a nightclub that boasted 'dining, dancing, dominoes'; I saw a child wearing a t-shirt emblazoned with the scarred and scary face of Marc Wilmots, star of the Belgian national football team – a man whose Flemish nickname is 'the Fighting Pig'; and a store selling glitzy designer dresses from Versace and La Croix was right next door to a dilapidated poodle parlour named, in English, 'Doggy Do'. There was a wig shop that offered a student discount; a tailor with a sign that beckoned 'this way for 500 trousers'; and a garden centre sandwiched between a strip club and a hostess bar. There was also lots of great beer and big portions of tasty food too.

I had some more after I got off the bus – a big dish of fish and prawns in creamy white wine sauce with a massive bowl of chips, plus a *coupe dame blanche*. The coffee came with a small jug of single cream and glass dish of whipped cream and several squares of chocolate. Sometimes during my stay in Flanders I wondered if I might not have traces of blood in my cholesterol.

After lunch I waddled off to have a look around the Museum of the Battle of the Golden Spurs. The Battle of the Golden Spurs is to the Flemish what Agincourt is to the English, Bunker Hill to Americans. The county of Flanders had been a semi-autonomous region of France since the ninth century, but in the first few years of the fourteenth century there was a growing movement for independence. When the Flemish rose up, the king of France, Philip IV, sent an army to crush them. The two sides met on the boggy water meadows outside Kortrijk on 11 July 1302. The Flemish army was largely made up of foot militia drawn from the local peasantry. The French force was led by 2,000 armoured knights drawn from the ranks of the nobility, mounted on huge warhorses, lavishly equipped and proverbially arrogant.

Pieter de Coninck, one of the leaders of the rebels, was the archetypal Fleming: stocky, rough-edged, stubborn, tough as teak and as down to earth as, well, a donkey. If he'd been born six centuries later he'd have been one of the local boys riding 'Valentino' Pélissier off his wheel, spraying mud in his handsome Gallic face. As it was he was fighting the blue-blooded French knights on foot armed with a weapon called a *goedendag*. The *goedendag* was a four-foot-long wooden pole with a heavy round steel head capped with a six-inch spike. You could stab or club with it. It was a weapon for men of strength and grim purpose, there was no finesse to using it. In Dutch *goedendag* means 'good day'. The name supposedly originated during the infamous Bruges Matins massacre, which preceded the Battle of the Golden Spurs. On 18 May 1302, Flemish rebels took over Bruges and marched around greeting everyone they met, killing anyone who replied with a French accent. When Samuel L. Jackson announced his intention to 'get medieval on your ass' in *Pulp Fiction*, this was the sort of stuff he had in mind. At the Battle of the Golden Spurs the French knights did what they always did – charged head on at the enemy in the expectation of sweeping them away. The Flemish, however, refused to budge. The battle became a slogging match, a gruelling test of stamina, strength and will on increasingly sludgy ground. This naturally suited the Flemish. After hours of fighting they prevailed. Over a thousand French knights were killed, their gilded accoutrements carried off as trophies by the victorious Flemings. It was the first time in history that mounted knights had been defeated by foot soldiers, a victory to ring down the ages. But, like Agincourt, it ultimately achieved nothing. The French returned a couple of years later and battered the rebels into submission. The Flemish once again found themselves under French rule and into the bargain were, humiliatingly, forced to pay a massive fine to the king of France. Over the centuries the county of Flanders would be tossed about from the French to the Burgundians, to the Spanish, then the Austrians, back to the French and on to the Netherlands until finally becoming part of Belgium. Foreign armies would march into Flanders and march out again leaving piles of dead behind, the soil fertile with blood, and the names of Flemish towns decorating the battle honours of their regiments. The victory outside Kortrijk remained throughout those times a glimmer of hope, lasting proof of what the Flemish could achieve. Indeed, the Battle of the Golden Spurs forms the centrepiece of Hendrik Conscience's novel *The Lion of Flanders*. The anniversary of the battle – now a Flemish national holiday – would become a rallying point for the patriotic movement that emerged in the late nineteenth century and found such a staunch supporter in Karel Van Wijnendaele. Cycling, as George Orwell almost said, is war minus the *goedendag*s.

After I'd looked round the excellent museum, and noted the comment by one outraged French visitor that the Bruges Matins – treated with some relish in the exhibition – was actually an act of 'ethnic cleansing' and not something to be celebrated, it was nearly time for the junior edition of Kuurne–Brussels–Kuurne to pass through the city.

I walked back into the town centre along the river Leie, past the Broel Towers that flanked a medieval bridge. There was a small toyshop where, 20 years before, I'd bought my daughter a little wooden doll with red hair, which stood on the mantelpiece in her bedroom for years. Glancing in the window at the soft toys I felt suddenly overwhelmed by the passing of time, the transience of existence and the looming spectre of death. Luckily I was dragged back from the brink of despair by the peep-peeping of the stewards' whistles.

As the race grew gradually nearer, its imminent arrival signalled by the rising pitch of the trilling, I found myself standing next to a small lady in her seventies who wore batwing glasses and a bronze-coloured down jacket that looked like it had been inflated with a foot pump. If you'd stuck a pin in it she'd have whizzed round the Grote Markt like a pricked balloon. She had white hair that had been given some kind of bronze rinse so that it glowed slightly in the grim light. She spoke to me in Flemish and when I explained to her I was English, blushed and covered her mouth, flustered by this unexpected turn of events. The juniors swished by and the old lady nodded with satisfaction at their efforts and went back into an apartment building above a swanky gents' outfitters selling expensive Italian suits.

With time to spare before the race proper came through I went off to get a drink at the Gainsbar, possibly the only temple of beer in the world named in honour of Serge Gainsbourg.

Though Kuurne–Brussels–Kuurne takes in around half a dozen hills in the Flemish Ardennes – all of which also feature in the Ronde – the last climb is over 50 kilometres from the finish and the race is generally won by a sprinter. Kuurne–Brussels–Kuurne doesn't have the prestige of the Omloop, it's only categorised as a semi-Classic, but a look at the list of winners demonstrates how seriously it's taken. There are a lot of big names on it: Jef Planckaert, Noël Foré, Eric Leman, Roger De Vlaeminck, Walter Planckaert, Museeuw, Boonen.

Less well known than any of these is the winner of the 1954 race, Leon Van Daele, a rider who, inadvertently, had a profound impact on the history of Flemish cycling. Van Daele came from Ruddervoorde in West Flanders. He won Kuurne–Brussels–Kuurne in 1954, was Flemish champion in 1956, and he took Paris–Brussels in 1957. He was still only 24 and his future looked bright. Then, in 1958, he joined Faema–Guerra (a team sponsored by the makers of an espresso machine). Faema–Guerra was the team of Rik Van Looy. In fact Van Looy pretty much was Faema–Guerra.

Van Looy, the Emperor of Herentals, was born in December 1933. He built his reputation as an amateur riding in the town *kermises*. He'd started aged 14. Even though he was an amateur, he was allowed to keep his prize money. The big teams didn't pay much attention to the results, but Rik measured success by his wallet, which got thicker and thicker. 'I needed money badly,' he'd say later. 'My parents were modest people. They could not afford to let me stay on at school so I went to work aged 13. I was just a lad with no skills of any type, so I got the only job I could – bicycle delivery boy for a newsagent.'

The bike was big, old-fashioned and heavy. Van Looy thought it must have weighed 50 pounds. It was fitted with a single gear, one so big the teenage Van Looy sometimes found pushing the bike easier than riding it. He persevered, though remained too nervous to ask his boss for a bigger sprocket. His idol was his namesake Rik Van Steenbergen, winner of the Ronde in 1944 and 1946. He had pictures of the great rider plastered all over his bedroom. In Herentals people knew of his obsession and when he wobbled past on the big bike they'd yell as if in radio commentary, 'Oh look, here comes Rik at a sprint . . . he's left the field far behind . . . he's closing on the line . . .' and other such witticisms. Later Van Looy would wonder whether his first name wasn't the thing that made him a rider. 'If my parents had called me something different things might not have worked out the way they did. The teasing didn't make me angry, it made me thoughtful. Why shouldn't I be a second Rik Van Steenbergen?' He saved up the tips he earned doing deliveries and bought a proper racing machine. Later he'd credit that big delivery bike with being his inspiration and building up his leg muscles.

Van Looy had an insatiable appetite for victory. Like Merckx he always rode to win. Even at his peak he would turn up for the post-Tour de France *kermis* races not simply to pocket his appearance money, as other big names did, but to carry off the cash prize too: 'Some riders think I shouldn't try in these races and let them have the cake. But for me to ride in that manner would mean I was no longer interested in cycling.' Van Looy would rather sit at home than race at half-throttle.

As an amateur Van Looy crossed the finish line first 113 times. As a pro between 1954 and 1969 he won 377 races at an average of 24 victories a year. Van Looy was the first rider ever to win all five Monuments, the first to win the eight great Classics (in those days considered to be the Monuments plus Paris–Brussels, Paris–Tours and the Flèche Wallonne). He was 23 when he won his first, the 1956 Paris–Brussels, and 35 when he took his last, the Flèche Wallonne in 1968. He was world champion twice. Originally Van Looy was known as Rik II (Van Steenbergen being Rik I) but as the victories piled up, surpassing those of his boyhood idol, he became 'the Emperor'. He might have gone down in history as the greatest Classics rider of all time but then, just as his career was winding down and he was thinking of retirement to the riding stables he'd had built near Herentals, Merckx appeared and started smashing all the records he'd set to smithereens.

Despite his success, Van Looy was not without his critics. Some felt he was a 'wheelsucker', constantly drafting, profiting from the work of others, relying on his sprint too much. He does not dominate like a true champion, his critics said. But that was not strictly true. In the 1962 edition of Paris–Roubaix, 'the Hell of the North', considered the hardest race on the calendar, Van Looy rode away and left all his rivals trailing far behind. He could do it if he wanted to, he seemed to be saying, he simply chose not to.

Van Looy was good-looking, always had time for the fans, and led his team in an autocratic manner. The Emperor won races and his teammates helped him. In return the Emperor distributed the prize money as he saw fit. Some journalists said that he was generous. The English rider Vin Denson, who spent 1965 in Van Looy's team, took a different view: 'When money went into Van Looy's pocket it never came out again.' Later he'd summarise more succinctly: 'Van Looy was a complete bastard.'

Leon Van Daele joined Van Looy at Faema–Guerra in 1958. But he clearly didn't understand the role of servant. In his first season – his first spring: Paris–Roubaix – the Emperor entered the velodrome in a breakaway group of four. Van Steenbergen and the Spaniard Miguel Poblet were with him, so was Van Daele. Van Looy licked his lips as his teammate lead out the sprint, but instead of pulling aside to let his captain hit the front Van Daele simply kept on going, leaving everyone else behind, raising his arms aloft in triumph as he crossed the line. Van Looy was furious. The Emperor was sleek and handsome and had been raised near Antwerp, a place the locals refer to without a hint of irony simply as 'the Metropolis'; Van Daele was a tall, horse-faced nobody from the West Flanders boondocks. How dare he? For his act of *lèse-majesté* Van Daele was kicked off the Faema–Guerra team.

This action was to have major consequences for Flemish bike racing. Van Daele might have been *persona non grata* at Faema–Guerra, but he had an influential fan – Aimé Claeys, owner of Flandria bicycles, whose original brandname, 'the West Flanders Lion', might have served as Van Daele's sobriquet. Claeys' firm had begun life at the family blacksmith's in Zedelgem before moving to a factory in Warneton near the French border. Aimé Claeys was eager to promote his bicycles in France, and the sudden availability of Van Daele persuaded him to start his own racing team. Van Daele was his main man, and he was soon joined by the aged Briek Schotte who came in as team captain and manager. Iron Briek Schotte would continue in the role at Flandria for close to a decade. Schotte was beloved but old-fashioned, and younger Flandria riders such as Roger De Vlaeminck and Jempi Monseré took to mimicking his rasping West Flanders accent and lampooning his habit of always referring back to the 1940s. When Briek said, 'In my day all we ate was grapebread,' it was all they could do not to burst into hysterics. De Vlaeminck would later wish he'd been more respectful. Monseré died too young to get the chance for regrets.

In 1959 the new Flandria team won 44 races, with Van Daele taking Ghent–Wevelgem and finishing third in Milan–San Remo. In 1961 he'd share victory with Fred De Bruyne (a rider with six great Classics victories to his name) in Kuurne–Brussels–Kuurne when the officials couldn't separate the pair in the photo finish. Unfortunately for Van Daele, as Flandria's success mounted so did the team budget. By the following year Flandria were so wealthy they were able to hire the greatest rider of the era, Rik Van Looy. And that, naturally enough, signalled the end of Leon Van Daele at Flandria.

* * *

With 15 minutes to go before the front runners of Kuurne–Brussels–Kuurne headed into Kortrijk for a three-lap circuit of the town, I finished my glass of Noir de Dottignies and went back to the spot I'd picked for the junior race. I was soon joined by my friend in the bronze anorak. She'd plainly been following the race on TV because, as she emerged from her front door, she looked at me and gave me a big toothy grin then shrilled, 'Jasper Stuyven! Jasper Stuyven!'

Sure enough Stuyven arrived a few seconds ahead of a small chasing group. The old lady got so excited as she watched him coming she began bouncing up and down on the balls of her feet and waving a hand in the air like a child at infant school who knows the answer to the teacher's question. As Stuyven passed she stepped out onto the road and yelled encouragement into his ear, then disappeared back into her apartment again. When she returned for the second circuit her mood was less exuberant. Stuyven had been swallowed up by a chasing pack that included Peter Sagan. When they swished by in a waft of sweat and embrocation fumes she still called encouragement at her hero, but there was a touch of nervous desperation in it. The old lady knew bike racing – she must have realised that Stuyven's failed breakaway had cooked him. There was a fair gap between the lead group and the main field and when a Trek–Segafredo team car pulled over opposite us, the old lady scuttled across the road and started speaking animatedly to the driver. I couldn't tell if she was asking him for information or giving him instructions on tactics, but I'm inclined to think it was the latter.

After the race passed through Kortrijk for the final time the old lady shook her head as if to rid herself of the madness, nodded at me and said politely, '*Dag, Mijn Herr,*' before returning to her home. I smiled as

I watched her go. To me this enthusiastic and knowledgeable old lady embodied everything that is great about Flemish bike racing.

I went off to watch the remainder of the race on TV in a bar attached to a bowling alley. Sagan proved too strong and fast for Stuyven and won the sprint comfortably. Afterwards he was presented with a big cuddly donkey then sat astride it quaffing from a goblet of beer the size of a man's head. Sagan is impressively hairy – not in some groomed hipster kind of way, but like a bass player from the Allman Brothers Band circa 1971. I imagine that if you got close to him he'd smell of patchouli oil and cheesecloth. He's a big man too, over six foot and muscular. If the Slovaks have a word for *flahute* then he'd define it.

4

A WEDNESDAY IN HELL

Le Samyn, 1 March

Le Samyn is a bit of an oddity. It's a Flemish-style race in the middle of the Flanders Classics season that takes place in Wallonia. It's down in Hainaut too, a province of Belgium rarely touched by bike races.

Le Samyn starts in a town called Quaregnon on the fringes of Mons and finishes in the aptly named Dour, a former coalmining town ringed with slag heaps. The route takes the riders out of the industrial wastes to the pretty farming country east of Ronse – a scene of much cycling acrimony, as we shall shortly see – around an area of short sharp gradients

84

known as the Pays de Collines, 'the Land of Little Hills', and then back again to coal country. For much of the route the roads are narrow, there are nasty crosswinds and the late-February weather can be cruel (the race was cancelled by blizzards in 1988 and 2005 – and, unlike British trains, bike races don't generally stop just because of a bit of weather) and to top that off there are 16 sections of cobbles. All of which has led to the race being dubbed '*Petit* Paris–Roubaix', though the hilly sections also suggest that, if not quite a Little Ronde, then it might certainly be a Diminutive Omloop Het Nieuwsblad.

It's not a well-known race, and the first prize in 2017 was just 8,000 euros (the winner of Paris–Roubaix gets 30,000), while the riders filling the bottom half of the top 20 get a couple of hundred each, but Le Samyn's hardness has given it a certain allure, especially for those with Paris–Roubaix aspirations. The list of winners includes Robbie McEwan, Herman Van Springel, Marc Demeyer and current Belgian champion, hero of Wallonia and three times Belgian Sportsman of the Year, Philippe Gilbert.

Another rider who'd won the race was Claude Criquielion, who came from nearby Lessines, birthplace of René Magritte. We'll return to the late lamented Criquie in a bit, because this seems like a good time to ponder the French-speaking half of Belgium's involvement in bike racing. Wallonia is home to Belgium's second oldest bike race, Liège–Bastogne–Liège (or Luik–Bastenaken–Luik as the Flemish call it), one of the five Monuments and, until recently at least, a race of equal prestige to the Ronde van Vlaanderen. Despite all this, pro riders from Wallonia are almost as scarce as those from Flanders are abundant. But that hasn't always been the case. Back in the early days of cycling the Walloons produced almost as many top-class competitors as the Flemish. Firmin Lambot from Florennes in Namur stands alongside Philippe Thys (who indeed lived in Florennes for much of his life) and Sylveer Maes as one of the greatest Belgian riders of the inter-war years. Lambot won his first Tour de France in 1919. France had barely recovered from the carnage of the Great War, only 67 riders entered and the road surfaces were so appalling only 11 of those finished. It was the first Tour where the yellow jersey was worn by the race leader (officially anyway – Thys claims he was given a yellow shirt to wear when he led the race in 1914) and Lambot was the first man to win it. The Walloon ace was said to lack star quality but was doughty, durable, canny on his bike and shrewd off it – the first rider ever to secure sponsorship from outside cycling, he was paid by the Kub brewery. He was helped to victory by a friend of his from Florennes, Léon Scieur, who finished fourth.

The 1920 Tour was completely dominated by Belgians, none of them Flemish. Thys won by nearly an hour, ahead of Hector Heusghem (from Ransart, a suburb of Charleroi). Lambot and Scieur (who'd won that year's Liège–Bastogne–Liège) were third and fourth. Another Walloon, Émile Masson, came fifth. Masson's son, Émile Masson Jr, born in the Province of Liège, would win the Flèche Wallonne in 1938, Paris–Roubaix in 1939 and the Belgian championship in 1946 and 1947.

The following year the Walloons continued to do well. The Charleroi-based Louis 'Iron Man' Mottiat (a double winner of Liège–Bastogne–Liège) won the stage into Le Havre, Scieur took the yellow jersey at Brest, Heusghem won the stage into Luchon and Mottiat the two stages after that. In blistering heat the race often slowed to touring pace and Scieur held on to the yellow jersey all the way to Paris. He was a huge man – memorably described as being 'as strong as steel and as healthy as a fish' – who it was said had not learned to ride a bicycle until he was 22 years old and then only because his mate Lambot had pushed him into it. He did well in most of the stages and at the end of the race took home a large pot of money, which he used to buy a garage and a coal haulage business. Heusghem came second, and a third Walloon, Hector Tiberghien from Hainaut, was fifth. He'd go one better in 1923.

Firmin Lambot won for a second time in 1922 at the ripe old age of 36 (he remains the oldest man ever to win the Tour), Masson took a couple of stages, Heusghem briefly wore the yellow jersey and the former coalminer Félix Sellier (from Spy) finished third. He'd win Paris–Roubaix three years later.

And for reasons that are hard to fathom, that was the end of the Walloons' golden era. Not that they didn't still produce the odd exceptional rider. Back when I first started going to races in Belgium in the 1990s Frank Vandenbroucke was the rising star. There were posters of him in chip shops and bars, t-shirts with his face on for sale at market stalls, old ladies had stickers proclaiming their devotion to him plastered on their shopping trolleys. FVB, as he was known throughout the country, had rock-star looks, raw talent and a cycling pedigree – his uncle Jean-Luc had finished third in the Ronde van Vlaanderen and won the prestigious Grand Prix des Nations time trial in 1980. Frank was born in Mouscron across the border from Roubaix, but grew up in Ploegsteert, a tiny enclave of Hainaut surrounded by West Flanders. He may have been a Francophone but his surname was Flemish and he was popular with fans on both sides of the divide. During a tumultuous career he won Liège–Bastogne–Liège, Ghent–Wevelgem, the Scheldeprijs, Paris–Nice and the points jersey in the Vuelta. Everything he did was compromised, however. Afflicted by a personality disorder, addicted to cocaine, Vandenbroucke failed numerous drug tests, saw his marriage fall apart, was disowned by the cycling establishment, attempted suicide and ended up dead of a pulmonary embolism aged 34.

And so to Claude Criquielion, a rider whose career was arguably best remembered not for the races he won, but for the one that he didn't. He was world champion in 1984, won the Flèche Wallonne twice and was the only Wallonian rider ever to have won the Ronde van Vlaanderen. It was the events in Ronse, West Flanders in the world championship road race of 1988 that people tended to remember, though. Criquielion was part of a two-man break with Canadian Steve Bauer. With only a few hundred metres to go and the two riders sprinting hell-for-leather towards the line, Bauer appeared to lean across and flick an elbow at

Criquielion, sending him into the barriers. The Walloon fell in a tangled heap. In an instant all the animosity between French- and Dutch-speaking Belgians was forgotten and the whole crowd began to howl and boo. Bauer did not profit from the crash; distracted, he allowed the Italian Maurizio Fondriest to burst through and take gold. Criquielion, meanwhile, picked himself up and, plainly fuming at what he saw as a direct act of cheating, refused to remount his bike. Instead, to wild cheers and the chanting of his name from the united Belgians, he dragged it across the line with one hand, waving the other in protest. Bauer was disqualified and had to be given police protection from enraged Belgian fans. Criquie threatened to sue him for $1.5 million, but his case came to nothing. The rage did not abate, however, and for decades afterwards Belgian fans turned up at races across Europe with banners calling for justice for their wronged idol. He died in 2015 without ever getting any.

This wasn't the only controversy there'd been at a world championship in Ronse. Back in 1963 Rik Van Looy had been looking for a third world championship victory to add to those of 1960 and 1961. The circuit for the race was flat as a pancake, ideal for the Emperor, and the powerful Belgian team seemed bound to help him gain a record-breaking third gold. What happened during the race has been the cause of discussion in Flanders ever since. No two people seem able to agree on what it all meant, or what motivated the protagonists. The facts are fairly simple, though. Over the last two miles a group of 28 riders were bunched together travelling at a speed of around 50kph. Attacks came and went but nobody seemed capable of splitting the bunch. Van Looy was somewhere in the middle and as the finish approached began making his way up towards the front, apparently feeling a little peeved at the lack of help he was getting from his teammates.

As the group entered the last 400 metres, Van Looy switched to his big gear and began forcing his way through the pack. He hit the front with 200 metres remaining. Sitting immediately behind him was another Flemish rider, Benoni Beheyt. The pair burned off the chasers, but as Van Looy began to ease up as the finish line approached, composing himself, perhaps visualising his victory lap in front of an adoring public, Beheyt suddenly kicked again and pulled up next to him. Shocked, Van Looy moved across the road to try to cut off the attack. He was too late. Beheyt slid past to take gold.

That at least is the basic story. Tommy Simpson claimed in his autobiography that Beheyt had grabbed Van Looy's jersey and pulled him back, a view that film footage appears to confirm (though it's such a faint tug even a Premiership footballer wouldn't fall down from it). Others felt Beheyt had simply had a rush of blood to the head, forgotten that he was supposed to be working for Van Looy, and seized a victory that seemed to have fallen into his lap. Film of the aftermath shows Beheyt looking strangely subdued for a man who'd just won a world title. Even on the podium he looks uncomfortable and embarrassed. Perhaps he realised he had driven a nail through his own foot?

Beheyt was a decent rider. He'd been a member of the Belgian team at the 1960 Olympics and had won the 1963 edition of Ghent–Wevelgem. In 1964 he'd win a stage of the Tour de France, take victory in the Tour of Belgium and win the Belgian national championships. That was his last year of victories, however. He rode for another four seasons but won nothing of any significance in any of them. It's alleged Van Looy made it known he would look unfavourably on any promoters who hired Beheyt. The appearance fees for track meets and *kermises* that pro cyclists relied on to make a living dried up. So did opportunities on the road as the Emperor tightened the screws on the peloton. Eventually Beheyt got the message and quit the sport aged just 27. Beheyt came from Zwijnaarde, a village just outside Ghent. Most villages in Flanders that had produced a world champion would have made something of it, but Beheyt doesn't even feature on the village website. The Emperor had airbrushed him out of history.

And if you're wondering what the story of Benoni Beheyt has to do with Le Samyn, stick around because there's a twist.

I set off for the unbeautiful south of Belgium from Ghent early on Wednesday morning. It was bone-chillingly cold and wet, a stiff wind skimming water off the surface of puddles and slapping you across the cheeks with it. It had been like that for three days. The fields of Flanders were filled with pools of water, the earth so sodden it seemed like it was melting back into the sea, the sky so heavy it appeared that it had been raining for ever and would continue doing so until the end of time. On the outskirts of Brussels damp rooks stalked about the watery fields like the harbingers of doomsday. The roads were as slick as vinyl, overflowing dykes and streams blending seamlessly with the land they were supposed to drain. It looked like a scene painted by the Ghent-born expressionist Albert Servaes. Servaes was born in 1883 and, like his fellow artists Gustave Van de Woestijne and Valerius De Saedeleer, came to be associated with the Flemish nationalist movement. His canvases are thick and murky, black and brown renditions of Flemish pastoral scenes in which bent-backed peasants toil in grey, sucking soil, or bow before faceless priests in rain-swept graveyards. They are so grim and tormented they make Edvard Munch look like *Toy Story*. I had always thought they were overwrought, but now I saw that if anything they were unrealistically uplifting.

At Brussels I changed onto a train bound for Quiévrain, a town on the French border that had once been on the main road from Paris to Brussels, leading some sarky French people to refer to Belgium as '*outre Quiévrain*'. The rain continued to fall as remorselessly as if Hemingway had written it.

Le Samyn was created in 1968 as the Grand Prix de Fayt-le-Franc, named after the municipality in which it started and finished. In 1970 it was renamed Le Samyn in honour of the winner of that first race, José Samyn, who died in an accident the previous year. José Samyn was born in Quiévrain, though he had French nationality through his father. He'd done his national service in France and won the French military cycling championship while he was doing it, which perhaps explains why the French territorial army team traditionally take part in the race.

José Samyn was a controversial figure. He'd won a stage of the Tour de France in 1967 and was tipped for great things, but in 1968 – the season he'd won the race named in his honour – he became the first rider ever to be expelled from the Tour for failing a doping test. He was suspended for two months. He came back strongly and joined the BIC team of Jacques Anquetil, but died after colliding with a programme-seller during a post-Tour *kermis* at Zingem in East Flanders in August 1969. He was 23.

Samyn wasn't the only promising rider of his generation to die young. The day before travelling south I'd gone over to Roeselare. In the town centre the rain whipped and lashed and the music traditionally played through speakers in Belgian shopping streets was mercifully blotted out by the rattling of signs and the sound of beer cans skittering down gutters. It took me several attempts to find the National Cycling Museum and when I did it was closed for renovation. By then I was so wet I fully expected that when I removed my hat a fish would fall out. I wiped the rain from my eyes and flung it aside indignantly like Oliver Hardy after Stan Laurel has emptied a bucket over him. I was about to mutter a string of xenophobic insults when I noticed the sign directing visitors to the temporary museum site in nearby Paterskirke.

The soaking proved worth it. The exhibition, *Cycling is a Religion*, was really wonderful: ingenious, creative, bold, tragic, ironic and just a little bit insane. The church setting was put to brilliant use. A wall of cycling jerseys acted as the altarpiece, the cross was made from bicycles, the communion chalices were cycling trophies and the Stations of the Cross marked with large photographs of incidents from bike races. My favourite was station number eight, *Jesus Meets the Women of Jerusalem*, which featured an old lady kissing a youthful Eddy Merckx. There were acknowledgements of the greatness of cycling, the suffering, the sacrifice, the glory, but also the sin. They had Tommy Simpson's world champion's rainbow jersey, a confessional box playing film of Lance Armstrong's interview with Oprah Winfrey, and a bicycle ridden by the heroic Jules Van Hevel, a Belgian army cycle messenger who in 1917 had been sent to convalesce in Britain after sustaining severe injuries on the Western Front and recovered sufficiently to twice win the Molinari Cup, a track race held at Stamford Bridge. Over in one corner of the church was a cabinet devoted to the life and career of Jean-Pierre 'Jempi' Monseré, the young Flandria rider who'd taken the Mickey out of Briek Schotte. Despite his French-sounding name, Jempi Monseré was a Fleming, the son of a factory worker raised in Krottegem, a rough working-class district of Roeselare near the Rodenbach brewery. He was given his first bike when he was 12 and soon showed that he had a natural gift for riding.

In 1964, competing in the aspirant category (the name given to under-23s), Jempi won not one but two Belgian titles. In Gullegem he finished first ahead of future Paris–Tours winner Noël Vantyghem. Later in the year, in Opgrimbie in Limburg, he found himself racing against one of the hottest young riders in Flanders, Rik Van Linden. Jempi pulverised him, winning the race by over five minutes. He didn't win all the time, however. That same year he was beaten into second place in a race in Ichtegem by a tall gangly lad riding his brother's bike – Roger De Vlaeminck. It's a measure of how strong that crop of young Flemish riders was that Jempi also found himself up against Walter Planckaert, Ronny De Witte and Eddy Peelman. De Witte won the Scheldeprijs and Paris–Tours while Peelman would win nine stages of the Vuelta a España. Planckaert we already know about.

In his first year as a pro with Flandria, Monseré won the Tour of Lombardy. It was a default victory. Jempi had finished second behind Dutchman Gerben Karstens who had completed the course at a record speed. Karstens had not done it unaided. He'd boosted amphetamines before the race and to beat the doping control got his *soigneur* to provide the urine sample. It was a cunning plan. Unfortunately for Karstens his *soigneur* had evidently felt the need for a bit of a sharpener too, and the test came back positive.

If that looked like a fluke win, the following year proved it wasn't. At the world road race championships in Leicester, on a flat and featureless course that seemed designed to demonstrate to the British that continental bike racing was a boring waste of time, Monseré took advantage of gusting winds and jumped away 800 metres from the finish to win ahead of Felice Gimondi. He was just 21, the second youngest rider ever to win the title after the mighty Karel Kaers of Vosselaar, who remains the youngest world champion of all time despite claims to the contrary made by Lance Armstrong.

Jempi was also a talented track rider and great things were expected of him. Tragically, in March 1970, while riding the Grote Jaarmarktprijs at Retie near Lille, he was hit by a car that had evaded the stewards and got onto the course. He died instantly. Tens of thousands attended his funeral in Roeselare.

As if that tragedy were not enough, in 1976 Jempi's seven-year-old son was knocked down and killed while riding a bike Jempi's old teammate and friend Freddy Maertens had given him.

How good was he? Roger De Vlaeminck, who was one of Jempi's closest friends, was emphatic in his praise, suggesting that if Monseré had lived he might have taken a bite out of the Cannibal: 'Merckx would have had a lot of trouble with him. Monseré was better than him, I think. He was even more of an all-rounder. He could sprint and climb very well. He was also cleverer.' Merckx himself put things more simply. Jempi, he said, 'had the face of a champion'. Briek Schotte, who managed the Flandria team, thought, 'He would have won every Classic.' As it was, Jempi Monseré took just one.

Quaregnon is a dozen miles south-west of Mons. The train stopped at one of those stations in Belgium where there's no platform and you have to jump down into gravel, like in the Wild West. Only three other passengers had alighted. One of them was a tall, young bloke with dark hair and an enormous backpack. He asked me if I spoke English. His name was Albert. He was a baker from Barcelona with a passion for bike racing, and a long-nurtured dream of leaving the dull confines of Catalonia, with its banal sunshine, mundanely glamorous street life and predictable insistence on brazenly exotic art and architecture, for a few months in Belgium. Even more remarkably than that, Albert spoke less French than I do. We walked together to the official start, outside the town hall – the real start was a few hundred yards away outside a Delhaize supermarket – chatting merrily about mud and snow and cobblestones, and watched the riders being presented to a smattering of people that barely justified the word 'crowd'. When I'd been at the museum in Roeselare the only other visitor had been a young Canadian woman with a tiny dog in a quilted raincoat. It turned out she was the wife of Guillaume Boivin, a rider with the recently formed Israeli Academy team. The couple were living in Ghent while he was racing. 'The big disappointment is they didn't get invited to ride Paris–Roubaix,' she told me. 'Guillaume's really kind of disappointed about that.' The Israeli team, which was made up of riders of 11 different nationalities from five continents, were at least in *Petit* Paris–Roubaix.

The race start was even less structured than I had been used to in Flanders. The Walloons are generally left-leaning and the area reserved for sponsors and VIPs had no discernible security to it, so I went in and asked the lady behind the counter if I could have a couple of programmes and a team sheet. In Flanders they'd charge you for those, if they'd let you have them at all, but she happily handed them over to me, unfazed by either my lack of credentials or my insistence on speaking only in the present tense. Albert also wandered into the press area, restructured his backpack and put on some waterproof trousers.

Albert had advanced technology that I didn't – a smartphone. Along with my pullout map from *La Dernière Heure* – French-speaking

Belgium's answer to *Het Laatste Nieuws* – this helped us identify a long section of cobbles near Dour that the race was going to pass across several times. I had already found out the number of the bus needed to get to Dour and had stored it on my own portable device – the Always be a Unicorn notebook.

'Can you ask these policemen where the bus stop is?' Albert asked after the far-from-*grand départ*. 'Yes,' I told him, 'I can ask them that, but I will only understand their reply if a) they speak very slowly and b) use words that I know.' The policeman I asked did neither of these things. He did something far better – pointed down the road and made a left-turn sign.

A bus for Dour turned up two minutes after Albert and I got to the stop. The journey lasted half an hour and took us through the sort of countryside and villages that will be familiar to anyone who grew up around pitheads anywhere in northern Europe. There are long straight streets of small redbrick houses, the conical peaks of slag heaps and, overall, a weird sense of desolation, as if removing coal from beneath the ground has somehow drained the warmth out of the place.

Coal and steel had once been the bedrock of the Belgian economy and the production of both was concentrated in Wallonia (though there were some pits in Flanders – mostly in the east of Limburg around the city of Genk, famous for its football team, where Kevin De Bruyne began his pro career). The mines and blast furnaces in the area around Charleroi, Liège and Mons – usually referred to as the Borinage or the Pays Noir – had been so productive around the beginning of the twentieth century that Belgium had briefly been (along with the USA, Britain and Germany) one of the four greatest industrial powers on the planet. But now all that was a thing of the past. Just as in Britain since 1980, pit after pit and steelworks after steelworks had closed. Unemployment in the Pays Noir is chronic. Belgium has the third highest rate of joblessness in western Europe and much of it is concentrated here.

In Dour we got off the bus just in time to see the women's race pass through, the riders coming up a narrow terraced street and swerving round a mini-roundabout before disappearing up towards what looked like it might be the town centre. After Albert had narrowly avoided being brained by a discarded water bottle thrown by an Australian cyclist with a blonde ponytail, we walked up in the direction of the race finish. Albert had some idea there might be a media centre with a TV screen on which we could watch the race. There wasn't, but there was a marquee where you could buy beer and sandwiches, and a chip van. Our arrival in the marquee caused some excitement and we were awarded two free glasses of Kwaremont ale for having travelled so far – presumably from Barcelona and Northumberland rather than Ghent and Mons, which was where Albert was staying.

Every time I went to the bar for beer after that and said, '*Deux* Kwaremont, *s'il vous plaît*,' the barman, a burly fellow with a balding head and the general look of a 1950s goalkeeper, said, '*Sept* Kwaremont,' and all the other people behind the bar – and this being the socialist republic of Wallonia there were far more employees than was really necessary – burst out laughing. It got a bit repetitious the second time you heard it, but everyone was so jolly and friendly I felt like I was somewhere in County Durham and so I laughed along with them. It is a strange truth that very often the grimmer and more rugged a place is, the bigger hearted and better humoured the people who live in it are, and the people of Dour seemed to be proving the point.

After a few beers Albert and I went and bought big cones of freshly cooked *frites*. I opted to top mine with *sauce andalouse*, but Albert rejected that in favour of mayonnaise, possibly because of some intra-Spanish provincial rivalry, or maybe because *sauce andalouse* tastes like a crisp manufacturer's idea of paella flavour. We ate the chips and had a couple more beers, which seemed a far more effective way of keeping out the cold than the 100-euro fleece I'd bought two days earlier in Ghent, and then headed off into the rain and the wind to watch the

96

race. We walked through empty streets and out into a countryside of derelict factory sheds and spoil heaps, splashing through puddles the colour of soot. The sky was the colour of a two-day-old bruise, the rain swirled around. Cars passed in a mist of spray. I've been to some rough-looking places but the outskirts of Dour in late February takes some beating. My daughter had been there a few years earlier to attend the annual music festival. When I asked her what Dour was like she replied, 'Shit.' My daughter has her mother's gift for brevity.

Albert and I found the stretch of cobbles the race was due to pass down. It was a mile long, straight and totally flat, but even walking on the cobbles was a nightmare in the rain. Craters of missing *pavé* had filled with water so we had no idea how deep they were. We picked our way along the muddy verge, past a police station housed in what looked like an old winding shed, to a midpoint that gave us a view up and down the road. A Dutch motorhome was parked nearby. After a few minutes the owner, a tall middle-aged man in a bright yellow cagoule, got out and started testing the depth of a few of the potholes. In a couple of them the water almost came over the top of his wellington boots. Any rider dropping into one would likely go over the front of his handlebars. The Dutchman looked down at the murky water then up at us and smiled ruefully. We had a chat. It turned out his friend's son was riding in the race. He went back into the motorhome and brought us a couple of the rider's publicity cards. Unfortunately by the time I got back to Ghent the water had soaked through my coat and the card had turned to papier mâché, so I've no idea who he was.

Standing in the rain we heard the helicopter approaching. The breakaway group of around eight riders swished and juddered past, slathered in mud, faces black as pitmen coming off shift. The big hazards for spectators were the team cars and, worst of all, a single-decker service bus that followed at the rear of the race apparently for no other purpose than to spray people at the roadside with filth. Albert unfurled a large golf umbrella he'd brought with him in an attempt to shelter us from the worst of the onslaught, but we were still picking soil out of our teeth.

After the race passed by our spot on the final circuit, the break still with a significant lead, we jogged back to Dour and found a place 30 yards from the finish line opposite La Maison du Peuple, a community centre with a bar that looked to be doing a roaring trade. We knew the leaders were getting closer when lots of middle-aged men with wobbly bellies beneath shiny shirts heaved out of the doors and rammed themselves against the barriers. The race announcer began calling breathless updates over the PA, counting down to the arrival of the lead group, giving the time gap to their pursuers. The rain fell and kept falling. With one minute to the arrival of the leaders people along the route began to bang rhythmically on the advertising hoardings, a great rumble that grew as the leading riders came into view up the slope of the main street between houses and down-at-heel shops. The competitors had swapped knackered bikes during the race. There were no numbers on the frames; those on their chests were so caked in dirt you couldn't read them. The commentary was drowned by the noise of the crowd. 'Van Keirsbulck,' somebody standing behind me croaked. I recalled that Guillaume Van Keirsbulck had won the Driedaagse De Panne a couple of years earlier and my friend Jim had said, 'Oh, hey, he's a right beast of a rider, that lad,' which was a big compliment from Jim. The rider who crossed the line with upraised arms certainly looked like a beast: big, burly with beard and hair caked in filth. It was Van Keirsbulck. In next day's *Het Laatste Nieuws* there was a piece about him. Like Jempi Monseré he comes from Roeselare and, guess what? He's the grandson of Benoni Beheyt.

* * *

Albert and I caught a bus straight back to the main station in Mons. Albert told me he was staying in Belgium for all the spring Classics.

He said he'd always wanted to come and watch them. Albert thought the big tours were all a foregone conclusion, too dull and predictable, while the one-day races could be won by dozens of different riders. 'I want to watch the Ronde van Vlaanderen standing on the Koppenberg,' he said. 'That is my dream.'

We said goodbye in Mons and agreed to meet up later in the season at E3 or the Ronde. I caught the train north to Brussels, sitting behind a bunch of American students, one of whom said, 'Soon Snapchat will be the only way anyone communicates with each other.'

I got back to Ghent a little after nine. My landlord asked where I'd been and, when I told him, shrugged indifferently. Despite their differences, there is no real animosity between the Flemish and the Walloons. Like commuters on the London Underground, they simply ignore one another unless some emergency arises.

Later, when I had a shower, mud came out of my ears. I'd been soaking wet since midday, frozen stiff and stood by the side of the road for several hours in one of the poorest, ugliest and most deprived parts of northern Europe. There's no doubt about it, it's one of the best, most romantic days I've had in all my years of watching sport.

5

HOLEY SOCKS AND A COOL HEAD

Dwars door West-Vlaanderen
Johan Museeuw Classic, 5 March

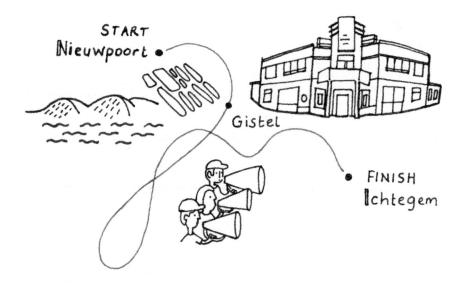

Sunday lunchtime in the teeming rain and cars swish past Gistel's Café O'Tourmalet as the overhead traffic lights vibrate in the swirling wind. Café O'Tourmalet is a large art deco building that wouldn't look out of place on a seafront esplanade, though it's several miles inland from the Flemish coast. Originally the café had an enclosed sun terrace and a big sign on the central tower above the main entrance proclaiming the name of the owner. Both are gone. Clusters of people in rainwear shelter in the doorways, waiting for the arrival of the Dwars door West-Vlaanderen Johan Museeuw Classic, shuffling from foot to foot, water dripping from hoods. Nobody says much.

Dwars door West-Vlaanderen ('Across West Flanders') was first run in 1945 as Omloop der Vlaamse Ardennen ('Loop of the Flemish Ardennes'). It retained that name until 1999 (well, more or less – sometimes it was called Omloop der Vlaamse Ardennen Ichtegem) when it was transformed into a two-day stage race, the Guldensporen-tweedaagse ('Two Days of the Golden Spurs' – in honour of the great battle). In 2003 the race had another day added and became Driedaagse van West-Vlaanderen ('Three Days of West Flanders'). Finally, in 2017, it went back to being a one-day race and got a UCI category of 1.1 and a new subtitle.

As all this messing about with the name and format suggests, Dwars door West-Vlaanderen has never been one of the great fixtures of the racing calendar. Despite that, it has been won by some top-class riders: Marcel Kint, Raymond Impanis, Noël Foré, Eric Leman and Frans Verbeeck. West Flanders legend Johan Museeuw, in whose honour the newest incarnation of the race is named, was victorious in 1995 and lived a dozen miles from the start line. Among the lesser winners my eye was drawn to the nicely named Brussels-born rider Kwik Van Kerckhove (1952) and to Norbert Callens (1949). Callens came from the percussive-sounding town of Wakken in West Flanders and became a footnote in cycling history during the 1949 Tour de France when he rode to victory on the stage into Boulogne-sur-Mer and took the race lead. Unfortunately there was some muddle over the presentation of his yellow jersey – either the lorry carrying it failed to arrive in Boulogne, or drove off before he was given one (accounts vary) – and Callens had to start the next stage wearing a yellowish sweater loaned to him by a Flemish journalist. By the end of the day he had lost the lead to Frenchman Jacques Marinelli and never got to wear the real yellow jersey.

Dwars door West-Vlaanderen is run on the first weekend in March, which means it clashes with the prestigious Paris–Nice and the Strade Bianche. The latter is a relatively new race with little history, but since it begins and finishes in Siena it has a patina of glamour that a ride through West Flanders is always going to struggle to match. Faced with a choice between Tuscany, a stage race with the romantic nickname 'the Race to the Sun', and a 203-kilometre slog through the wind and rain of Belgium, most of the top riders – even the Flemish ones – head south. The point was driven home by the Friday edition of *Wielerkrant*, which had a photo on the front cover of Flemish Limburger Tim Wellens in a t-shirt walking through a palm-fringed park in Monaco with his pet French bulldog, Georgette. The Lotto–Soudal rider would finish third in Siena that weekend, behind Greg Van Avermaet and winner Michał Kwiatkowski. Fleming Tiesj Benoot was eighth. Philippe Gilbert, Oliver Naesen and Yves Lampaert were riding in Paris–Nice.

The starting line-up for Dwars door West-Vlaanderen, therefore, featured a lot of second-string riders from the bigger Belgian teams – Lotto–Soudal, Quick-Step, Cofidis, Wanty–Groupe Gobert – and a bunch of riders from smaller local set-ups with unlikely monikers including Pauwels Sauzen–Vastgoedservice (whose website described them as 'one of the biggest players in sauces in Europe'), Veranclassic–Aqua Protect (two companies, one that makes conservatories, the other bathroom fitments), Tarteletto–Isorex (pâtisserie joins forces with a firm that manufactures plastic compounds) and, my particular favourite, the Netherlands-based Monkey Town Continental, which turned out to be sponsored by an indoor play area chain.

It was not the sort of field likely to attract the glory-seeking cycling fan, but in the previous few days there'd been a rumour going around that Museeuw's former protégé Tom Boonen might make an appearance. Tommeke, as Boonen was affectionately known, was recovering from injury and needed miles in his legs before his final tilt at winning another spring Classic. Was it possible he'd forego the warmth of the south for a ride from windswept Nieuwpoort to Ichtegem via the bumpy Heuvelland in the freezing rain?

A family – a mother, father and two small boys – had taken shelter in the doorway next to me. I asked the dad if he thought Boonen would ride today. He shook his head. 'I don't think so, but I'll ask my wife. Her brother is in the Quick-Step team.' He conversed in Flemish with his wife. At the mention of Boonen the two small boys started bouncing up and down and chirruping as if they'd just heard Santa Claus coming down the chimney. But their mum wrinkled her nose and shook her head. 'No, no, not today. He's not ready. Maybe next week.' The boys piped up in protest but to no avail. I tried to cheer them up by saying that Stijn Devolder was definitely on the starters' list. It didn't work. We all shrugged at one another and went back to staring silently through the sheets of rain in the direction of the invisible sea.

The lack of any positive reaction to Devolder's name didn't surprise me. I'd encountered it quite a few times in Flanders, which was odd because the rider from Kortrijk was a double winner of the Ronde van Vlaanderen – in 2008 and 2009. He'd also won a couple of Tours of Belgium, the Driedaagse De Panne, three national road race titles and the national time trial championship twice. All of which might have generated rather more than the sort of 'oh him' expression that seemed to be the standard reaction to any mention of his name. Devolder had been a *domestique* deluxe at Quick-Step when he'd had his golden moments. People in Flanders were happy for him, but not that happy. Devolder was one of those odd sportsmen and women whose successes are chalked down to luck, yet who for some reason never draws the kind of warm-hearted appreciation the victorious underdog might expect. With Devolder there was little misty-eyed talk of a fairytale come true. His career had tanked too. Since the end of the 2010 season, when he'd fallen out with Quick-Step, he'd notched just one major victory – the national road title, and that had been in 2013. Devolder kept swapping teams and talking of a fresh start, but nobody seemed to be listening. Ultimately, as the reaction of the little lads demonstrated, Devolder's real problem wasn't who he was, but who he wasn't: Tom Boonen. I felt a bit sorry for him. Though that might have had something to do with where I was standing. The Café O'Tourmalet had an air of chill melancholy about it that chimed with the weather. A chalkboard propped against a wall advertised the dish of the day, but the interior was dark. Placing a hand against the window and peering in I could see that the tables still had cloths on, there were empty glasses strewn across the bar tops and waiters' clothes tossed over chair-backs. A few dried-up pot plants stood in the windows. It had the forlorn look of somewhere once loved but then abandoned in a hurry.

It was a far cry from the photos I'd been looking at earlier in the week in the Wielermuseum de Gistelse Flandriens. They had shown the Café O'Tourmalet in its 1930s heyday: open-topped roadsters in the car park, the owner standing proudly out front, spiffily dressed in plus fours, a short-sleeved sports shirt and argyle socks, hair slicked back like a crooner in some big band, or filling a glass of beer from the shining chrome pumps inside, the bar top as gleaming as his lopsided smile. Local boy made good Sylveer Maes had built the café in his home town with the money he'd made winning the 1936 Tour de France and named it after the Pyrenean climb on which he'd burned off his great rival, Antonin Magne of France.

'One of the greatest, for sure,' said the tall, squarely built and avuncular pensioner who'd kindly let me into Gistel's small cycling museum (even though it was officially closed for the winter), smiling at a photo of Maes standing next to a cow on the family farm on the outskirts of the little West Flanders town. Rain was lashing the windows of the museum, housed in a restored grain shed near to an impressive Victorian windmill. I'd been standing outside hopefully gazing in for 15 minutes before the old chap came out and found me. He was working in the town archive next door and, taking pity on a bedraggled foreigner, ushered me into a long gallery filled with bookshelves and filing cabinets where several other retired gents were sitting at long tables busily collating information on record cards, and from there through a side door into the room we were standing in surrounded by photographs and artefacts from the lives of two of Gistel's most famous sons, Johan Museeuw and Sylveer Maes.

Only 90 riders had entered the 1936 Tour. Maes, winner of the 1933 edition of Paris–Roubaix, took yellow in the Pyrenees and held on to it for the rest of the race. Magne attacked hard in the Alps but the man from the flatlands of Gistel held grimly on and, when the Frenchman – who seemed to have little support from his team – punctured, gained nine minutes on him thanks to the help of fellow Fleming Félicien Vervaecke. Almost as brilliant in the mountains as Maes, Vervaecke overhauled Magne to take second place overall. However, he was then handed a ten-minute time penalty, some claim because his mother gave him a bottle of beer on one of the climbs on the road to Pau, though a more plausible explanation is that he had borrowed a bike with derailleur gears, which Henri Desgrange had outlawed for pros because it made life easier for them – something the great man could not countenance. Whatever the reasons, it dropped Vervaecke back to third and irritated the Belgian team.

In 1937 the Flemish attacked hard from the second day onwards with Marcel Kint, Vervaecke and Maes in the thick of the action. The great Italian Gino Bartali gave the Flemish a battle in the mountains, but the tough Vervaecke stuck with him. On the way down from the Col du Télégraphe, Albert 'the Sock' Hendrickx from Kalmthout in Antwerp crashed and nearly died. As the race went on through the Alps, Bartali led from Maes. The man from Gistel attacked on the mountainous stage to Digne and took the race lead. Psychologically and physically wrecked, Bartali abandoned in Marseille leaving Frenchman Roger Lapébie in second position. On the stage to Bordeaux, Maes punctured and Lapébie broke away. Maes enlisted a couple of Flemish *touriste-routiers* to help in the pursuit. (Amateurs they may have been, but the pair could ride. One of them, Gustaaf Deloor, had won the first two editions of the Vuelta a España; the other, Adolph Braeckeveldt from East Flanders, had won the Flèche Wallonne.) Since assistance by non-team members was banned under the Tour de France rules, Maes was handed a time penalty. This proved to be the final straw for the Belgian team. They believed French fans fed up with Belgian dominance had been throwing pepper in their faces, and were annoyed that a proposed team time trial in Marseille, which they would have expected to win, had been suddenly dropped from the race for no good reason. Vervaecke's penalty from the year before still rankled. Hendrickx's near fatal accident added to the general displeasure. Furious at what they perceived as typical Francophone slyness, the team – including yellow jersey Maes – withdrew. Would he have won again? Probably. As it was, Lapébie took first place over seven minutes ahead of Mario Vicini of Italy.

Because of the international situation, not one of Italy, Spain or Germany sent teams to the Tour de France in 1939. The Flemish dominated. Maes attacked brilliantly on the horrendous track that led up Col d'Izoard to build a 17-minute lead and claim yellow. He never lost it. Lucien Vlaemynck (from West Flanders, riding for Belgium's B team) was third overall and Edward Vissers from Antwerp fifth. Belgium's B team took the national prize with the A team finishing third. Flemish riders also took the first three places in the King of the Mountains competition, with Maes first, Vissers second and Albert Ritserveldt from the Flemish Ardennes third.

'Sylveer was one of the greatest of all time, for sure,' the old man in the museum said. He spoke excellent English with a humorous inflection. 'Good on the flat and even better in the big hills. And not only talented but also with a scientific approach that was not so usual for those days.' He gestured to a cabinet housing a strange-looking peaked leather hat with a Belgian flag stitched on the front. 'Now this I say was the first air-conditioning unit.' The old man continued, 'It is made from . . . what is it you call the things with which you wash windows?' Chamois leather, I suggested. 'Yes, yes,' he said. 'Chamois leather. This helmet is made from it. Maes would soak it in a bucket of cold water before a hot stage then put it on his head. As the water evaporated it cooled him, you see? To us perhaps not so clever, but his equipment was hi-tech for those times.'

On the wall opposite there was an elaborate chart over five feet in length that recorded the performances of the riders in the 1939 Tour using a different coloured yarn to mark each man's progress stage by stage. 'The women in towns all across Flanders made these charts each year,' my guide explained. 'But then wives stopped mending their husband's socks and so there was no longer wool in the basket to do it with and they stopped.'

I wasn't entirely sure why they'd used yarn in the first place – coloured crayons would have done just as well – but West Flanders had a tradition of textiles, weaving and lacemaking, so perhaps using tapestry to record things came naturally.

'I will leave you to look round. Don't touch anything, please,' the old man said, disappearing back into the archives.

I watched a film of Sylveer Maes thrashing up the dirt roads of the Pyrenees and the Alps and being mobbed in the Parc des Princes, studied the photos, the cases of medals and trophies and the old bicycles he'd ridden and later endorsed. One of ten children raised milking cows and furrowing spuds, Sylveer Maes was from typical Flemish cycling stock, yet he had a star quality about him, a self-confidence and ease. He was a snappy dresser and a good deal more polished than the traditional image of the Flemish rider. I wasn't sure Briek Schotte would have worn houndstooth checks and diamond-patterned sweater vests.

Remarkably Sylveer wasn't the first man from West Flanders named Maes to win the Tour de France. That honour had fallen to Romain Maes from Zerkegem the year before. Like Sylveer, Romain came from a huge family – he was the 13th child of 15. And like Sylveer he too used his winnings to open a café named in celebration of his Tour de France exploits, In de Gele Trui (In the Yellow Jersey) located near Brussels-Nord station. Extraordinarily, given the close-knit world of Flemish cycling, the two Maes were not related, though they became good friends and rode together on the track.

Unlike Sylveer, Romain wasn't a celebrated rider. Aside from a stage in Paris–Nice and another in the 1939 Tour de France, winning La Grande Boucle was the only major victory in his long career. Not that he wasn't a little unlucky. Many felt he'd crossed the finish line first in the 1936 edition of Paris–Roubaix, but the judges enraged the crowd by awarding victory to Frenchman Georges Speicher instead. Misfortune also befell Romain two years later at the conclusion of Paris–Brussels. He was over 100 metres ahead of the chasing group but stopped when he crossed the line in the velodrome, apparently unaware that he had another lap of the track to do. He realised his error too late and was pipped to victory by Marcel Kint.

Romain was short and thickset with dark wavy hair. Henri Desgrange thought him a solid 'ball of muscle'. Like Ritten Van Lerberghe, the Death Rider of Lichtervelde, Romain Maes seems to have raced on the edge, gambling everything on smashing the opposition. Unfancied at the start of the 1935 Tour, Romain might have been expected to act as watercarrier for some of the other riders in the powerful Belgian team, but on the first stage he got the stroke of luck that so often seemed to elude him when he raced. On the road from Paris to Lille he made a solo break and had built up a two-minute lead when he arrived at a level crossing in the mining town of Bruay and (shades of the Death Rider) sneaked across just ahead of the train. His pursuers were thwarted as heavy goods wagons rumbled slowly past adding over a minute to the Fleming's lead. He won the stage and took the race leader's jersey. He would defend it all the way to Paris in a display of such fierce tenacity he was nicknamed 'the Yellow Demon'. Romain Maes got great support from his Flemish teammates: the climber Vervaecke, Jules Lowie (we'll get to him later) and Sylveer, of course. Romain would win the stage into Paris just as he had won the first stage and burst into tears when he was presented with his yellow jersey. He was a popular winner, a beloved outsider.

I was studying an old moped that Johan Museeuw's father, Eddy, had used to pace his son on his training runs along the coast from Ostend to De Panne – a one-and-a-half-hour ride on which the crosswinds were so powerful that mastering them required the skills of a yachtsman as well as those of a cyclist – when the old man popped his head in the door again. 'Have you seen everything now?' he asked. I had a feeling he was perhaps worried that someone might turn up and tell him off for letting me in and so I said I had, thanked him profusely for his kindness and headed back out into the rain. I walked back along Gistel's long, meandering main street. Past cafés, lawnmower repair shops and stores selling surgical support stockings. A lady who looked to be in her eighties emerged from a terraced house on the other side of the street. Wrapped in waterproofs and wearing a see-through plastic headscarf, she unhooked, from a nearby downpipe, the sort of raw-boned old bike that village postmen used to ride, wheeled it into the road, hopped on it and pedalled off into the gnashing wind, head bowed.

I trailed along behind her until I found a café opposite the bus station that had an artificial coal fire burning and Irish coffee on the menu. I asked the waitress if she knew where Sunday's race, Dwars door West-Vlaanderen, was going to pass through Gistel. 'It doesn't come through here,' she said. 'It did once, but that was years ago.' After a moment I realised she thought I was talking about the Ronde. She had no idea what Dwars door West-Vlaanderen was. Luckily the old couple sitting opposite did. They said the race would pass the Café O'Tourmalet, down at the end of the street, in the opposite direction from the museum.

I sat and drank my Irish coffee looking out across the wet brick houses of the town. Though it was only 20 minutes by bus from Ostend, on a foul day in late winter Gistel felt a long way from anywhere.

Johan Museeuw was born in nearby Varsenare in 1965, and brought up in Gistel. He'd built a house here for himself, his wife, Veronique, and his son, Gianni. He loved the flat polders and the rolling sand dunes and the feeling of the wind buffeting him as he rode. When asked whether, after retirement, he'd move back from Italy to West Flanders, Museeuw replied 'of course' in a tone that suggested to have done otherwise would have been an act of madness.

Throughout the 1990s and into the new millennium you saw Museeuw's name, his image, across Flemish Belgium printed on caps and jackets and t-shirts, even on the hoods of Babygros. He was as ubiquitous in that era as Boonen is now. On the slopes of the Kemmelberg during Ghent–Wevelgem in 1998 I stood next to a dark-haired young woman who held her baby aloft as Museeuw approached and whispered his name into the child's tiny ear like somebody reciting a prayer.

Museeuw's background was different from other great Flemish riders. He was an only child and his father had a successful car dealership selling Peugeots.

Museeuw rode from an early age, but his focus was more on cyclocross than on road racing. His father had been a professional cyclist but there had been trouble with money. Wages weren't paid regularly. After he rode in the Amstel Gold Race and came second he went home, thought about it and quit.

Eddy Museeuw had been a good rider, a pure sprinter. He'd won 42 races as an amateur and signed as a pro with the happily named Okay-Whisky team, riding alongside one of the last great *flahutes*, Frans 'the Flying Milkman' Verbeeck. But his experiences left him, if not completely bitter towards pro cycling then certainly suspicious of some of the people involved in it. At first he kept his son away from cycling altogether. Johan played football for Gistel. A left-sided striker, he was good enough for local top-flight team K.V. Ostend to express an interest. But by then Johan was riding cyclocross. He'd gradually transition to the road, but Eddy remained cautious. He didn't want his son caught up in the sort of hype that had ruined the careers of so many young Flemish cyclists. He brought him along slowly, maintaining a focus on cyclocross. Johan's first major road race as an amateur was Ghent–Staden. He came fifth. Belgian national team coach Dirk Baert was impressed. He selected Johan for the Belgian amateur squad and took him to France for two races. The experience was a disaster. 'I was totally blown apart. Just couldn't keep up with them,' Museeuw recalled. Determination saved him. In his second season with the national amateurs he finished second in a number of races, beaten only by the leading amateurs of the time, Russia's Dimitri Konyshev and Michel Zanoli – a Dutch rider who'd die of heart failure aged 35, a tragedy linked by some to EPO.

Eddy's wariness and Johan's early focus on cyclocross were a blessing. Johan's lack of profile as an amateur road racer kept him away from the spotlight. Unlike many other talented young Belgian cyclists of the 1970s and 80s, Museeuw did not labour under the 'new Eddy Merckx' tag that blighted the lives of the likes of Eric Vanderaerden, Edwig Van Hooydonck and many more.

Museeuw turned pro in 1988. He had stayed one more year in the amateurs than was strictly necessary – another example of family caution. Johan was working at his father's garage, and he was reluctant to give up that job for the uncertainty of the pro's life, especially as the pay was often worse. At least he had a safety net. When Eddy had quit racing he'd started working as a motor mechanic and built up a business. So when his son was offered a pro contract by the leading Belgian ADR team, Eddy said to try it for a while and if it didn't work out Johan could come back and work in the garage business with him.

When Museeuw joined ADR in 1988 he raced alongside veteran Flemish riders Eddy Planckaert, Frank Hoste, Dirk Demol and Fons

De Wolf (the latter one of the legion of new Eddy Merckxs). The team was managed by José De Cauwer from Temse in East Flanders, a former pro who'd finished third in Le Samyn.

That year saw Museeuw's baptism in the Ronde – he would ride in it every year thereafter until he retired after the 2004 race. It was a brutal day of torrential, icy rain and multiple crashes. 'That was a hard race,' Museeuw recalled. 'I was just a helper then. I worked really hard for Eddy and the team. And, of course, Eddy won, so everybody was happy.' (Eddy himself, as we have already heard, was positively ecstatic.)

In 1989 American Greg LeMond, recently recovered from the gunshot wounds he'd suffered in a hunting accident, joined ADR and won the Tour de France by eight seconds from Laurent Fignon. It should have heralded a great future for the team, but instead the chronically underfunded outfit promptly split apart acrimoniously. Museeuw found himself at Lotto. A vacuum had been left by the retirement of leader Claude Criquielion and the 25-year-old Fleming took over the number-one role.

Lotto were the Belgian team of the moment, managed by Jean-Luc Vandenbroucke, Frank's uncle. Johan won races for them, but the sort of financial problems his father had warned him about quickly surfaced. Museeuw had a bad crash two days before the world championship in Benidorm, damaging his pelvis. It took a long time to heal. The race was won by Gianni Bugno. Museeuw thought he might have had enough to take it, but watched from his hospital bed instead. Lotto reacted badly to the injury and slashed Johan's wages to the minimum, equivalent to around £500 a month. He felt let down. He'd ridden for them for three years, won Tour de France stages and the Belgian national title.

In 1993 he moved to Mapei–GB. The wage cut at Lotto had hit him badly, poisoning his relationship with the Belgian team. Some thought the Lotto team – which was not the strongest – had held him back, but Johan denied that. He didn't like to blame others and knew that his teammates had ridden as hard as they could in his service. Lotto were constrained by money. While a big Dutch team might pay all its riders a minimum of £80,000 per season, most of the Lotto riders were on less than £20,000. The poor pay in Belgian teams – often sponsored by relatively small local companies without the financial clout of the global brands who supported other European teams – was a longstanding complaint, though Iron Briek Schotte had thought it beneficial: for wasn't hunger what Flemish racing was based on? You didn't make a *flahute* with cream cakes and feather cushions.

Museeuw might have got an even fatter contract at Gatorade or Carrera but considered them 'too Italian'. Mapei were part Belgian. The *directeur sportif* and his assistants were Belgian. Museeuw spoke multiple languages, but he remained a home-loving boy. If he couldn't be in Flanders he could at least take a bit of Flanders with him.

Museeuw's training regime was notoriously brutal. Mapei–GB teammate Wilfried Peeters once said, 'Ninety-five out of 100 riders couldn't deal with it.' The training runs regularly went on for six-and-a-quarter hours. Often they were muscle-numbingly fast. Museeuw ignored hills and wind. 'Why slow down,' he declared, 'when you can pedal harder?'

Johan never complained. He regarded bike racing as his work. In some ways it was easier than a proper job. His training regime lasted from nine till two, while his father worked from eight till five. Racing days were longer and harder, but Johan didn't mind – it was the life he'd chosen. The one thing he hated was being away from home so much. He was Flemish to his core. After he won the Ronde in 1993 he told people he'd ride for three more years then retire in 1996. Some days he dreamed of going back to cyclocross. Erik De Vlaeminck tried to persuade him to devote himself to it again, and it would have meant spending more time in his beloved Flanders, but something drove him on. When 1996 came around he said the same thing again – he'd ride for three more years.

Museeuw was sometimes criticised for being too cautious, almost timid in races. The attitude was seen as an extension of his public image. Shy and self-contained, he preferred riding to talking. He did not make predictions, he did not brag, or insult his rivals. He kept his own counsel. Museeuw was said to be monosyllabic and wary. He always rejected that suggestion, calling it 'a good story for journalists'. What was undoubtedly true was that Museeuw shied away from the limelight. He was not an attention-seeker like his friend the Italian sprinter Mario 'the Lion King' Cipollini. He hid in the Mapei team bus before races, avoiding the hullaballoo, emerging late.

To me he seemed typically Flemish – bright, chatty, with a nice line in self-deprecating jokes that tended to underline rather than undermine his self-confidence. When asked if his 17 rides in the Ronde was a record, he replied, 'I don't think so. Perhaps. It could be!'

In fact Briek Schotte had started more, but finished fewer. They called Schotte 'the Last of the Flandriens'. They gave that title to Museeuw too. Perhaps they'll say the same of Boonen.

The Sunday after visiting the museum I returned to Gistel. I took an early train from Ghent to Ostend. The station in Ostend had been totally flattened and replaced with the sort of portacabins they have at big construction sites. The bus station was across the road and utterly without shelter. Mrs Thatcher once said that anyone who was still taking the bus at 30 could consider themselves a failure, and the Flemish government seemed eager to ram that point home by forcing bus users to stand in the open getting soaked. To add to the sense of abandonment and futility the computerised signboards indicated that no buses were due for the next three hours. Luckily I had a paper timetable I'd picked up on my previous visit and that proved far more accurate. The bus arrived five minutes after I had.

It was still raining heavily and the Flemish canals looked likely to spill over the flat countryside we rode through. The breeze was on the concrete side of stiff and whenever the bus got caught broadside it shuddered so heavily it felt like it might topple over.

Outside the O'Tourmalet the rain kept lashing down. But more and more people arrived to watch the race: a couple of teenage girls with a Lotto–Soudal flag, men in Tarteletto–Isorex beanie hats, groups whose matching jackets marked them as members of various local cycling clubs, some armed with megaphones to better hurl instructions at the passing field, and a couple of cycling WAGs, one in a green fun-fur gilet, Burberry baseball cap and fashionably ripped jeans, carrying a Chihuahua under her arm.

The race came past a shop selling equestrian supplies and a car dealership – in the teeming rain and howling wind, the riders' raincapes flapped like sails. They didn't seem to be racing hard, but in the conditions just staying upright required a major effort. Down the wide dual carriageway, swinging right at the traffic lights, they were gone in less than 30 seconds. The Flemish fans ran to their cars – if they drove fast enough they could catch another glimpse a few miles away. The man whose brother-in-law was a teammate of Tom Boonen said he couldn't squeeze me into his car, 'But ask one of the other guys. They'll do it.'

I could see the bus for Ostend coming down the long road, however. There was a stop just opposite. By the time I'd got on board a minute later, all evidence of the race had gone.

After close to five hours of riding in conditions that made Le Samyn look positively balmy by comparison, a field of 164 riders had been sliced down to just 39. Dutchman Jos van Emden crossed the finish line in Ichtegem first, ahead of Silvan Dillier of Switzerland and Dane Lasse Norman Hansen. Jasper De Buyst was fourth and Guillaume Van Keirsbulck, who seemed to like the rain, fifth. Stijn Devolder was 31st.

The bus took me back through the flat country where Johan Museeuw had trained as a boy. As an amateur Museeuw had struggled in the mountains, barely making it over most of them, always in the last group. He improved in the hills as a pro, but he was no Sylveer Maes and could never match riders such as Frenchman Laurent Jalabert. It left him at a massive disadvantage when trying to win the coveted green points jersey in the Tour de France, and he never did manage it.

Not that he had any regrets. 'For a Flemish rider, winning the Ronde van Vlaanderen for the first time is better than winning the Tour de France,' Museeuw commented. It was sometimes said that a Fleming only loved what he could see from the bell tower of his village church, and however flat the surrounding countryside was, you couldn't see Paris from Gistel.

6

IT'S A FAMILY AFFAIR

Omloop van Wetteren, 11 March Omloop van het Waasland, 12 March Nokere Koerse, 15 March

Wetteren had the look of a place abandoned after a failed party. There were beer cans on the public benches, broken glass around the rubbish bins, a couple of beanie hats lying in puddles, and damp beer mats with card scores scribbled on them strewn across the pavement. It was Saturday lunchtime and if there was life going on it was plainly elsewhere.

After a fruitless tour round the main square I went into the library to ask about the statue of local cycling ace Achiel Buysse. There was some confusion, until the librarian worked out who I was talking about (Buysse is pronounced to rhyme with 'purser' not with 'toys' or 'looser'). She didn't know anything about the statue, but she thought that maybe the old boys reading the newspapers in the reference section might. It turned out one of them did, a man in a corduroy jacket who explained exactly where it was before adding something in Flemish that made the librarian laugh. 'He says that it is easy to miss and that it is not very good anyway,' she said, raising her eyebrows comically. 'But maybe that is just his opinion.'

The bit about the sculpture being easy to miss proved true, largely because a group of burly Dutch bikers had parked their Harley-Davidsons all around it before taking up position outside a nearby café where they were drinking glasses of De Koninck and scowling fiercely. I'd also have to concede that the second part proved sadly accurate too. The sculpture of Achiel Buysse is made out of scrap metal objects – the rider's head is a rake – and stands about four feet high. It's tucked into the angle between a couple of walls, and somebody had abandoned a child's pink bike with two flat tyres next to it, as if they thought it was a sign saying 'dump your bike-related rubbish here'.

It seemed an underwhelming tribute to the first man to win the Ronde van Vlaanderen three times, especially in a town that has been the race finish point for close to 30 years. Buysse was born in Lochristi in 1918, but brought up in Wetteren. As a teenager he'd inherited a bicycle from his grandfather – but it was a women's model and his mother disapproved of him riding it, perhaps fearing that pedalling round on something that lacked a crossbar would lead inevitably to him wearing dresses. Achiel was undeterred, however, and entered his first race in nearby Wetteren-ten-Ede, winning it in a sprint on the ladies' bike. His first prize was 20 francs and he returned home elated, only for his mother to give him a clip round the ear when she found out what he had been up to.

Buysse turned pro in 1938 with the French Dilecta–Wolber team. He won the Scheldeprijs in 1939. When the war came he continued to ride and, because of his status and his ability to win prizes in local races, seems to have had a fairly easy time of it, even travelling to Paris to race. The Ronde, meanwhile, carried on during the conflict with the encouragement and assistance of the occupying Nazis. Buysse won the race in 1940 and 1941 – when the finish line was in Jan Broeckaertlaan in Wetteren – and again in 1943 when the race ended in Ghent. A tall, slender man with a vaguely vulpine look (there's some resemblance to Vladimir Putin), Buysse was a sprinter, arguably at his best in races that did not exceed 200 kilometres. When he competed in the Ronde he'd tell friends and family that if he was still in touch with the leaders after the climb of Kwaremont then they should stand in the finishing straight and cheer him on, and if he wasn't they should stay at home. Since only Belgians rode in the wartime editions of the Ronde, Buysse's victories are clearly compromised. He was obviously a decent rider, though, and proved it after the liberation by winning the Scheldeprijs for the second time in 1948, a year that he also won Kuurne–Brussels–Kuurne and the Belgian national championship. He might have won more races too, but in Sleidinge in 1950 he was knocked off his bike by a motorcyclist and fractured his skull. He came back, but his nerve had gone and he retired shortly afterwards. He died in Wetteren in 1984.

The statue was a disappointment, but luckily I hadn't come to Wetteren just for that. There was a race in the town that started at two o'clock. The Omloop van Wetteren was a typical small Flemish race, a 105-kilometre event open for elites, z/c (*zonder contract* – unsigned riders) and *beloften* (under-23s). It was one of half a dozen such criteriums being held in Flanders that March Saturday. The others were at Betekom, Haringe, Grandglise, Meulebeke and Sint-Maria-Lierde. And they were popular. Between them these little races had attracted a total of 614 entrants, drawn from across Flanders and the Netherlands. At Wetteren there would be 161 starters.

The excellent Wielerbond Vlaanderen website listed Café Tonneke as the riders' check-in point. I managed to find it without too much difficulty, despite making a detour into a vast supermarket car park to take a photo of an estate vehicle with the words 'Kok Fresh Since 1989' painted on the side. There was a buzz of activity around the café, which was at the entrance to Wetteren's rather nicely old-fashioned-looking football stadium. I walked along the road to an area of parking bays filled with motorhomes. Some were old, the white paintwork turned sepia, others brand new, glossy and decorated with the names of the racing teams who'd arrived in them. Through the window of one I saw a rider in full kit eating sandwiches with two elderly couples who must have been his grandparents.

A teenage rider with long dark hair, a goatee beard and the pallid appearance of someone who really ought to have been in the basement of a comic book store playing Magic: The Gathering was sitting on a wicker picnic chair while his dad rubbed embrocation into his calves. His mother paced nervously about nearby.

The Goma team from Oosterzele emerged from a motorhome, five big lads plus their team manager. It seemed amazing they'd managed to drive here without the thing bursting at the seams.

In a café near the indoor tennis centre, just beyond the finish line, an elderly man and young rider sat opposite me, on high stools. The rider was handsome, with chiselled features. Newly checked-in, he held his racing numbers in one hand and an espresso in the other. He and the older man spoke intently about the race in French. The older man kept telling the rider to eat the two chocolate biscuits that came with the coffee 'for the energy, for the energy!' But the younger man waved the idea away.

The road where the race started and finished was busy with traffic – most of it heading into a vast Carrefour supermarket. Stewards whistled madly in an attempt to communicate to shoppers that if they went in now, they might not get out again for a couple of hours.

Marshals with green flags drove up and down the course, yelling from megaphones at any vehicle that seemed likely to stray onto the course and disrupt the race. The music began its electro-booming summons to the start.

The boy from the comic shop basement went by on his bike. His outfit and his cycle were entirely black and unmarked by any sponsor's name or logo. It dawned that he was that rarest of all beasts, a sporty goth. I imagined it must be tough explaining to his friends why he'd exchanged a morbid afternoon hanging morosely around a shopping precinct drinking super-lager and thinking about death for riding round and round a small Flemish town for two and a half hours. Most of the riders were in teams or pairs but the goth – perhaps typically – seemed to be utterly alone (but then, aren't we all, when you, like, think about it, right?).

For the first time in what seemed like years it had stopped raining, and though cloudy and overcast it was warm enough to shed a coat. Cars were parked all along the road leading from the start/finish line out into the East Flanders countryside. Boot doors were open, fold-out chairs placed strategically close to cool boxes.

Parents with small children walked past chatting and laughing. An elderly female steward in a director's chair lit a cigarette and waved a greeting to a man passing by on a mobility scooter. Birds chirruped in the hedgerows, daffodils nodded. Having got the motorhome up onto chocks that keep it perfectly level, the Goma team manager, a huge man with the face of a ranch foreman in a 1970s TV western, sauntered off to the start line, hands tucked in the waistband of his jogging pants like it was a gun belt. A woman in a leather trench coat, stonewashed skinny jeans and tan Cuban-heeled boots clicked past clutching a heap of team jackets. A rider in a red top hopped off his bike and pissed in a roadside ditch. Police cars started to arrive.

I found a park bench on a little triangle of grass opposite a 1970s estate of brick terraces with white stuccoed upper floors and grey roof tiles. It afforded a good view down the road the riders were going to come along. I was soon joined on it by three elderly Flemish ladies with rasping accents and twinsets. They spoke no English but cheerily laughed and joked with me and offered me slices of cake from their picnic basket. They reminded me of my great-aunts in Teesside, doughty northern matriarchs whose prime aim in life was to ply men with unhealthy foodstuffs until they keeled over and were finally out from under their feet so they could get some washing done.

The race came round every ten minutes or so. At the sound of the stewards whistling everyone leapt to their feet. The elderly chap who was sitting on a fold-out chair a few yards away bustled across the street to get a better view up the road. The peloton thundered past with a rattle of gears, trailing Deep Heat fumes. There was a bit of shouting and a smattering of applause but the biggest excitement of the day greeted a tubby man with two Chihuahuas who walked along the pavement to mass cooing. The dogs were hardly bigger than mice and I wondered if he wasn't tempted to whirl them round his head like a bolero. When the police cars and race marshal's vehicle that marked the back of the field had passed, we all sat down again. The three ladies spent the time in between laps by filling in the pages of puzzle magazines, occasionally laughing with satisfaction at the completion of a word search, or tutting at the impossibility of some clue in a general knowledge crossword.

On the second lap a small group broke away and built a lead of maybe 20 seconds on the main bunch, but by the third lap the field was back together again, strung out in a long chain. Several riders had already been dropped off the back, unable to keep up with the pace. I watched out for the goth rider, who seemed to be sticking with the rest fairly easily. His father stood near me at the roadside yelling instructions to him as he flew past, though it was hard to believe he could hear any of them.

A woman with two Dutch barge dogs, white jeans, knee boots and peroxide blonde hair stopped for a chat. She had a rider's jacket over her arm. I wondered if the three ladies had a relative riding in the race, some lad from next door, or the boy who helped out in the village shop. But I'd come to realise that women don't follow bike racing in Flanders simply because they have some emotional investment in a rider. They were not here to give support to some bloke. They were here because they liked bike racing.

After the third lap the three Flemish aunts and I were joined by a younger woman with short black hair and a turquoise anorak. She folded out her garden chair, which was bright green and covered in pictures of palm trees, pineapples and parrots. After she'd chatted for a couple of laps she got up, folded her chair and moved off further down the road. The three older women, like me, were reluctant to abandon the bench to watch the race but kept doing so anyway. After the sixth lap we came back to find our fears had been realised and two other women had snatched part of the bench for themselves. Space became a little constricted, and after getting up to brush cake crumbs off her slacks one of the aunts inadvertently sat back down in my lap, which caused a good deal of raucous chuckling.

I decided it was time to find another vantage point and, after bidding goodbye to the Flemish aunts, walked up the road through the village of Massemen and out into flat countryside, green pasture land and what looked like a vineyard. There was a horse box for sale, a couple of billboards advertising tarts and waffles, a hand-painted notice that said 'Beware – Potatoes' and another that pointed the way to a farm selling 'giant chicory'. I found a junction in the course. The narrow side road the riders came down had a dike at one side and was flanked by pollarded willow trees. A stiff crosswind coming from the right swept across the riders and then smacked them in the face when they turned left at the top of the road. Despite that the riders came

123

past hard, the gears clicking as they prepared to hit the long straight that led into Wetteren. I sat on a bridge over a shallow stream and watched as a young rider from the Brema team based in Vilvoorde abandoned with four laps remaining, his Superman socks apparently no help. His family were parked nearby and came over to see what the problem was. His mum, concerned that he was hurt, checked his legs for cuts and abrasions; his father, more bothered by thoughts that he may have had problems with his gear ratios, began fiddling about with the rear wheel.

I walked back up to the Café Tonneke where I found the photo-finish van – which looked like it might work using string and a box Brownie but actually had two men inside with a laptop. The lap counter was more what my daughter would call 'analogue': tin numbers on a timber frame operated by a young lad so eager to change them over that one of the stewards had to literally hold him back by his coat to prevent him going too early and confusing the back markers.

With the finish approaching, the PA system was cranked up full blast, the soundtrack to the race moving seamlessly from an electro-pop version of 'Zorba's Dance' through announcements detailing the local sponsors – billiard halls, DIY stores and purveyors of Austrian blinds – and on to The Romantics' hit 'What I Like About You'.

The race ended in a mass sprint. On the narrow road only those who had already muscled their way to the front had any chance. Benjamin Verraes from Moortsele took first prize, followed by Tom Verhaegen and Jens Moens. The Dutch rider Thijs de Lange was fourth. Beyond the finish line the families had joined the riders. Backs were patted and commiserations offered to the sound of Creedence Clearwater Revival's 'Bad Moon Rising'.

Criteriums like the one in Wetteren are the universities of Flemish cycling. They create the unique style of Flemish racing. The young Flemish riders learn their craft there. There is an art to mastering the unique conditions – the greasy cobbles, the cinder paths, tight turns, the sudden gusts of wind across the flat fields, the narrow lanes and hazards of public roads. The first thing Flemish riders learn is the importance of correct tyre pressure. If the tyres are too hard they won't adhere to the slippery surface of the cobbles, and the shockwaves of the jolting will be magnified to a point where it seems it will rattle the rider's teeth loose. But if the tyres are too soft the rider risks punctures. Flemish racers learn quickly to adjust the pressure according to the conditions of the road and the weather.

Criteriums in Flanders hit the road at top speed from the dropping of the start flag. Part of the reason the Flemish like to ride off the front is that it allows them to see ahead. The paths that run alongside cobbled stretches of road and ease a rider's passage are narrow – riders have to cycle along them in single file. Any rider who misses his chance to jump onto one is forced to stay on the cobbles, sometimes for hundreds of metres. The Flemish don't let riders who miss the chance cut back in. Anyone who tries is likely to get a forearm smash in the chops. The rider who fails to jump onto the path when the opportunity arises is left with two choices: hammer along on the cobbles or drop to the back. Either way his chances are knackered.

In an urban race with short laps like the one I'd just watched, constantly being in the front group of a dozen or so riders is vital. There are lots of tight corners and right-angle bends into narrow streets. The riders at the front can go into them quicker and come out of them faster. In the congestion behind, riders at the back often find themselves coming to a complete standstill. Stopping and starting, constantly having to accelerate back to racing speed, saps energy from the legs. When it comes to cornering, controlling their machines on poor surfaces or reacting fast to avoid hazards such as traffic islands or tram tracks, the Flemish racers quickly become experts.

Getting to the front and staying is hard, though. Even before the start riders are trying to shove their way into a prime spot. Ankles are kicked, shins scraped. It's the sort of environment that favours the big and the aggressive, a world of shoulder charges and bunched fists. It's no place for the fainthearted. Brian Robinson, the first British rider to win a stage of the Tour de France and a fixture of the pro circuit in mainland Europe from 1954 to 1963, told his biographer Graeme Fife that racing in Flanders was 'all rough and tumble, grunt and growl, there was nothing friendly'.

This approach was exemplified by the most Flemish of all teams, Flandria. It did not sit well with some purists. The English chronicler of European cycling during the 1960s and 70s, Noel Henderson, was very sniffy about them, commenting on the 'elbowing and jostling . . . where physique counts and pride is taken in one's ability to intimidate'. Flandria, Henderson suggested, were never a team to play fair if they could play dirty instead. He wrote, 'The Flandria sprint has only one guiding principle: get to the line first! If that means boring, switching, chopping, elbowing, leaning or intimidating in any way possible, what does that matter?'

The fastest of all Flandria's sprinters was Eric Leman, a three-time winner of the Ronde van Vlaanderen in the early 1970s. Henderson was unimpressed: 'There is little skill or finesse about Leman's sprinting. His one thought in the last 50 kilometres of a major race is to find the right wheel to follow, to follow that wheel safely without ever losing contact with the front of the race, and then to unleash all of his carefully stored energy in one tremendous jump . . . Just one frantic effort and anyone in the way better move out of the way quickly.'

Eddy Merckx, for one, seemed to agree with Henderson's line. After the Cannibal crashed on the finishing straight into Saint-Étienne during the 1972 edition of Paris–Nice with Leman in close proximity, he said that he would never contest a sprint again if he thought the Fleming was anywhere in the vicinity.

The Flemish, of course, would have expected such complaining. Indeed they might have taken it as a compliment. They were the scrappy underdogs, and if the French and Italian fancy dans didn't like it, well, they'd just stick it to them harder.

* * *

The next day at Ghent–Dampoort station there was a grey-haired middle-aged man pacing up and down the platform waiting for the train to Antwerp. He was wearing silver lamé pants, silver patent leather shoes, a blood red shirt and a canary yellow tie. It seemed a tad elaborate for ten o'clock on a Sunday morning. He looked like he might be in a showband that plays 'popcorn music' covers at one of those dancehalls you often see in the hinterland of small Flemish towns. Popcorn is, more or less, the Belgian answer to northern soul. It was massively popular back in the 1970s and still has its adherents today. It's cheesier and more eclectic than northern soul, mind, and, among the 1960s r'n'b stompers and Motown knockoffs, you're likely to find yourself swaying about to something by Edmundo Ros, Mel Tormé or Googie René.

It was a 20-minute train journey north to Lokeren. The sun was beating down and in front of the station the flea market was in full swing, people eagerly sifting through the sort of stuff they threw out 20 years ago but now realise they can't possibly live without. Sadly, there seemed to be a total absence of Breville electric pie-making machines.

I walked into the centre of town past a cluster of giant chrome rabbits. When I'd first come here in the mid-1990s my friend Steve had memorably remarked, 'Bloody hell, you wouldn't want to bump into one of them when you were pissed.' That description still holds true. At the time I had no idea why the giant rabbits were there, but I've since learned that right up until the 1960s a vast number of Lokeren's inhabitants were employed scraping the fur off rabbit skins to make felt for the hat trade. Photos suggest it was as grim a job as it sounds, and it was typical of the sort of work that went on in Flanders. Little wonder that people saw bike racing as an escape.

I bought an iced brioche from a little bakery and sat in the sunshine opposite the town hall while riders signed in, coming down the steps with their racing numbers then standing on the pavement fiddling about trying to attach them to their jerseys.

Mingled in with the race riders were a whole lot of other blokes on bikes. The crowd at any cycling event in Flanders is not complete without its quota of spotty teenagers and barrel-gutted OAPs dressed in replica cycling kit, mounted on expensive machines, often with race numbers attached, desperately hoping to be mistaken for anyone from Rik Van Looy to Sep Vanmarcke. I used to think they were ridiculous, but I'm less judgemental now. Most of them arrive on bicycles and often they've covered quite a distance. They are quite different from the sort of people who wear replica football shirts to matches. I mean, I bet none of them have run to the stadium dribbling a ball, or scuttled along waving an arm above their head calling, 'Give it to me now, Dazza! Deliver it, mate! I'm open. I'm open!' or fallen theatrically when an elbow came within a foot of their chin.

Usually these cycling imposters are content to pose around at the roadside filling the air with talk of group sets and gear ratios. Sometimes they take things a stage further, loitering around the start until a group of pros pass by on a warm-up run and inveigling their way into the pack. If you sarcastically wave to them, they will wave back with the distracted air of men with their minds on weightier things.

On occasion they take things even one step further. In the late 1990s I had stood on the Kemmelberg, a fiercely steep hill a dozen or so miles south of Ypres, and watched a lone rider in the gear of the Lotto–Mobistar team appear on the lower part of the slope a few minutes after the leading group had ridden past. From the exertion on his face it was plain he was making a heroic solo effort to catch the breakaway. A murmur passed through the crowd. Who was this noble rider? No one was sure. 'Andrei Tchmil,' someone ventured. 'No, too short,' came a response. 'Maybe the Planckaert boy?' All along the verges the crowd applauded and yelled encouragement at this exhibition of apparently superhuman effort by the mysterious loner. Then, when he reached the top of the hill, the rider suddenly and surprisingly stopped, dismounted, sat down on the grass and began chatting amiably to some blokes standing nearby. Even by the standards of professional cycling fans this was a monumentally cheeky performance.

Wandering away from the start line in Lokeren I saw a silver Suzuki SX4 with big photos of Oliver and Lawrence Naesen plastered across the back window. I had a suspicion it must belong to the brothers' mum and dad and I later discovered that I was correct. The Naesens hail from Berlare, a small town in East Flanders a dozen miles from Lokeren. Berlare has some historic importance – in 1798 it was the first place in Flanders to rise up against the French Revolutionaries who had annexed the region three years earlier. The rebellion lasted two months and was eventually crushed with Flemish dead estimated at 15,000. From a cycling point of view Berlare is significant too – it was the birthplace of Fred De Bruyne, one of the best Flemish one-day riders of the late 1950s. The Omloop used to pass through their town when the Naesen boys were kids. Oli, the elder brother, got his first racing bike in 2005, the year Tom Boonen won his world title. He was signed with the French Ag2r–La Mondiale team. It was the younger boy, Lawrence, a rider with the smaller Belgian outfit WB–Veranclassic–Aqua Protect, who was competing today.

The 190-kilometre Omloop van het Waasland is not a Classic, but it is a far bigger deal than yesterday's event in Wetteren. It has been held since 1965. Niko Eeckhout from Izegem – a double winner of Dwars door Vlaanderen, and a four times champion of Flanders – won three times on the trot in the first decade of the twentieth century, and past winners include Walter Planckaert. The race has also been won twice by Geert Omloop, whose name suggests he was destined to be a cyclist.

There was a field of 160 riders assembled for the start in Lokeren, including a couple of Israelis, a handful of Norwegians, a Finn and an Albanian. Some of the big teams were present too. There were a couple of riders from Cannondale, some from Cofidis. Pre-race was the usual mix of crap music and stilted questioning – further confused by the fact that the teams were all different sizes: some had only a couple of riders, while others had 18 or 20. Before the race set off a middle-aged woman in a jogging suit asked me what was going on. When I told her, she shook her head in amazement. 'So many riders,' she said. 'What a big event for a small town like Lokeren.'

I caught the train to Sint-Niklaas and from there took a bus to Kemzeke, 16 kilometres north of Lokeren, where the race finished with several circuits of the town. The bus headed out into the flat and marshy Waasland, past a large long pond where a coarse-fishing competition was in progress and a garage with a sign reading 'Home Sweet Home' above the up-and-over door.

I arrived to find the little town of Kemzeke in party mood. The year 2017 marked its 900th anniversary. There was not much to the place – an elegant eighteenth-century town hall, an austere brick church and a smattering of unambitious-looking cafés, most of which were shut – but it was heaving with people, the majority of whom seemed to have been drinking for several hours. The finishing straight was long and flat, flanked by redbrick houses. The adverts pinned to the fences along the finishing straight were for wet fish shops and paintball centres. The photo-finish van was the one that had been on duty in Wetteren. It was operated by a firm called Ardiles. Presumably not the Argentina and Spurs footballer, Osvaldo, though given his managerial record you wouldn't rule it out. Near a busy bar stood a bookmaker's table, operated by a middle-aged man and woman. A whiteboard carried odds for today's race and the following Saturday's running of Milan–San Remo. The man was in charge of the odds, occasionally wiping some out and rewriting them with a black magic marker. His wife handled the cash, which was in an old-fashioned steel lockbox.

The pavement was already lined with fold-out chairs and stools, and nearly every shop windowsill had a couple of people sitting on it. The upper-floor windows of the houses were open and people occasionally poked their heads out and shouted back into the room, reporting what was going on, which wasn't much.

I stood and stared down the finish straight. I said earlier that the Omloop van het Waasland is a minor race, which is true, but it has a small and significant part in cycling folklore. It was down this street in 1978 that Eddy Merckx, tired, sick with a virulent stomach complaint and wearing the unfamiliar white jersey of the C&A team, had ridden his last few hundred metres as a pro. He finished twelfth.

I wandered around looking for something to eat, but Kemzeke seemed to be just about the only town in Flanders that didn't have a chip shop, and I rejected the idea of a kebab, or a visit to the sort of burger van that wouldn't be out of place parked by an English non-League football ground. The beer wagon only had one beer and that was Jupiler, the ubiquitous, gassy Belgian lager. I found myself pining for Dour – not a feeling I'd expected. The Ford Mustang Club of the Waasland had provided all the stewards' cars, which made for a whole lot of rumbling engine noise and, coupled with Kemzeke's large jet ski showroom, hostess bar and Harley-Davidson dealership decorated with Confederate flags, suggested that this was the redneck capital of Flanders. I wasn't all that surprised. I grew up in rural Yorkshire and I know the strange power Lynyrd Skynyrd exercise over the bucolic mind.

The riders did eight laps around Kemzeke, turning left just after the finish line and then re-emerging 20 minutes later at the top of a long wide street that crossed the main road at a junction flanked by a newsagent's and an Egyptian pizza shop. I found a free windowsill on a flank of the pizzeria and plonked myself down on it. A few minutes later I was joined by a couple who must have been in their eighties and both walked with the aid of sticks. They had brought Lidl carrier bags to sit on. The man, who wore a natty spotted shirt beneath a blue fleece, spoke to me in Flemish. When I told him I was English he and his wife greeted the news with some wonder. The old man began telling me something that sounded heartfelt, grabbing my wrist for emphasis. The only words I could understand were 'Tommy Simpson'. This is generally a positive thing in Flanders. Simpson made his home in Ghent after lodging for a while in the city with the dearly beloved Beurick family at Café Den Engel. The landlady fed him boiled spinach and horse steaks cooked '*au bleu*', advising him to soak up the blood with his chips. It was a singular diet, but it clearly worked. In 1961 Simpson outsprinted Nino Defilippis of Italy to the finish line in Wetteren to become the only British rider ever to win the Ronde van Vlaanderen. 'Major Tom' is generally more fondly remembered in his adoptive homeland than he is in his original one, where less allowance is made for the taint of drug use. The Beuricks' son Albert, who became Simpson's great friend, once said, 'When Tom came to Belgium he was just a normal working-class boy. But he was a gentleman. After his death everybody was very sad. My mum, for example, said he was like one of her sons. He was one of us, he was from Ghent.'

'Tommy Simpson,' the old man said again. And we both nodded and smiled at one another and I told him that Simpson was born in the north-east like me. And we nodded and smiled again. Major Tom came from Haswell in County Durham. His father was a pitman and the family had relocated to Nottinghamshire when Tommy was still at school. Simpson had a reputation – in Britain at least – for being spiky. His sense of humour had a scathing, sarcastic edge to it that some members of the UK cycling fraternity thought betrayed arrogance, though a more charitable interpretation might be that it masked insecurity. Whatever, there's little doubt that Simpson was a resourceful and ambitious man. He endeared himself to the Belgians by playing on caricatures of Britishness – wearing a bowler hat and carrying a brolly, for example – that were far from the realities of the England he'd grown up in. Sadly, although he came from a tough working-class northern background and made his home in Flanders, Simpson was no *flahute*. Small and slight, there was a frailty to him, an anxiety. He was not strong enough, too prone to illness, to finish near the front in the great Tours, while in the one-day races, as an outsider, he sometimes seemed to have been isolated by the politics of the peloton, where nationality or language group could sometimes transcend team loyalty. Yet despite that, Major Tom won four Classics (Milan–San Remo, the Giro di Lombardia and the brutal 350-mile Bordeaux–Paris, as well as the Ronde), took Paris–Nice in 1967 and was world road race champion in 1965. He was famous enough in Britain then to be voted BBC Sports Personality of the Year, but the discovery of amphetamines in his pockets and among his possessions after he died on Mont Ventoux during the 1967 Tour de France changed all that and he was almost written out of our country's sporting history. Following his death, professional road cycling's general popularity in Britain plummeted and it became a fringe sporting interest, strictly for the hardcore, only reviving with the success of the Ghent-born Sir Bradley Wiggins.

Simpson's legacy is looked on a little more sympathetically now. 'They're going to put up a statue to Tommy Simpson in Haswell next year,' I told the old man. He smiled uncomprehendingly. I smiled back. And then in the inevitable lull in the conversation the old man indicated that he wanted to borrow the team sheet I'd bought for one euro in Lokeren. I handed it to him and he took a look down it, then pointed with a bony finger to the name Joeri Stallaert and gave me a thumbs-up sign. Stallaert, 26, from Denderbelle, a dozen miles south-east of Lokeren, rides for the small Belgian team Cibel–Cebon and had won the junior edition of the Ronde van Vlaanderen in 2009, which marked him out for a greatness that he'd yet to achieve – though he finished second in the Omloop van het Waasland in 2015.

The race flashed past. A small breakaway group of half a dozen riders had a lead of several minutes when they reached Kemzeke, but by lap six that had been nibbled away to 55 seconds. The peloton came down the long sloping main drag leading to the crossroads like an express train, a spread of riders from Tarteletto pulling them on, despite the fact they had a man in the break.

By lap seven the field had closed up again. On the final lap they burned down the main street to yells, applause and drumming on advertising hoardings. Fittingly the sprint was won by a man named Wouter Wippert, a Dutch rider with Cannondale. Michael Van Staeyen from Ekeren came second, another Netherlander, Barry Markus, third. The old fellow's tip, Joeri Stallaert, was fourth.

* * *

Stallaert and the rest didn't get much time to recuperate. It was only three days till the next pro-race on the Flemish calendar, Nokere Koerse. The start of that race was in Deinze, a city south of Ghent. Even by this early stage of the season I'd hit a wall with race starts. The milling around, the horrendous music, the inane questions, the terrible temptation to drink 9 per cent abv beer at ten in the morning, had worn me down. Besides, it has to be said that Deinze is a pretty drab place despite its location on the banks of the river Leie. When I'd mentioned it to my landlord, he'd shrugged: 'I think I drove through it one time, maybe.'

Deinze was the birthplace of Rudy Dhaenens. Dhaenens had become world champion in 1990 but was then forced to retire the following year due to a heart condition. This was an example of what cycling fans muttered of as 'the Curse of the Rainbow Jersey' – more or less cycling's equivalent of the Bermuda Triangle, albeit that so far no world champion

1. The Beast of Eeklo, Roger De Vlaeminck, one of the few people in Flanders who thinks Tom Boonen isn't all that.

2. Rik Van Looy, wearing the rainbow jersey, with Andre Darrigade in 1961. No mud (literal or metaphorical) ever stuck to The Emperor.

3. The Flying Milkman Frans Verbeeck finds yet another painful way to lose to Eddy Merckx, Paris-Roubaix 1972.

4. Odiel Defraeye (centre) surrounded by the statutory bunch of blokes in hats after winning the 1912 Tour de France.

5. The always nattily attired Karel van Wijnendaele (left) chats with Sylveer Maes (seated) at the 1939 Tour de France.

6. Paul Deman (leading) won the Ronde in 1913 and Paris-Roubaix in 1920, narrowly avoiding a German firing squad in between.

7. Ritten van Lerberghe looked, and sometimes behaved, like he was appearing in a silent comedy film.

8. Gaston Rebry (centre) stops for a drink during the Tour de France. Unfavourably clement conditions hampered his chances.

9. The peloton judder across the muddy cobbles and past the slagheaps on a glorious day in Dour.

10. With Albert at Le Samyn just before we discovered that an umbrella is inadequate protection against the spray of passing team cars.

11. The author standing in the pouring rain outside Sylveer Maes' café, waiting for a five-second glimpse of Stijn Devolder.

12. One lap to go in the Omloop van Wetteren and the tension at the finish line is palpable.

13. Johan Museeuw, 'The Last of the Flandriens', a man as at home as a willow tree in the flat, windswept West Flanders landscape.

14. A mattentaart – kind of what would happen if a cheesecake and a pork pie had a baby – and beer. All the nutrients you need.

15. A Slovakian family wave their national flag as the Het Nieuwsblad inflatable fights with a church. Another boring day in Belgium.

16. Regulars at De Nieuwe Pulle put down their billiard cues for a sighting of Peter Sagan in Ghent-Wevelgem.

17. The mighty Karel Kaers, the youngest ever road-race world champion and the only rider ever to win the Ronde by accident.

18. Georges Ronsse sporting the classic face-paint of the Flemish ironman.

19. A demonic-looking Eric Leman (left) with Briek Schotte after winning the 1970 Ronde. The ubiquitous fan in the Martini cap looms.

20. The Boss, Rik Van Steenbergen, after winning the rainbow jersey at Waregem in 1957. A statue commemorating the victory mysteriously disappeared.

21. The President and the Cannibal. Godefroot (Flandria jersey), Van Impe (polka dots) and Merckx (Molteni jersey), with French president Valéry Giscard D'Estaing in 1975.

22. De Kuipke on the day of Omloop Het Nieuwsblad. The author is somewhere on the left next to a man with a Jasper Stuyven brolly.

23. The 'Three Musketeers': Maertens (yellow jersey), Demeyer (third from left) and Pollentier (fifth from left), with the Flandria team at the 1976 Tour de France. The Ogre (Maertens) wears yellow. He'd finish in green.

24. Flemish hero Tom Boonen struggling to look pleased with the prizes at Kuurne-Brussels-Kuurne.

25. A shoe shop in Mol wishes local boy Tom Boonen 'a week of golden cobbles'.

26. E3 Harlebeke. Oliver Naesen leads, but is about to suffer the inevitable consequences of being the author's tip for victory.

27. Guillaume van Keirsbulck sadly too preoccupied to enjoy the scenery.

28. The moment that sent beer and loose change flying: Sagan, Van Avermaet and Naesen crash to the deck during the Ronde.

29. A human pyramid in Het Nieuwsblad caps forms on the Kapelmuur for the Ronde van Vlaanderen.

30. Tasteful Flemish cobble porn – hard-core fans prefer them much dirtier and damper.

31. The fearsome Koppenberg claims another bunch of victims. In 1987 it was removed from the Ronde van Vlaanderen until it learned to behave itself.

32. Flemish cycling bookmakers at Noekere Koerse. Imagine all the money they've paid out on results that were subsequently overturned by doping scandals, and chuckle…

33. Oude Kwaremont, Ronde van Vlaanderen, 2015. Bike races show why somebody needs to invent a Shazam for flags.

had completely disappeared on a clear day with not a cloud in the sky. At first the evidence for some sort of weirdness looked impressive, even in purely Flemish terms. Stan Ockers was killed in a crash at the velodrome the year after winning the world title jersey and Jempi Monseré died while wearing it. Freddy Maertens failed to win a race when he wore it in 1982. It all looked like it might mean something, but then a statistical study published in the *British Medical Journal* in 2015 revealed that between 1963 and 2013 winning the world championship road race had had about the same effect on the holder's fortunes as winning the Tour of Lombardy. And nobody talked about 'the Curse of the Race of the Falling Leaves'.

The start area of Nokere Koerse was filled with groups of people photographing team buses and absent-mindedly sifting through the discounted team baseball caps in the merchandise tents. Nokere Koerse is defined as a semi-Classic, but I couldn't find a programme or a team sheet, even when I wandered illegally through the press area and used the journalists' toilet.

Mindful of the lack of food in Kemzeke earlier in the week, I decided to take some with me this time. I went into a supermarket near the inflatable arch marking the race start. There was a sandwich bar at the back. I asked the girl serving behind the counter for a shrimp baguette. 'Do you want everything in it?' she asked. I said I might as well. And watched as she coated the shrimps with lettuce, endive, tomatoes, cucumber, coleslaw, potato salad and hardboiled eggs. At one point she picked up her mobile phone and I wondered if she was going to sling that in as well, but it must just have been a text. The completed baguette was at least 18 inches long and its contents would easily have fed a family of four. 'You get a drink, a bag of potato chips and a rice tart as part of the meal deal,' the girl told me. By the time I'd packed the food in my bag I could hardly lift it.

I went to Deinze's bus station, which is tucked away under the overhead rail lines, and caught the bus out to Kruishoutem. For some reason it was packed with schoolchildren, though it was term time and seemed a bit early for lunch. The driver set off but then got snarled up in the traffic jam created by the race. We lurched forwards in small increments then came to a halt. The driver turned off his engine. The teenage boys began to punch and nip one another. The girls started to argue over YouTube clips. The temperature mounted. The bus smelled of adolescence – celebrity-endorsed perfume, acne cream and those deodorant sprays that are marginally more offensive than the odour they're supposed to mask. Five minutes passed. Ten. Phones trilled Beyoncé ringtones. The boy behind me began a burping contest with himself. I started to worry that my shrimp sandwich would go off before I had chance to eat it.

Eventually the race passed across the junction at the top of the narrow street we were trapped in and we set off again, past signs advertising the Tequila Radio Station and hypermarkets selling bricks and tiles. DIY is almost as popular as bike racing. Every Belgian has a brick in his stomach – an expression so popular that I have yet to meet a Belgian who doesn't at some point quote it to you while pointing out a patio that looks like it was assembled by the Incredible Hulk when in one of his moods and tell you that, yes, for sure, he did all the work himself.

After leaving Deinze the race headed off through Oudenaarde and Kerkhove before completing eight 15-kilometre circuits round Nokere and Kruishoutem. The famous hill at Nokere, the Nokereberg – sometimes referred to as 'the Poggio of Nokere' in honour of the hill at the finish of Milan–San Remo – is the key point in the race.

My intention was to change buses in Kruishoutem and get another bus to Nokere, but the delay in Deinze had scuppered that idea. But it was a lovely day and when I looked at my map the walk didn't seem that long – three miles, maybe four. 'I can do that in an hour,' I told myself. I'd get myself a pitch on the slopes of the Nokereberg, eat my sandwich in the sunshine. If I was lucky there'd be a nice café along the route selling Witkap Stimulo or some other likely Flemish beer.

I set off up the hill out of Kruishoutem, a short sharp pull that ended on a stretch of flat upland; the road flanked on one side by a deep drainage ditch, on the other by flat expanses of arable land. Mr and Mrs Naesen were parked slap on the two-kilometre marker. They had a large flag on a tall pole extolling their sons' virtues and were sitting in fold-out chairs eating salad.

Nearby was a massive mobile home with 'Big John' emblazoned on the front. The gap between the two words suggested a couple named Big and John, or a large man named John who spoke very, very slowly. When I passed it on the way back a massive bloke was sitting on the rear steps wearing a straw Stetson.

The countryside between Kruishoutem and Nokere is very pleasant, flat and green with large fields of leeks and cabbages, edged by willow trees. The sky above was wide and blue and it seemed that whatever direction you looked in you could see the spire of some village church. If there's such a thing as *La Flandre profonde*, then this was surely it.

Near a garden filled with more peacocks than is strictly necessary – i.e. one – I fell in step with a Flemish couple who'd decided the sunshine warranted matching red shorts. They were carrying chairs and an icebox and aimed to get into Nokere and establish a pitch on the Nokereberg before the race started its circuits. I told them that was my plan too. We walked along chatting in English about the race.

Nokere Koerse was first staged in 1944. Eighty-two riders entered. The winner was Marcel Kint. Back then Nokere Koerse (which means, like it sounds, Nokere Course) was known as the Grand Prix Jules Lowie in tribute to the rider from Nokere who won Paris–Nice in 1938 and was an integral part of the powerful Belgian team that dominated the Tour de France in the late 1930s. Photos show Lowie's gala reception in Nokere after his return from Nice. A man of medium height with narrow eyes and dark hair in a widow's peak, Lowie, dressed in white and clutching a vast bouquet of flowers, is surrounded by a dozen or so fans. These were the men who would organise the race that bore his name. Lowie appeared in the Grand Prix Jules Lowie at least twice, but his best finish was fifth in 1946.

Although the race was not a Classic it was prestigious enough to have attracted Tour de France winners Bernard Hinault, Greg LeMond and Bernard Thévenet. And the winners' board had many great names on it – Kint, Schotte, Sercu, Van Springel, Maertens, Demeyer. Frans De Mulder, who came from nearby Kruishoutem and won the 1960 Vuelta a España, had been victorious in Nokere in 1963.

Another winner had been Wim van Est, and my companions were just telling me that the Dutchman, who'd begun his bike-riding career as a tobacco-smuggler, was nicknamed 'the Executioner of Heike' because of his powerful sprint finish, when we arrived at the one-kilometre marker to find our way into Nokere barred by an elderly steward with wild hair and a jacket that looked like it had been borrowed from a 1950s train guard. My new Flemish friend exchanged words with him in Dutch, which gradually escalated in volume. His wife joined in and after a final hostile exchange they turned on their heels and walked back along the road we had come along. Naturally, I followed them. 'What's the problem?' I asked. 'They say you can't go into the village unless you have a ticket,' the man said. I pointed out that there was a lot of stuff in Flemish on the website which I couldn't understand but was likely on this very topic. 'So all the tickets are sold?' I asked.

'No, no, you could buy one off him but he wanted a stupid amount of money, a dumb amount.'

'How much did he want?'

'Five euros each.'

'Five euros!?' I said, incredulous because it seemed like a small price to pay to me, especially since I'd walked three miles to get there. The Flemish couple, however, took my astonishment as a sign that I was in full agreement with them. 'Yes,' the man said. 'Five euros! Five euros! They must think we are crazy.' He made a looping gesture with his index finger next to his temple. 'To watch cycling is free,' he continued. 'Always. How can they charge money? These people ... these people...' He couldn't think of a suitable word in English, but I had a feeling that if this was Britain he'd have said, 'They are worse than the Nazis.'

I could see his point. It seemed odd to have to pay five euros just to enter a village. I wondered what would have happened if I'd caught the bus. Would they have forced me to pay up before letting it through?

On the other hand, it was only five euros. I thought of sneaking back, but I felt I couldn't out of solidarity with the Flemish couple, and so instead I consoled myself with the fact that we had made a stand against the encroaching forces of commercialism, and that I had a foot-and-a-half-long shrimp baguette in my bag and it was now lunchtime.

I walked along with the Flemings until I found a tree to sit under and bade them farewell. My shrimp sandwich was delicious and drew admiring glances from passers-by and calls of *'bon appétit'* and its Dutch equivalent *'eet smakelijk'*. The Flemish like food and are always keen to see what you are having. Flanders is one of the few places where people eat over your shoulder.

As I was wiping the mayonnaise off my fingers – and shirt, and jeans – the race arrived. The Rodania car – which preceded many Flemish races, blaring out its advertising jingle for the Swiss watchmaker whose international sales office is in Flemish Brabant – was followed by a smaller car extolling the virtues of Ename (a type of beer, not a colonic treatment) and a truck pulling a portable advertising hoarding for a firm that makes conservatories.

The peloton swirled past. Immediately it was gone and life went back to normal. Tractors and wagons bundled across fields and down the narrow lanes; trucks with the name Potato Queen painted on the side of them drove past along the main road. I walked back towards Kruishoutem, catching the second circuit near a feed station just outside the village. At the feed station the riders grabbed the cloth bags and more or less instantly rifled through them, tossing aside stuff they didn't want like kids ripping through a party bag. Energy bars flew out in all directions. A burly chap a few yards down from me, who was squeezed into Lycra like liver sausage in a tube, rushed out and picked them up. By the time the field had passed he must have nabbed at least half a dozen.

An old man came and stood beside me. I asked him who he thought would win. 'No idea,' he said and looked up at the sky. 'But it's a sunny day, we're out of doors and I have a beer, so who cares?' That was the thing with cycling – unlike most other major sporting events this was one that actually came to you, even when you were miles out in the countryside. If you weren't that interested in the sport, it was still a welcome break from the grind, a day out.

I moved around between laps, ending up on a roundabout in Kruishoutem. The riders came down the long straight hill into the little town and then made a sharp right turn down the main street. There was a steward with a warning flag standing in the middle of a traffic island, and as the riders hurtled past him I feared for his life. One slip and they'd wipe him out.

Unlike their counterparts in Nokere, the locals in Kruishoutem had made little effort to cash in on visitors. Most of the cafés were shut. There were vans selling ice cream and burgers, and a stall selling chocolates, where a man dressed as the Easter bunny was sipping from a can of Red Bull and talking into his mobile phone in a voice that sounded far too deep for a rabbit. The race went past to cheering and applause one final time and then people headed off home to catch the final stages on TV.

The finish was a slightly bad-tempered affair. The Flemish rider Kris Boeckmans, who'd nearly died in 2015 after a crash in the Vuelta, and

Frenchman Justin Jules, who'd served time in prison for the manslaughter of his stepfather, got involved in a scuffle a kilometre or so out in which shirts were pulled and threats uttered. Nacer Bouhanni of France won the sprint from Britain's Adam Blythe, who'd been based out in Flanders since his amateur days. The old boy from Kemzeke's pick, Joeri Stallaert, came third.

7

SHOW ME THE MONEY

Dwars door Vlaanderen, March 22
E3 Harelbeke, March 24

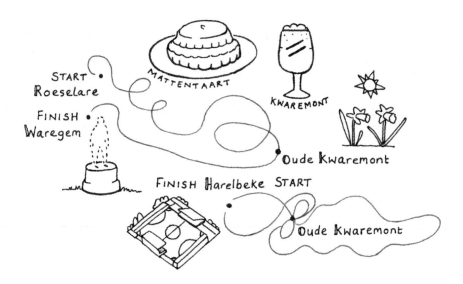

The Nokere Koerse was closely followed by the Handzamme Classic. The Handzamme Classic (which, confusingly, wasn't actually a Classic at all) had originally been a stage of the Driedaagse van West-Vlaanderen, but then, in 2010, you might say it went off on a solo breakaway. So far it has not been reeled back in, and since the Driedaagse van West-Vlaanderen is now also a one-day race, it seems unlikely it will be in the future. Although the UCI had given the race semi-Classic status it was

142

a low-key affair, which set off from the beach resort of Bredene and wiggled along the coast before finishing after just under 200 kilometres, usually in a bunch sprint, in Handzamme. As at Nokere, Adam Blythe was beaten for speed in the final 50 metres, this time by Norwegian Kristoffer Halvorsen.

During the hiatus in the Flemish cycling season that followed Handzamme, spring arrived. The rain gave way to warm sunshine. Daffodils popped up and danced in the breeze, cherry trees blossomed and the temporary fencing, beer tents and hospitality marquees of the Ronde van Vlaanderen sprang from the warm Flemish earth. We were nearing the start of Flemish Cycling Week – a whirl of five races that sent Flanders into such giddy excitement nobody seemed to notice that it actually went on for nearly a fortnight. Flemish Cycling Week culminates with the Ronde, which by this point was creating such a tingle of excitement it was an effort of iron will not to put three exclamation marks after it.

The great race was 12 days away and the banners advertising its imminent arrival strung across the streets of towns and cities along the route seemed as much a harbinger of the new season as gambolling lambs and frolicking bunnies. Indeed, I suspect that if Charles De Coster had written his tale of sixteenth-century Flemish trickster Tijl Uilenspiegel today it would have opened with the line, 'In spring in Flanders when the posters for the Ronde go up.'

My friend Steve had come up from his home in Luxembourg to join me for a few days' watching bike racing, drinking beer and complaining about football. Steve was the man who had introduced me to pro bike racing back in the mid-1980s. He had a picture of Sean Kelly on the wall of his flat in Tottenham. In those days I was so ignorant of the sport I'd thought the reason Kelly was wearing a green jersey was because he was Irish. These days Steve is less enchanted with the sport than he'd been then, the legacy of the apparently endless doping scandals that had ripped cycling apart since the fateful day in

143

1998 when Flemish grandfather Willy Voet, a *soigneur* with Festina, was stopped by French customs officers on the border near Lille driving a car stuffed with more drugs than Woodstock. (Voet had a fair few drugs stuffed in himself, I should add. Shortly before arriving at the border he'd pepped himself up with an injection of '*pot belge*' – a drug stew containing amphetamines, cocaine, caffeine and heroin.) Steve was hoping that a few days spent watching at the roadside might rekindle his love for bike racing.

We got the train to Oudenaarde and did enough denouncing of drug cheats on the journey to make Lance Armstrong's ears burn. Oudenaarde was now the finishing point of the Ronde, a role it had taken over from Meerbeke in 2012 and which it seemed unlikely to relinquish in the foreseeable future. Since the Centrum Ronde van Vlaanderen, the impressive museum devoted to the great race, was also in Oudenaarde, the pretty little town had some claim to being the epicentre of Flemish cycling. But this has not always been the case. When I'd first visited Oudenaarde in 1997 it had been a quiet backwater; the only foreign tourists were British military history buffs eager to visit the battlefield just outside the town on which the Duke of Marlborough had scored one of his great victories over the French back in the early eighteenth century.

At the tourist office just off the *markt* Steve and I enquired about the bus to Oude Kwaremont, a key point in the day's race, Dwars door Vlaanderen. The lady behind the counter glanced to left and right and lowered her voice. 'I'm not sure,' she said. 'I'm not actually a fan of bike racing.' In Oudenaarde this was pretty much like a Catholic priest saying he didn't really hold with all that Holy Trinity nonsense. She asked a colleague.

The bus left from Tacambaroplein, a square named in honour of a battle fought by the Belgian Legion in Mexico in support of the Emperor Maximilian, an Austrian prince who'd been put into power by the French while the USA was distracted by the Civil War. Maximilian's wife, Empress Carlotta, had previously been known as Charlotte and was the daughter of the Belgian king, Leopold I. The entire enterprise was a shambles. The Belgian Legion, made up of 1,500 volunteers, had assembled at Oudenaarde in 1864. Only half of them came back. Maximilian was shot by a firing squad of Mexicans loyal to the elected president, Benito Juárez. Carlotta returned to Belgium, her nerves shattered by the whole experience, and was eventually locked up in an insane asylum by her father, a man with the empathy of a rattlesnake and considerably lower morals.

The bus wobbled out into the countryside, the hills of the Flemish Ardennes rising up to our left. We passed through the village of Melden, where you could see the steep, straight cobbles of the Koppenberg – the most notorious of all the climbs in the region. The bus driver seemed not to know where or what Kwaremont was, but we guessed he was just baffled by our pronunciation. Eventually, panicking that we had already gone past the hill, we rang the bell and hopped off to find we had landed in exactly the place where the road leading to the ascent started.

Dwars door Vlaanderen marks the start of Flemish Cycling Week. The name means 'Across Flanders', though naturally enough the race isn't straight, nor does it in fact cover much of Flanders. In reality it wriggles about like a worm with a tummy rash, starting in Roeselare in the west, veering about through the Flemish Ardennes and then hooking back to Waregem. The race traditionally has plenty of hills (between 12 and 14) and plenty of cobbled stretches, such as the Haaghoek and the Holleweg.

Dwars door Vlaanderen had first been run in 1945 when it went from Sint-Truiden in Limburg over to the east of Brussels to Waregem in East Flanders. Back then it was called Dwars door België ('Across Belgium'), a name it kept until 1999, by which stage it had ceased to cross any French-speaking territory. From 1946 until 1964 it was a two-day stage race, which went from Waregem into Limburg or Liège on the first day, and back again the next. Since 1965 it's been a one-day affair that's left out Limburg altogether (in fact poor old Limburg seems to have been more or less entirely ignored by the cycling Classics) and avoided the Flemish coast too.

The list of winners is pretty much a who's who of Flemish cycling: Schotte, Impanis, Foré, Godefroote, Leman, Museeuw and Boonen all feature, though there are some notable absentees, including Van Looy, De Vlaeminck and Maertens. Recently, though, the big-name riders, the spring Classic contenders, have tended to take it easy in the race, treating it as a light warm-up for the rigours ahead at the Ronde. As a result the list of recent winners includes decent but hardly world-renowned riders, such as Omloop van het Waasland specialist Niko Eeckhout – who has won it twice. In 2011 Nick 'the Bomb from Bevel' Nuyens won Dwars door Vlaanderen and then rode off with the Ronde too, something that Johan Museeuw also did in 1993. It was something Flemish cycling writers, always eager for Ronde omens, kept track of.

The winner of the first edition of Dwars door Vlaanderen was Rik Van Steenbergen (or Rik I, as he came to be known after the emergence of the young man he'd inspired as a teenager, Rik Van Looy).

Earlier in the week I'd gone in search of a sculpture of Van Steenbergen near the finish line in Waregem. It was here that Van Steenbergen had won his third world title in 1957. For once I had fairly detailed directions for finding the statue, but the spot where it should have been was empty. There was a tourist information point in the town hall. The woman behind the counter had stand-alone hair and severe glasses worn on a chain. Her blouse looked like something a starchy headmistress would have worn in a 1970s sitcom. I told her I was looking for the statue of Rik Van Steenbergen that was supposed to be located between the shopping precinct and the arts centre. 'Maybe I'm being stupid – but I can't see it,' I said.

'Ah, yes, Rik . . . Van . . . Steen . . . bergen,' the lady behind the desk said. She rolled the name round her mouth as if she didn't care for the taste of it. 'I'm afraid the statue has been taken away,' she said, 'for . . . restoration purposes.' Her tone suggested she hoped it never came back. In some ways I could see her point of view. These days people want a sporting superstar to be a role model, and an example to children. Rik wasn't a role model for anyone unless you had an ambition to win a fortune, gamble it away, boost amphetamines and end up paying the rent by appearing in erotic films. (Yes, I know. Me too.)

Van Steenbergen is one of the greatest cyclists Flanders has produced. He won the Ronde for the first time when he was just 18, and was the only man apart from Merckx and Italy's Alfredo Binda to take the world road race title three times. Yet it is hard to see quite how he fits in with the Flemish legend. He was tough, for sure, and beefy and powerful, but he was hardly the simple home-loving farm boy who would come back from winning a Monument, give the bouquet of flowers to his mother, pop out to milk the family cow then rush off to Mass. Cycling fans called him 'the Boss', which hinted at shady dealings as much as it honoured his talent.

Van Steenbergen was born in Arendonk near Antwerp in 1924. He'd first come to public attention thanks to the efforts of Karel Kaers. A tall, hefty, rugged *rouleur* with legs like tree trunks, Kaers started racing aged 14. He was Belgian champion in 1937 and won the Ronde more or less by accident in 1939 (he'd planned just to ride half of it as a training run for Paris–Roubaix, but when he found himself in the lead heading over the Kwaremont he barrelled on to the finish). Kaers' most remarkable performance, though, came in the 1934 world championship road race in Leipzig. On a flat course he harnessed all his raw power to surge home ahead of the field. He was just 20 years of age.

During World War Two there was still track cycling in the famous Vélodrome d'Hiver in Paris. Kaers rode there and told anyone who would listen that there was a young lad in Belgium who was destined for greatness. Remember the name, he said: Rik Van Steenbergen. Even in those days journalists were sceptical of Belgian claims for their young riders. Before there were hundreds of 'new Eddy Merckxs' there were dozens of 'future Sylveer Maes' or 'junior Georges Ronsses'. Kaers, though, was adamant, and his cycling credentials, allied to his strapping physique, made him hard to ignore.

Van Steenbergen came from a poor family and, like Fausto Coppi and Rik II, the Emperor of Herentals, he began his working life on a bike as a butcher's delivery boy. Kaers was one of his customers. The big Flemish star took a shine to the young lad and gave him an old bike frame and a pair of his training wheels. Van Steenbergen made his debut at the Antwerp Sportpaleis shortly afterwards.

The Boss was tall at six feet, three inches and weighed around 13 stone, a big brute of a bloke to be riding a bike. Indeed, he was bigger and heavier than the world heavyweight boxing champion of the time, Rocky Marciano. Despite his size, though, Van Steenbergen was a man at ease in the saddle. He was elegant and fast, with deep reserves of stamina. He could produce an explosive sprint finish after hours of riding and was equally at home on the polished wood of the velodrome or the slick wet cobbles of Flanders.

The Boss began riding a bike seriously during World War Two, after the Belgian army requisitioned his car. He quickly found an advantage in racing. When he was allowed to travel to Switzerland to compete he smuggled back some Swiss watches and sold them on the black market.

That was Van Steenbergen. He was cunning, crafty and always had an eye to the main chance. He was a hustler. If there was money to be made, he would make it, no matter what it involved. The 1946 world championship was held in Switzerland. It poured with rain all day. Van Steenbergen was in a breakaway group of three riders as the race entered the final lap. Alongside Van Steenbergen was fellow Fleming Marcel 'the Black Eagle' Kint, who'd won the world title eight years earlier in

Valkenburg, and the Swiss Hans Knecht, one time amateur champion of the world. Kint was past his best and Knecht had no professional reputation to speak of. Van Steenbergen seemed a certain winner. Instead, he came in third. Later he offered vague excuses about being exhausted from riding at the front too long, of not seeing Knecht when he sprang past him to take victory. Observers were unconvinced. The result was marked down as suspicious by the press, though no official inquiry was ever made. Had Van Steenbergen 'sold' the race to the home nation's rider? Many thought so, and it wouldn't be the last time.

In 1949 Van Steenbergen suffered another defeat that seemed odd, on the Tour de France stage that ended in the Bordeaux velodrome. Sprinting to the head of a small bunch, Van Steenbergen raised his arms in triumph as he crossed the line. There was still a lap to go, however. Local favourite Guy Lapébie – Roger's younger brother – took the victory. The Belgian press wondered how an experienced rider like Van Steenbergen could make such a beginner's error. Had he sold another win to a local?

In 1956 in the Roubaix velodrome Van Steenbergen mysteriously lost out in a six-man bunch sprint that saw Louison Bobet win the Hell of the North. People muttered of Van Steenbergen bargaining with others in the final kilometres, turning the race into an auction.

Even when he won – and he did win, a lot – Van Steenbergen's career never seemed far from the tramlines of controversy. There was his victory in the 1949 Flèche Wallonne, for example. Fausto Coppi had broken away and was heading for what seemed like a comfortable victory when Van Steenbergen and his compatriot Ward Peeters managed to slipstream a following car, which effectively towed them back into contact with the great Italian. Van Steenbergen outpowered Coppi in the sprint. Had the driver deliberately helped him? Many thought so.

The perpetual air of conspiracy damaged the Boss's reputation internationally, but he remained hugely popular in Flanders. Mobbed by fans, he'd sit for hours after races signing autographs. His brilliance was beyond dispute. How many races he won is a matter for conjecture. Certainly it seems to have been in four figures, with some writers saying he won 1,300 on the track alone. In Copenhagen in 1949 he took the world road title ahead of Coppi and Ferdi Kübler, two of the giants of the age and both at their peak (though rumours circulated that Van Steenbergen again had bribed them to let him win). In the Danish capital seven years later he saw off his young shadow Rik Van Looy and Dutchman Gerrit 'the Pedalling Fool' Schulte, who had won the title from Coppi in 1948, and the following year he beat out Bobet and André Darrigade in Waregem.

Ultimately Van Steenbergen was motivated by one thing only – money. Glory meant little to him, and the feeling among cycling writers was that he entered the big races only in order to increase his appearance fees in the *kermis* races and track meetings. One contemporary described him as 'a fabulous cyclist with the soul of a mercenary'.

He seems to have made just one really concerted effort in a Grand Tour, the Giro d'Italia of 1951. Rik I was at his heavily muscled peak. He might not have had the build for a mountainous race like the Giro, but he had the power and – when he put his mind to it – he had the class and the character too. Van Steenbergen saw off Gino Bartali early and then battled with the great Fiorenzo Magni up and down the high mountains, wrestling the pink jersey from him, only to lose it again a few days later. Several times he looked to be done in and broken, only to fight back when it was least expected. Eventually Magni crossed the finish line one minute and 46 seconds ahead of him. To finish second in a field that included not only Magni, Coppi and Bartali but also Frenchman Bobet (who'd win the Tour de France three times) and Hugo Koblet of Switzerland (a winner of the Giro and the Tour) showed exactly what Van Steenbergen was capable of. But as far as he was concerned it was too much effort for not enough reward. Cycling was how the Boss put food on the table. You couldn't eat a heroic reputation.

Van Steenbergen made a fortune from appearance fees in track and *kermis* races. He was always on the lookout for a paid ride, or a chance to earn easy prize money. If he had an overnight stop in a town on his way to an engagement he'd seek out the nearest race and compete in that. In one memorable 48-hour spell Van Steenbergen raced in the Belgian Congo, Copenhagen, Paris and Liège. He won all four events. It was said that he travelled two million kilometres during his career in search of pay. The French cyclist-turned-journalist Jean Bobet wrote, 'At any race he would want to know the start time, the address of a restaurant, the gear to use and how he would be paid. For the rest, jokes and civilities, no time was wasted.'

Just about the only time Van Steenbergen raced for more than the money was in the Flèche Wallonne of 1958. He was 33 years old and there was talk in the Belgian media that Rik Van Looy was now a better rider than the first Rik had ever been. Incensed by the impertinence of the young usurper, Van Steenbergen trained by riding 1,000 kilometres in a week, driving his usual training partner to lock himself in despair in his bedroom claiming illness. He then destroyed Van Looy in the hills of the Ardennes and walked away satisfied.

Noel Henderson wrote that Van Steenbergen was the antithesis of Louison Bobet, who was all class and no character. While Jacques Anquetil's lieutenant, the affable Raphaël 'the Big Gun' Géminiani, said the Boss was, 'A typical cold Fleming, not saying much and with a cloud of boredom over his forehead. He wandered the world with his bars and his saddle, ready to race anywhere against anyone.'

In many ways Van Steenbergen resembled the itinerant Mexican middleweight in Leonard Gardner's classic boxing novel *Fat City*, who travelled by bus from town to town carrying a cheap suitcase containing his gloves, boots, shorts, robe and protective cup. Van Steenbergen was a man for hire, but his skill could not be overestimated.

Van Steenbergen made no bones about his drug use. 'The stars had to look fresh in every race, and they couldn't do that without stimulants,' he told one reporter. Later he clarified his comment by saying he only took drugs when he wanted to win a race, 'not like the riders nowadays' – a rare example of his attempting to take the moral high ground.

It was a very different world, of course. Amphetamines such as Tonedron were available across the counter in any chemist's in the 1950s and early 1960s. Tonedron – nicknamed 'Tonton' ('Uncle') in France – was sold as a pick-me-up and medicinal tonic, or to help people lose weight. Most cyclists – including Tommy Simpson – doubled, tripled or quadrupled the recommended dosage. As Van Steenbergen suggested, drug abuse was commonplace, thriving in a system where riders were paid appearance money. The more they raced, the more they earned, so they booked themselves for everything available. The agents who made the bookings and took 10 per cent of the fees had little interest in an athlete's health. When the riders appeared, they earned. But appearing was not enough. The stars also had to give the paying public their money's worth and entertain them. It wasn't enough simply to be good, the rider had also to be memorable. That's why Tommy Simpson would appear on the track in his bowler hat, playing up to his English gentleman persona to amuse the fans. The track meets in particular had something of professional wrestling about them.

It's doubtful the riders knew the health risks they were taking when boosting themselves with speed, or even injecting morphine into their calves to ease the torturous pain of racing two or sometimes three times a day. And even if they did, given that the alternative for most of them was back-breaking work on a farm for little pay, would they have done anything different? Few people who rode in that era seemed to think so.

Van Steenbergen liked money. And he accumulated a great deal. By the mid-1950s, as he turned 30, Van Steenbergen was living just outside Antwerp in a vast house with a swimming pool and a couple of tennis courts. He trained hard daily at the Sportpaleis velodrome, acting as his own mechanic and doing without the traditional services of a *soigneur*.

Maybe he was too down to earth to bother with such things, or maybe he just didn't like shelling out his hard-earned cash.

In the afternoons he'd hang out in the café Karel Kaers had bought near the velodrome, playing cards with local industrial workers. For all his personality faults, Van Steenbergen had no airs and graces, which was one of the reasons the straight-talking Flemish liked him. He played then for small stakes, though gambling would later become a besetting vice and lure him into deep waters.

Ultimately Van Steenbergen earned a fortune but frittered it all away, got in hock to Belgian gangland characters over gambling debts, and was reputedly jailed for ferrying a suspect package across the Dutch border. His marriage fell apart. In 1969 he appeared in *Pandore*, an erotic Belgian film, cast as Dimitri, a middle-aged Greek who dallies with a young Belgian woman named Peggy played by Diane Dee (whose film credits included *Take Me, I'm Old Enough*). His later years were stabilised by marriage to an English woman. When he died in 2003 his funeral attracted Belgian cycling royalty – from Rik Van Looy to Tom Boonen via Eddy Merckx – as well as the Belgian Prime Minister and the president of the IOC.

There is another statue of Van Steenbergen in his native Arendonk. So far it hasn't been taken away.

* * *

Steve and I marched up Oude Kwaremont, where Karel Kaers had made his famous break in the 1939 Ronde, at a fair old lick, past a bar with a sign outside that read in English 'Train hard. Crying victory. Being happy' and round a chicane that cut between steep banks topped by clumpy willows. It was a longer climb than the Molenberg but with the same lurching camber that made it more or less impossible to walk without affecting a limp – and though the cobbles were more even they went on for a lot longer, covering not just the ascent but the flat hilltop stretch that followed it. Alongside that stretch of the route – and the baby's heads were notably lumpier here – a temporary wooden terrace had been put in for ticket holders at the Ronde. If I'd been a rider I'd have been tempted to jump on that and pedal along it.

The sun was beating down and after watching the race pass on the tarmacked stretch of the hill known as Nieuwe Kwaremont, we repaired to the famous In 't Palet café, where we sat at a table drinking Kwaremont beer, watching the race on a big-screen TV and refuelling on freshly baked *mattentaartjes*, fist-sized flaky pastry pies filled with curd cheese. They're delicious, if slightly puritanical compared to most Flemish desserts – I mean, where's the chocolate, the kirsch-soaked cherries and brandy-laced whipped cream?

After a couple of drinks we went outside to watch the women's race pass under the inflatable Kwaremont arch. I've often remarked on the idiocy of those spectators who manage to knock riders off their bikes by stepping out to take a photo, or leaning over the barrier to get a view at just the wrong moment. I have a little more sympathy for them now, because on the slopes of the Kwaremont I almost became one myself, stooping to pull my bag out of the concrete guttering into which the riders were swerving to avoid the jarring cobbles and almost headbutting eventual winner Lotta Lepistö of Finland.

Chastened after my lucky escape, I went back into the bar with Steve and watched the men's race unfold to the noisy chatter of cycling fans. A breakaway of 15 riders had built up a lead of around 45 seconds. Belgian champion Philippe Gilbert was in among them, so was 2015 winner Jelle Wallays from Roeselare. The riders came up the cobbled hill at real speed, apparently not inconvenienced in the least by the 12 per cent gradient. There was a decent gathering of spectators but the applause was appreciative rather than exhilarated, though there were shouts of encouragement for the aggressive Gilbert who was driving the bunch.

A few minutes later on the Paterberg, Gilbert kicked again, dropping everyone with the exception of Australian Luke Durbridge, Alexey

Lusenko of Kazakhstan and his Flemish teammate at Quick-Step, Yves Lampaert. Lampaert, a 25-year-old from Izegem who'd missed most of the 2016 season after his girlfriend accidentally rammed a shopping trolley into his ankle and damaged his Achilles tendon, broke away from the other three a few kilometres from the finish and, with Gilbert refusing to help chase him down and Durbridge and Lusenko too suspicious of each other to team up, he crossed the finish line in Wevelgem 39 seconds ahead of them. Gilbert won the sprint for second. The best of the rest for the Flemish were the Naesens' boy Oliver, placed sixth, and Tiesj Benoot, who combined pro riding with his economics degree studies at Ghent University, in seventh.

In the following day's *Wielerkrant* there was great delight at Lampaert's unexpected victory. He was a throwback to the good old days – a farmer's son who was happy to be photographed standing on the running board of his dad's tractor. He appeared modest and unflashy. Even the champagne he was pictured spraying all over his teammate Gilbert came from Lidl. While Lampaert's trolley-wielding girlfriend talked up Lampi's chances in Paris–Roubaix to the gathered media, there was little time for the rest of the riders to relax. Two days later it was the E3 Harelbeke, possibly the only international sporting event to be partly named after a motorway.

For those of you who are interested in this sort of thing – and, frankly, who isn't fascinated by the history of motorways? – the system of pan-European highways was developed by the United Nations Economic Commission for Europe from 1950 through to 1975, in an attempt to link up European nations in the same way that the interstate highways system did for US states. The new roads were all given the designation 'E' for Europe (except in Britain where they were totally ignored) and it has to be said that they have some fairly random start/ finish points. The E05, for example, goes from Greenock near Glasgow all the way to Algeciras in southern Spain, while the E10 goes from Shannon in the Republic of Ireland to Saint Petersburg.

The E3 was given its name in 1950 and ran from Lisbon to Helsinki. After 1975, however, the UNEC surrendered control of the roads to the European Union, who set about reorganising the whole system. The name E3 now refers only to the stretch of the original E3 that runs across Normandy from Cherbourg to Carentan. The road from Arras to Antwerp, which passes near Harelbeke, was renamed the E17. The E3 Harelbeke therefore not only finds itself named after a motorway, but named after a motorway in another country.

The race was inaugurated in 1958 and originally ran along the route of the E3 from Harelbeke to Antwerp and back again. It was unimaginatively called Harelbeke–Antwerp–Harelbeke until the early 1960s when it was renamed just as unimaginatively the E3–Prijs Harelbeke. Like Dwars door Vlaanderen, the E3 nowadays follows a looping circuit that takes in most of the major sites of the Ronde, only in this case in reverse order.

Though it covers much the same ground as Dwars door Vlaanderen, the race run a few days before it, it's undoubtedly a much bigger deal. Tom Boonen has won the E3 five times, Fabian 'Spartacus' Cancellara three, Johan Museeuw twice, while big names Sagan, De Vlaeminck, Maertens, Verbeeck and Van Springel all feature on the list of winners. The Emperor of Herentals, Rik Van Looy, has won it as often as Boonen. There are some less well-known Flemish names on the winners' list too, including the evocative Arthur Decabooter – who was nicknamed 'El Torro', possibly because the Flemish diminutive of Arthur is 'Tuur' – and Willy In 't Ven, who sounds like a Yorkshire delivery man.

Freddy Maertens' win in 1978 was proof that financial shenanigans within the peloton had not ended with Van Steenbergen's retirement. Pierre Lano, a Harelbeke carpet manufacturer and future mayor of the town, had been married the day before the race and apparently offered Maertens a bonus of 80,000 Belgian francs if he brought him victory as 'a wedding present'. Maertens broke away on Oude Kwaremont in the company of Netherlander Jan Raas. They were so far ahead of the pursuers it was effectively a two-horse race, but Maertens was eager to make certain of a bonus and the favour of his boss and promised 40,000 Belgian francs to the Dutchman if he'd let him cross the finish line first.

Belgian riders have shown poorly in the E3 in recent years; the last podium finisher was Boonen in 2012. Since 2007 they've only had six podium places compared to 14 in the Ronde. It's the kind of thing that vexes the journalists, but most fans don't seem too bothered. Then again, they don't have a daily cycling supplement to fill.

Steve and I caught the train to Harelbeke for the start of the race only to find that the team presentation was inside the football stadium and was ticketed. I hoped the Flemish couple from Nokere hadn't turned up too. It might have tipped the chap over the edge. Unable to witness the interviews we were forced to mill around photographing the team buses with the rest of the hoi polloi until the race departed, slowly, through a 1970s estate. After that it was back to Oudenaarde again.

Away from the really big names of Flemish cycling there are a host of others who have won Classics but whose names these days would only likely be known in their home town or village. Rik Wouters, winner of Paris–Brussels and Paris–Tours, came from Baarle-Hertog, an island of Belgium that's entirely surrounded by Holland – indeed some houses and businesses actually straddle the border. At one time Dutch law dictated that restaurants in the Netherlands closed earlier than those in Belgium – which in Baarle-Hertog meant moving tables to continue eating. Willy Brocklandt, winner of Liège–Bastogne–Liège, came from Bellegem; Walter Boucquet, winner of the Grand Prix des Nations, from Meulebeke; Jos Huysmans, winner of the Flèche Wallonne, from Beerzel; Frans Melckenbeeck, winner of Liège–Bastogne–Liège, from Lede; Daniel Van Ryckeghem, winner of the Frankfurt Grand Prix, from Meulebeke; Valere Van Sweevelt, winner of Liège–Bastogne–Liège, from Kuringen.

Because of the success of men like Schotte, Van Steenbergen and Van Looy, a rider like Germain Derycke from Bellegem barely gets a mention when great riders of the 1950s are discussed. Yet Derycke won Paris–Roubaix, Milan–San Remo, the Ronde and Liège–Bastogne–Liège – four out of the five Monuments. Add to that the Flèche Wallonne, Dwars door Vlaanderen, a stage of the Tour de France and silver and bronze medals in the world championship road race and you have the sort of career that would have made him a national hero in Britain. In Flanders he was an also ran.

Oudenaarde's own unsung Flemish hero is Eric Van Lancker, of the un-PC nickname 'the Moroccan' because of his dark skin. Van Lancker won the Amstel Gold Race in 1989 and Liège–Bastogne–Liège the following year. Van Lancker was modest and unassuming. He didn't believe in showing off. 'There are some riders you see in the papers every day, even though they never do anything – I am against that,' he said.

Van Lancker had been a cycling fan since childhood and had named his favourite marble after Roger De Vlaeminck. To Van Lancker's way of thinking De Vlaeminck talked too much but he liked the way the Beast of Eeklo sat on his bike. Before turning pro Van Lancker was working for Belgian railways drawing up work schedules and offering moral support to drivers who'd witnessed suicides. He was earning £500 a month on the railways and took a 25 per cent pay cut to turn pro with the Belgian Fangio team in 1984.

Van Lancker lived at the foot of the Tiegemberg – another of the famous climbs of the Flemish Ardennes – and trained on the hills, never letting up until his average speed was 30kph. During the season he took things easy. His father-in-law mowed the lawn for him, telling him that using a lawnmower was 'bad for his legs'.

In 1990 Van Lancker became the first Belgian to claim victory in Liège–Bastogne–Liège for 12 years, the nation's longest ever winless run. In honour of his victory he was presented with a gear cog, pedal and chain gilded in 18 carat gold. I imagine it's sitting on his mantelpiece even now.

* * *

We caught the bus out to Berchem. It had gone about a mile when it pulled into a stop and my old friend Albert from Barcelona got on. He'd started working at a youth hostel in Brussels and had been using his spare time to ride part of the Ronde route on an ancient borrowed bike. He showed us a photo on his phone. 'You went up the Eikenberg on that thing?' Steve said, clearly impressed.

On Oude Kwaremont there was already a far bigger crowd than there'd been for Dwars door Vlaanderen, and the corporate hospitality was up and running. In the hope of catching an early part of the race we walked along the road that heads out towards Ronse. We could hear the helicopters overhead but by the time we made it to that section of the course, the stewards were folding up their chairs and stowing their flags.

We walked back to the village again past a mobile home with a massive satellite dish and a flag pole outside displaying the banners of Flanders and Lotto–Soudal. After the superteam of Quick-Step, Lotto–Soudal (sponsored by the national lottery and a foam and adhesive maker) are generally the second best of the Belgian teams and, on roadside evidence, the most heavily supported. That's probably because they've been around in various forms since 1984 (Lotto are the oldest sponsors in the peloton) and been pretty successful (the team won 40 races in 2015). But despite the cheering fans, so far this season they'd had a terrible time of it. The hacks at *Wielerkrant* had already begun talking about a team in crisis.

Ahead of us a middle-aged bloke with over-elaborate jeans and an East Midlands accent said to his mate, 'I went to the Oval last year. Don't know anything about cricket. Never came out of the hospitality tent. Could barely walk by the end,' as if it was something to be proud of.

We forced our way into the packed Café In 't Palet, loaded up on *mattentaartjes* and beer and squeezed into a back room with a TV in it. Oude Kwaremont is about 40 kilometres from the finish of the E3, and the last cobbled climb of the race. People watched in relative silence until the field hit the nearby Paterberg, at which point things started to get rowdy as Peter Sagan suffered the first of what would become his regular misfortunes that spring. Knocked over in a pile-up, the world champion quickly remounted and set off in pursuit only to realise his bike had been damaged. He abandoned soon afterwards.

As the race sailed up towards the base of the Kwaremont there was a seven-man break that included Greg Van Avermaet, Philippe Gilbert and Oliver Naesen, who was rapidly becoming my favourite rider. We rushed outside and found ourselves standing next to a big Flemish lad dressed as a panda. The noise levels on the slopes were ten times greater than they'd been earlier in the week for Dwars door Vlaanderen, and the reason for the excitement quickly became plain as Naesen, Gilbert and Van Avermaet came into view. Naesen had attacked on the lower part of the climb and blown Luke Durbridge, Sep Vanmarcke, Lukas Pöstlberger and Laurens De Vreese out the back. And by the way the trailing quartet were rocking as they came up 15 or so seconds later it was plain they weren't coming back.

We watched the denouement back in the bar. From seeing the Naesen family in Lokeren and on the roadside outside Nokere I'd developed a bond with them, and when Oli was the first to launch the sprint I could barely restrain myself from howling at the screen. Sadly he just didn't have the speed and Van Avermaet and Gilbert both passed him, the Olympic gold medallist Van Avermaet winning by a wheel.

Naesen's third place was the best result of the 26-year-old's career, and the following day *Wielerkrant* was talking about him as a future star. I thought about his mum and dad driving their two sons to *kermis* races all over Flanders for year after year in their little Suzuki. All the times they'd sat on the roadside with their banners, or sheltered in the car from the rain; all the miles they'd driven, the injuries they'd nursed and the defeats they'd rallied after. There were thousands of ordinary people making those kinds of sacrifices in Flanders, collecting the riders' jackets, handing them drinks, cutting their grass, hiring somebody to take their place at work, making them special meals. The cyclists and the team management were just the visible part of a vast network of support built on affection and love.

8

THE BULLDOG AND THE RED GUARD

Ghent–Wevelgem, 26 March

The first time I'd seen Ghent–Wevelgem, back in 1995, the race was ridden on the Wednesday slap bang between the Ronde van Vlaanderen and Paris–Roubaix – a position it had occupied more or less since its inception. The riders had been presented in the Kuipke velodrome in Ghent and the race had set off from the broad main street outside. But just as Kuurne–Brussels–Kuurne no longer goes to Brussels, and the Ronde van Vlaanderen makes no real attempt to actually tour Flanders, so Ghent–Wevelgem abandoned Ghent in 2003. It had also shifted its position in the calendar to the Sunday before the Ronde. Neither of these things would have been so bad had not the organisers chosen to start the race in Deinze. I had seen enough of that city, so I elected to head down to what looked like the most exciting part of the race – Ploegsteert, near Comines.

Steve had returned to Luxembourg feeling less jaded about cycling than when he'd arrived, and Albert was working at the youth hostel, so I got the train south from Ghent to Wervik alone. It was a warm day and I had a decent café picked out for my lunch. However, when I got to Menen, a dozen or so miles to the east of Ypres, the train unexpectedly terminated. A large sign by the platform announced '*Wegens Spoorwerken is er geen treinverkeer mogelijk. Er zeen vervangingsautobussen voorzien.*' In any language the phrase 'a temporary bus replacement service is in operation' spells disaster, but I took the bus that was waiting and got off in Wervik, a sprawling market town slap on the French border. I'd nursed a vague hope that there might be buses from Wervik to Comines and there were, but never on a Sunday.

Everything was not lost, however, as Wervik had a number of other attractions. The National Museum of Tobacco was sadly shut, but the men in the Grooten Moriaen café were happy to offer directions to the statue of cyclist Joseph 'Jef' Demuysere. Demuysere was born in Wervik in 1907. Early photos show Jef with the characteristic barge-like body of the *flahute* standing by his bike in his parents' garden. He has fair hair, a broad nose and the sort of Jaggeresque lips that often seemed a feature of Flemish riders. He was nicknamed 'the Flemish Bull'.

The statue had been unveiled on the centenary of Demuysere's birth, sculpted by local artist Willy Calis. Calis had done a fine job, though his decision not to show the cyclist's legs, cutting him off at mid-thigh, was unusual. The statue depicted Demuysere in his cycling gear, an inner tube strapped around his torso like a bandolier, his goggles pushed up onto the top of his head, his belly button exposed. The rider's expression conveyed a mixture of exhaustion and relief.

Demuysere had ridden mainly for French teams, including the nicely named Génial Lucifer (who made bikes and motorcycles), and his career had been a good one. He'd finished second, third and fourth in the Tour de France, taking the mountain jersey in 1931, and come second twice in the Giro d'Italia, both times bested by the great Alfredo Binda. He'd been Belgian national cyclocross champion and, in 1934, had won Milan–San Remo, the first Belgian to claim the Race to Spring since Odiel Defraeye in 1913, and only the third in the race's history (the first was Cyrille Van Hauwaert). Demuysere's achievement in winning Milan–San Remo shouldn't be underestimated. Italians dominated the Primavera and Jef was the only foreigner to win the race over a 40-year spell that began in 1914 and was finally ended by Rik Van Steenbergen in 1954.

Satisfied, I walked back through Wervik, past a bar named the Special One and a memorial to the soldiers of the British Expeditionary Force who had fought a holding action along the canal here in 1940 as their comrades fell back to Dunkirk.

It was a sunny day and I sat on a bench waiting for the replacement bus to arrive with a couple of Chinese tourists who were heading in the opposite direction to Ypres. I had the Saturday issue of *Wielerkrant*. There was a preview of Sunday's race, almost inevitably speculating on whether Tom Boonen still had the sort of sprint finish you need to win. We had entered the heart of the Flemish racing season, where an event had barely finished before the speculation about the next one began. 'After the race is before the race,' as West Germany manager Sepp Herberger might have said if he'd been a cycling *directeur sportif* instead of a football coach.

Perhaps because of its traditional position between the Ronde van Vlaanderen and Paris–Roubaix – the two toughest races on the calendar – Ghent–Wevelgem is relatively flat, heading out into West Flanders down towards the seaside resort of De Panne and then looping back along the French border. There's a bit of fiddling about in the rural Heuvelland (which means 'hill country' in Dutch) where the steep climb up the Kemmelberg supplies the obvious point for a breakaway, and the backroads round Ploegsteert are pretty rough. Mainly, though, it's the sort of not too arduous race that sprinters enjoy.

Ghent–Wevelgem had first been run in 1934 under the auspices of the newspaper *Gazet van Antwerpen*, whose owners probably felt it needed a bike race of its own to compete with *Sportwereld* and the Ronde. Wevelgem was chosen as the finishing point in honour of Gaston Rebry, one of the great Flemish riders of the inter-war years. Rebry was born in a village just outside Wevelgem and lived in the town. He had a puppyish face, large dark eyes and a penchant for big-checked baker-boy caps and shawl-collar cardigans that brought a hint of the jazz age to rural Flanders. In 1931 Rebry had won Paris–Roubaix and finished fourth in the Tour de France. In 1934 he got a spring triple, winning Paris–Nice, the Ronde and Paris–Roubaix, the latter only after the first man across the line, Roger Lapébie, had been disqualified on a technicality – riding a borrowed bike that didn't have a race number on it (perhaps Lapébie's victory in the 1937 Tour de France after the mass Belgian withdrawal had a hint of poetic justice to it). Rebry won the Hell of the North for a third time the following year, only the second man in history to do so. The record would eventually be surpassed by Roger De Vlaeminck and, later, Boonen.

Originally Ghent–Wevelgem was run in September – it moved to the spring in 1947 – and was an amateur race on a flat circuit of around 120 kilometres that started outside Sint-Pieters station in Ghent. Its first outing was won by East Flandrian Gustave Van Belle. In 1936 the course was lengthened to 168 kilometres, and professionals were allowed to enter. After World War Two and following his retirement Rebry became the race director. In 1945 he presided over what must have been the longest photo-finish debate in history, Robert Van Eenaeme eventually being declared the winner a full ten days after crossing the line. It was the racer's third victory, a record at the time, and one he now shares with Rik Van Looy, Eddy Merckx, Mario Cipollini and, inevitably, 'Tornado' Tom Boonen.

By the 1950s the race had enough prestige – thanks in part to Rebry's involvement – to attract the likes of Fausto Coppi and Gino Bartali as entrants. In 1964 Jacques Anquetil became the first French victor. There were various changes of course and tack during the subsequent decades and, in 1977, the race expanded to an epic 277 kilometres – Breton hardman Bernard Hinault won that edition – before reverting to the more usual length of just over 200 kilometres.

While the other big Flemish race events have increasingly opted to race over the same territory, Ghent–Wevelgem has at least tried to make itself a bit different. Since 2015 there's been an attempt to tie the route in with the World War One battlefields it traverses. The race has been rebranded as 'Ghent–Wevelgem – in Flanders Fields', the posters decked out with poppies. The organisers said they wanted to commemorate the start of the Great War. I'm not sure how I feel about that. Is it a genuine tribute or simply opportunistic? I tend towards the latter view, but then again, maybe 30 years of writing about professional sport and watching corporate sponsors' logos getting slapped on everything has made me cynical.

Whatever, there's little doubt that Ghent–Wevelgem has attracted a high calibre of riders. The winners' board highlights that. Van Looy is there, Schotte, Kint, Impanis, Van Springel and Maertens, not to mention Boonen. There are a lot of big-name foreign riders on the board too – as well as Anquetil, Hinault and Cipollini there's Francesco Moser, Sean Kelly and Jan Raas. In 1974 the largely unsung Englishman Barry Hoban won it.

Though it doesn't have the same reputation for ferocity as some of the other Flanders Classics, Ghent–Wevelgem can also suffer from rough weather. Freddy Maertens' victory in 1976 came in sleet, snow and brutal cold. 'Fat Freddy' hit the front on the slopes of the Kemmelberg and powered away from the field, but the conditions were so bad, the head wind so strong, his solo break lasted barely half an hour. He was swallowed up by the pursuing pack, but outsprinted them all at the finish.

There's been controversy too. In 2005 Nico Mattan from Izegem won after allegedly using the Van Steenbergenian subterfuge of drafting behind a publicity car to catch breakaway Spanish rider Juan Antonio Flecha.

After over an hour spent picking my way through *Wielerkrant*, the replacement bus arrived. It was packed. I squeezed into a seat next to a large, rustic-looking chap who said he came from Ypres, and whistled tunelessly throughout a journey that took rather longer than it should have done because the driver got lost and had to stop to ask passers-by for directions.

Although there were still several hours until the race arrived in Menen there was some sporting excitement in the town already. Next to the station the local dog-training club was hosting an international 'control by voice' (category 3) competition. Luckily the stewards had not begun whistling yet or the whole thing might have descended into chaos.

I wandered off and took a look at a roundabout filled with a celebratory pyramid of pastel-coloured bicycles and then found my way to the splendid Tea Room Decroos, which billed itself as being 'renowned for *tartes de Menin*' (Menin is what the French-speakers call Menen). Practically every small Flemish town has its own speciality confectionery. Ghent has its edible snowballs, Kortrijk the apple and apricot *kalletaart*, while in Veurne you can order a Veurnse Slaper, possibly without puerile sniggering. The Menen tart is said to date back to the sixteenth century and contains apples and jam. This sounded a bit too healthy for me and so I opted instead for the *pannenkoeken met advocaat*, which were cooked to order by a charming grandfather in a floral pinny and came with a steepling pile of whipped cream, enough chocolate curls to fashion a small wig and sufficient advocaat liqueur to make me wobble slightly when I got up. All of which convinced me that it was time for a drink, and so I went across the road and found a bar that had a big-screen TV showing the race and Duvel on the beer list.

The man sitting at the bar next to me wore a windowpane check sports jacket and the cheery blurred expression of someone who'd been enjoying himself for some while. He began talking to me. I alerted him to the fact that I could not speak Flemish but far from deterring him this actually seemed to spur him on. Men get to an age when they really don't want to hear anyone else's opinions any more, they just want to express their own, fully and at length.

One time in Ypres's football stadium I had stood next to an old boy cast from the same iron mould – face like an amiable turnip and wearing those big council work boots with soles as thick as breeze blocks. The minute the game kicked off he started talking to me in rasping West Flanders Dutch. I told him I was English and couldn't understand. 'Ah, *Engels*,' he said and carried on talking just the same. As the game went on and the home side collapsed so spinelessly they may as well have fielded 11 amoeba, the old chap became more and more animated, slapping my arm and pointing at some or other player and hurling out his exasperation.

At the final whistle, as we walked towards the exit, he delivered a bitter summary of everything we'd witnessed, then got on his bike and, with a wave, disappeared off in the direction of the Cloth Hall. I imagined he went home to a wife, who had made a big stew and some mashed potato with leeks, and she'd say, 'How was it then, luv?' And he'd say, 'Total bloody shambles. Again! I was stood next to this lad from England and he totally agreed with everything I was saying. And if he could see it, how the hell the manager can't is an absolute bloody mystery.'

This was how it was with the man in the bar in Menen. As the riders pedalled through the clouds of dust that rose from the gravel roads of 'Plugstreets' (the name British soldiers had given to Ploegsteert during World War One – they'd also called Ypres 'Wipers') and the cameras picked out a current star like Greg Van Avermaet, the man in the check sports jacket would wave at the wall-mounted TV and say something incomprehensible that concluded with the words '. . . Freddy Maertens . . . Roger De Vlaeminck!' I had no idea what he was saying, but anyone who has ever hung around elderly sports fans will guess that it was an unflattering comparison between the modern age and the time when the speaker was himself in his athletic prime and everything was done properly. 'Boonen, Gilbert – don't make me laugh. This modern lot aren't fit to fill Walter Godefroot's *bidon*. The Bulldog of Flanders, now he was a rider. And a MAN!'

You could have heard such laments at any time, though they were likely at their loudest among Flemish cycling fans back around 1967. By then the Boss, Rik Van Steenbergen, had left the building and Rik Van Looy, the Emperor, was on the verge of abdication after a radiant late flourish. The incident at Ronse in 1963 may have irreparably damaged the career of Benoni Beheyt, but crushing the upstart who had stolen 'his' world title only seemed to spur Van Looy on. In 1964 he won 24 races and the following year 42, including eight stages of the Vuelta a España, in which he finished third overall. Many felt Rik II could have done better in stage races, pointing out that though he didn't seem like a man for the big climbs, he'd actually won the King of the Mountains jersey in the 1960 Giro d'Italia. Perhaps he preferred the easier pickings. He won the Tour of Sardinia three times and hoovered up obscure one-day races such as Rome–Naples at every opportunity. Unlike Van Steenbergen, who squandered his fortune on gambling and alcohol when he retired, the Emperor used his money wisely, setting up a horse-riding school in Herentals. He talked often of retirement but kept on pushing. In 1965 he won five out of six stages of the Tour of Sardinia, gifting the other to his protégé Ward Sels, and told journalists he would quit in two years. Four years later he was still racing.

In 1967, aged 34 and regarded by everyone as past his best, the Emperor was part of the winning break in Paris–Roubaix, narrowly missing out to Jan Janssen in the sprint. Witnesses say that he received the loudest cheer of the day when he was awarded his silver medal. It was perhaps acclaim tinged with regret, for the fading of Van Looy had plunged Flemish cycling fans into despair. They believed the glory days were over, that football, thanks in part to television, was about to usurp bike racing and that the younger generation were a bunch of milksops whose easy lives and full stomachs had left them incapable of enduring the sort of agonies that Briek Schotte swallowed as if they were a hot broth on a cold day.

That things didn't turn out that way takes us back to Flandria.

After Van Looy departed, taking his faithful servants, the Red Guard, with him, the Flandria team had to be completely rebuilt. Previously it had featured a mix of Flemish and Italian riders, now it became exclusively Flemish. The lesson of having all efforts focused on Van Looy had been absorbed and the team no longer worked for a single star. Instead it featured multiple specialists capable of winning all kinds of different races. The new squad was built on Flemish virtues of toughness, tenacity and commitment.

In 1967 Flandria signed a rising star of Flemish cycling who exemplified those virtues. Walter Godefroot was bronze medallist in the 1964 Olympic road race, and claimed 131 races as an amateur. Born in Ghent in 1943 he was stockily built, with a boxer's flattened nose and curling ears and a pugnacious expression that earned him the nickname 'the Bulldog of Flanders'. During his career he'd win ten stages of the Tour de France and take home the green points jersey in 1970. He was formidable in the Classics too, wining Liège–Bastogne–Liège (1970), the Ronde (1968, 1978), Paris–Roubaix (1969), Bordeaux–Paris (1969, 1976) and the Scheldeprijs (1969), notching a total of 155 wins as a pro. He'd won Ghent–Wevelgem in 1968.

Godefroot was notoriously dour and had no romantic attachment to cycling – he'd originally hoped to become an Olympic gymnast. Bike racing was simply how he made a living. The result of his ambivalence was a Kiplingesque approach to the sport that saw him barely celebrate his achievements and react to even the unluckiest of events with little more than a shrug.

Godefroot was a reluctant trainer, yet he was ferociously competitive and pushed himself so hard that he'd often end a race by doubling over and throwing up. For a chunky Flandrian he was surprisingly good in the mountains, and in the 1973 Tour de France defeated Merckx and Lucien Van Impe in a mountainous stage from Nancy to Mulhouse.

Godefroot's greatest victory came in the 1969 Paris–Roubaix. The field was astonishing: it included Roger and Erik De Vlaeminck, Merckx, Van Looy, Van Springel, Felice Gimondi, Anquetil, Poulidor, Rudi Altig and world champion Vittorio Adorni. It was a day of rain, hail, snow and turbulence. Punctures were frequent, echelons formed against the crosswinds and cracked apart on the ruinous *pavé*. Around the 180-kilometre mark the Bulldog began launching attacks, shedding Van Looy with the first of them. In the final 28 kilometres he burned everybody off, opening up a gap of over a minute, riding at a furious pace, flying into bends and bumping over the slippery cobbles like a man with a death wish. He finished two minutes and 39 seconds ahead of second-placed Merckx, who was so impressed he would later say that Godefroot was the only man he could never beat in a direct fight for victory.

171

Like the De Vlaemincks and other top Flemish riders of that era, Godefroot had no liking for Baron Eddy and butted heads with him at every opportunity.

Godefroot's arrival in the Flandria team was followed by other key signings: Eric Leman in 1968, Roger De Vlaeminck in 1969. Initially the new Flandria focused attention on the one-day Classics rather than the Grand Tours, and heaped up wins. Soon their ambition increased. Flandria strengthened still further and began to go after victory in the Tour de France. In 1972 they'd recruited Dutchman Joop Zoetemelk, who finished second in 1970 and 1971 (he'd win it eventually, in 1980, but by then he was riding for Peter Post at TI–Raleigh). Zoetemelk joined his compatriot Evert Dolman. Dolman would win the Ronde in Flandria's colours in 1971 but left the following year and his career was dogged by doping allegations (he would later claim that he was the victim of a witch hunt).

So, by the early 1970s, the Flandria team contained both De Vlaemincks, Walter Godefroot, Eric Leman, Johan De Muynck, Ronny Van Marcke, Frans Mintjens and, all too briefly, Jempi Monseré. It was a line-up of galacticos.

By that time Lomme Driessens had, after some behind-the-scenes skulduggery, supplanted the unfortunate Briek Schotte as the main manager of the team. Godefroot had little time for Driessens, once commenting of the *directeur sportif*'s thick skin and pathological inability to understand when he was not wanted, 'If you kick him out the door, five minutes later he'll be climbing in through the window.'

Rarely seen without a big cigar in his mouth, Driessens involved himself in every aspect of the riders' lives, even visiting them at home so he could check on their wives' cooking. Like many old-school cycling managers Driessens had eccentric views on diet and believed that one of the keys to success in cycling was eating quantities of minestrone soup.

Van Looy worked with Driessens and liked him, but according to Godefroot that was only because Lomme the Liar's non-stop blarney was good at attracting sponsorship money and boosting the Emperor's appearance fees.

Whatever anyone thought of Driessens, with him at the helm, aided by the ever loyal Schotte and the recently retired rider Noël Foré, Flandria continued to impress. When top riders like the De Vlaemincks left they were swiftly replaced. Between 1972 and 1973 Driessens signed Marc Demeyer, Freddy 'the Ogre' Maertens and Michel Pollentier. The young trio became great friends. They shared a fondness for practical jokes (they once locked Driessens in a sauna and went off drinking, returning hours later to find him, in Maertens' words, 'as red as a lobster'). The press called them 'the Three Musketeers'. The lives of all of them would be characterised by *palmarès* and controversy.

Van Steenbergen's use of drugs was seen by some as characteristic of Flemish cycling. Britain's Brian Robinson felt that Belgian riders took more drugs than the French, Italians and others because the testing was not as thorough in Belgium, particularly in the *kermis* races. 'In Belgium it was obvious – because the syringes came out in big races,' he told his biographer, Graeme Fife.

I'd heard about that myself. A friend of mine who'd ridden at semi-pro level in Britain in the 1970s recalled an English city criterium at which the organisers had hired a big-name Flemish pro to take part: 'For most of the race we were going along nicely beside him. I thought, "What's all the fuss about this fella? He's nothing special." Then we're coming up to the bell for the last lap and he just reached round into the pocket at the back of his jersey, pulled out a syringe and banged it into his thigh. A minute later he was off, travelling that fast he could have caught a pigeon.'

Whether Robinson's assessment is true or not is hard to gauge. Performance-enhancing drugs have, of course, been part of cycling almost since the beginning of pro racing. The great French rider Henri Pélissier – winner of the Tour de France in 1923 – spoke to journalists of using cocaine, chloroform and a variety of 'pep' pills, saying, 'We are running on dynamite!'

Drug testing seems to have been haphazard throughout pro cycling – doping controls weren't introduced to the Tour de France until 1966, and even then the riders protested about it. Van Steenbergen wasn't the only great rider of his era to talk frankly about his drug use. Fausto Coppi admitted taking '*la bomba*' (a mix of amphetamines used by the Italian military) and famously responded to the question of whether he had ever used drugs by saying, 'Only when it was necessary.' When asked how often that was, he answered, 'All the time.' 'Maître' Jacques Anquetil, meanwhile, was cynical on the point, mocking the idea that you could 'ride the Tour de France on mineral water'. The Ghent-based Tommy Simpson allegedly bought his amphetamines in Italy, arguing that they were better than the pills available elsewhere. It's also worth noting that Ghent University was one of Europe's leading scientific institutions for anti-doping and developed a number of the tests that would unmask the wrongdoing of some of Flanders' finest riders.

Whatever the truth of the notion that the Belgians were the worst offenders when it came to doping, there is no denying that they – and the Dutch – often fell foul of the doping controllers. In 1974 Godefroot and Maertens both tested positive for a previously undetectable stimulant derived from piperidine. In 1977 the chemists at Ghent developed another new test, for the previously invisible Stimul (a drug used to treat attention deficit disorder and narcolepsy by heightening alertness and alleviating fatigue). The Italian and French cycling authorities seem to have alerted their riders to the change in situation. The Belgian authorities, meanwhile, chose not to. Godefroot, Maertens, Merckx, Pollentier, Walter Planckaert, Willy Teirlinck (from Flemish Brabant, winner of five stages of the Tour de

France) and Bornem-born Karel Rottiers were all caught, though naturally most of them vigorously denied any wrongdoing, with various wild counterclaims. Among the least relevant of these was the Cannibal's assertion that one of the French dope-testers was a pervert who enjoyed watching cyclists urinate.

The strangest of all the 1970s doping scandals involved Flandria's Michel Pollentier. Michel Pollentier's name sounds French but he grew up in the West Flanders farming town of Diksmuide, where much of the butter you see in Belgian supermarkets is made. Though he'd win the Ronde in 1980, the tall, slightly built, fair-haired Pollentier was not a Classics specialist like the rest of the Flandria roster but a man built for the Grand Tours. He finished second in the 1982 Vuelta and in 1977 won the Giro d'Italia, a victory that earned him the Belgian Sportsman of the Year award.

Pollentier came into the 1978 Tour de France wearing the Belgian champion's jersey and with a reasonable expectation of finishing it in yellow. He won the famous mountain stage to Alpe d'Huez and took the race lead. A few hours after he'd crossed the finish line in triumph Pollentier entered the doping control centre. His strange behaviour quickly aroused the suspicions of one of the officials, who asked the Fleming to remove his shirt. When Pollentier did so it became apparent that he had been attempting to pass off clean urine as his own, by squeezing it from a condom concealed under his armpit down through a rubber tube attached to his penis. Flandria's excuses for this fiasco are worth hearing, if only for comedy value. They claimed that an exhausted Pollentier had wet himself close to the finish and, unable to produce urine of his own, panicked and tried to use someone else's instead. I think you'll agree that for a man apparently exhausted, dehydrated and in a tizzy, Pollentier had acted rather resourcefully. Flandria would later claim that the whole thing was a stitch-up by the French, who did not want a foreign rider to win the race. The team would also claim that the decision to expel Pollentier from the Tour for failing to provide a urine sample was 'controversial', though few other people thought so.

In fairness to Pollentier he seems more able to deal with reality than his former employers. He would confess later on to doping throughout his career (he also tested positive in the 1980s) and say that the drugs taken while racing had so severely affected his health that he'd been treated for the side effects for several years by a doctor in Ostend.

Scandals aside, the 1970s saw Flemish riders win race after race – Flandria amassed 103 victories in 1977 alone. What had seemed like the end of Flemish cycling was actually the start of a new golden era. And the man in the noisy sports jacket in the Menen café was in little doubt that its glister would never be surpassed.

The TV screen in the café was showing us Van Avermaet leading a breakaway of 20 or so riders, including the ominous Sagan, up the cobbled slope of the Kemmelberg. The bar staff had decided not to switch the music system off, so snatches of Eurosport's Dutch commentary became none too convincingly mashed up with Blackstreet's 'No Diggity'. About 15 minutes later the Olympic champion attacked again. The bunch fractured – only Norwegian Søren Andersen, the previous year's winner Niki Terpstra of the Netherlands, Sagan and Bruges-born Jens Keukeleire stayed with the Belgian. The lead cranked up second by second. I decided it was time to abandon my friend at the bar and go out and watch the race for real. He showed no desire to follow me but, as I bade him farewell, patted me on the arm and unleashed a final volley of thoughts that concluded, 'Frans Verbeeck. Frans Verbeeck!' – the latter delivered like a prize fight announcer introducing the heavyweight champion of the world, only with the addition of the phlegmy Dutch 'R' and 'K' so percussive it sounded like a steam hammer striking a steel rivet: '*Frrrrrrrans VerrrrrrbeeeeecKa!*'

Ah, yes, Frans Verbeeck, 'the Flying Milkman'. Poor Frans, I feel like writing, because if it seemed the De Vlaemincks and Godefroot lived in the shadow of Eddy Merckx, well, they were in need of sunblock and sombrero compared to Frans Verbeeck.

Verbeeck was born in Aarschot, but his family soon moved to Wilsele, where his father ran the village dairy. The Flying Milkman's career got off to a false start. He began as a pro in 1962, and won the 1964 Ronde van Vlaanderen 'B race' (for members of the reserve line-ups and independents; Dutchman Jo de Roo was another notable victor), but quit after the sixth stage of the Vuelta later that year. Like Johan Museeuw's father, Eddy, with whom he'd ride later, Verbeeck was sickened by the feudal financial system of cycling that seemed to make the top riders monumentally wealthy while keeping the rest on wages that saw them fall below the poverty line. Disgusted, he walked out and went to work as a milkman with his dad.

Verbeeck showed no interest in cycling for a couple of years, but gradually his passion for the sport was rekindled, first by watching races, then by managing a small Flemish team. By the summer of 1968 he was back riding in races for elite unsigned riders (*zonder contract*) like the Omloop van Wetteren. He came back as a pro the following spring.

In his peak years Verbeeck rode for one of Flanders' other great teams, Watney–Maes (the English brewery, famed for the pissy weakness of its ale, was part of the giant Maes brewing empire based at Alken in Flemish Limburg). Watney–Maes was just as Flemish as Flandria. Its line-up included Walter Planckaert, Eddy Verstraeten (a winner of Omloop van het Waasland), Staf Van Cauter and the mellifluously named Englebert Opdebeeck.

Verbeeck was such a fanatic for winter training he made Briek Schotte look like a dormouse. He only allowed himself a fortnight off a year and went on 300-kilometre rides even in the summer when racing was at its height. To prepare for the 1969 season he took a heavy bike with a mighty fixed gear and ploughed up and down a sand-covered hill in the woods near his house. At first he couldn't get to the top without falling off, but by the end of the winter he was capable of doing it 40 times on the trot without a pause. He hit the roads too. He never missed a single day of training no matter what the weather, astonishing his fellow pros by going out in blizzards. Unlike most riders he did not go south to train in winter, preferring to slog away in Flanders in the darkness and the freezing sleet. Sometimes when conditions were really bad he'd borrow an old solid-framed bike from the village postman and ride on that. Verbeeck reasoned that, 'If I couldn't outclass Merckx, I'd out-train him.'

His hard work generally came to nothing. In 1973, for example, he finished second behind Merckx in Ghent–Wevelgem, second behind him in the Amstel Gold Race, and in Liège–Bastogne–Liège clung on grimly to the great man's wheel in a two-man breakaway only to lose to him in the sprint by a couple of centimetres.

At times Verbeeck's obsession with beating Merckx cost him victories. In the 1974 Ronde, when he was so fixated on what the Cannibal was up to, he let Cees Bal escape to win. In 1975 Merckx won Milan–San Remo while Verbeeck won the E3. Both men came into that year's Ronde van Vlaanderen in fine form, Merckx buoyant and telling reporters he intended to win by a distance. As it was he finished 30 seconds ahead of the trailing Verbeeck, who at the end was utterly disconsolate: 'What can I say? He was too fast.'

The Milkman continued to get close, but not quite close enough, and never won one of the Monuments. In the Classics (in those days the Monuments plus Paris–Brussels, Paris–Tours, Het Volk, Züri–Metzgete, the Amstel Gold Race, Ghent–Wevelgem and the Flèche Wallonne) he finished on the podium 12 times but won just four (Het Volk twice, the Amstel and the Flèche).

That Verbeeck kept going is a real testament to his guts and determination. The psychological crushing of constantly striving and failing to beat Merckx would have broken lesser men. Or less stubborn ones, at least.

I left the café and headed back towards the station where there was a long flat straight flanked on either side by flat-fronted brick houses. I took up a position opposite a bar called the Nieuw Pulle, which boasted of having a billiard table, next to a group of men whose mullets, white socks and medallions suggested they were on their way to a 1980s theme night and would kick off if the DJ didn't play any George Benson.

The five-man escape group came down the long straight into Menen 15 seconds ahead of the chasers, Sagan at the front, pulling the others with him.

After the rest of the field had flashed by I went and found another bar with a TV. The breakaway group's lead had expanded by the time they left the outskirts of the town. Shortly afterwards Van Avermaet kicked again and only Keukeleire went with him. Sagan had been knocking himself out powering the group forwards and when the fresh split occurred looked round to see what Terpstra and Andersen were doing. The Dutchman and the Norwegian stared back at him blankly. Sagan was an old-school rider who competed in every race, but the Slovak's reputation was working against him now. His finishing kick was so feared that nobody but his own teammates would ever help him, and they couldn't keep up. It had been the same for Boonen when he was at the top of his game. His teammate Stijn Devolder had profited, riding away to those two apparently unheralded Ronde victories while the eyes of all the other riders were trained on Tomeke.

With Sagan unwilling to expend more of his energy towing his reluctant companions back into the lead group, the two Flemish riders got clean away. The sprint was a foregone conclusion, the Olympic gold medallist simply too fast for the younger man. And so Van Avermaet became the first rider since Jan Raas in 1981 to win the Omloop Het Nieuwsblad, the E3 and Ghent–Wevelgem in the same year.

It was a good day for Keukeleire too. He'd burst onto the pro scene in 2010, winning the Driedaagse van West-Vlaanderen, Le Samyn and the Nokere Koerse in his first season. Big things were expected of him – if not a new Eddy Merckx, perhaps he would prove to be a little Johan Museeuw or a mini-Boonen? But since then the results just hadn't come. He was now 28 and even the Flemish press seemed to have given up on him. A podium finish in a Classic was something to build on, and he'd pushed Sagan into third, which was hardly a bad day's work.

9

THE DEVIL AND MEESTER MAERTENS

Driedaagse De Panne–Koksijde, 28, 29, 30 March

On the Tuesday after Ghent–Wevelgem I found myself standing in an upper-floor window of Zottegem Stadhuis. Zottegem, to the south of Ghent, is a town of 25,000 inhabitants and one of at least a dozen 'gateways to the Flemish Ardennes'. It once had a famous brewery that made one of the world's greatest cherry beers – but that closed down some years ago. The *frituur* in the town square that sold portions of snails and chips has gone too. Thankfully the church with its elaborate chiming clock has survived. Zottegem is a typical small Flemish town. In the evenings a group of teenage boys take it in turns to ride mopeds up and down Heldenlaan, the long main street. At nine o'clock they all go home. And so does everybody else. Zottegem is a sleepy place where everything appears on the verge of closing for the day, even at ten in the morning.

Today, though, things were different. Heldenlaan was the finishing straight for Flemish cycling's last remaining stage race, Driedaagse De Panne–Koksijde – the Three Days of De Panne–Koksijde.

As its name suggests, the race is run over three days and four stages, one of them that rarest of Flemish events – a time trial. The Driedaagse feels like a bit of an afterthought, dreamed up to plug a gap in March's racing calendar before the Ronde van Vlaanderen and give the Flemish public something to focus on beyond the endless speculation about Sunday's big race. Many of the top contenders opt out of it and go training around the Flemish Ardennes instead. Only a few of the men who might be in with chance in the Ronde had entered this year's edition – Philippe Gilbert, Luke Durbridge and Alex Kristoff, the latter looking way below the form that had seen him win glory in Oudenaarde in 2015.

The Driedaagse has been running for 40 years. The first edition in 1977 was won by Roger Rosiers from Vremde, a one time Molteni teammate of Merckx. The fiery Limburger Eric Vanderaerden, who spent most of his career smouldering like a tractor tyre on a farm bonfire, dominated the race in the 1980s, probably just to deny his arch-enemy Sean Kelly (who'd won in 1980) the opportunity. Museeuw, Van Petegem and Devolder were other Flemish Ronde winners who'd also taken first prize in the Driedaagse. Italy's spring Classics specialist Michele 'the Little Lion of Flanders' Bartoli had won it too. Perhaps more typical of the victors was Gustaaf Van Roosbroeck, a near-miss rider from Hulshout outside Antwerp. During a long pro career – from 1969 to 1980 – Van Roosbroeck won Driedaagse De Panne, Kuurne–Brussels–Kuurne, Nokere Koerse, Dwars door Vlaanderen and the Scheldeprijs, but never took a true Classic.

The Driedaagse De Panne–Koksijde used to start in the football stadium of Excelsior Mouscron in Hainaut, but nowadays it begins at the seaside in De Panne. On the first day the race set out from the coast heading east and went looping around the Flemish Ardennes taking in 11 climbs, including the Ronde staples Berendries and Tenbosse. The riders had even gone up the famous Muur at Geraardsbergen *twice*. On the first ascent Philippe Gilbert attacked and fractured the field. On the second climb he'd gone again; this time nobody could stick with him and he'd ridden off alone. There was still 16 kilometres to the finish and those waiting in Zottegem were in two minds over whether Gilbert's move was bold and, well, Merckxian, or simply crazy and doomed. The chasing group were mounting a ferocious attempt to pull him back, gradually clawing back the seconds, but the Walloon just would not give in. His courage and his stubbornness were the subject of approving nods among the waiting crowds in Zottegem.

Ten minutes before the race arrived there were several thousand people crowding along the pavements of the streets leading to the main square. More were arriving by the second. The windows above the shops and bars along the course were full of eager faces. A local priest had snaffled a prime spot for himself on the balcony of an apartment overlooking the photo-finish wagon. A gang of likely lads in elaborate jeans and Ralph Lauren polo shirts had scaled a memorial to the Great War dead. A middle-aged fan walked past wearing a faded cap in the colours of the Belgian tricolour bearing the legend 'Supporters Club Frank VDB'. The problem with Flemish names like Vandenbroucke is they don't always fit on a hat. Indeed, some of them you'd struggle to get on the side of a Zeppelin.

On the corner a group of corporates from KBC Bank stood in a three-sided shelter of green canvas, drinking Jupiler lager and taking glances at their skinny-suited reflections in the window of a florist. Many sports have executive boxes, this was an executive hide. The chap from the local *ijssalon* walked through the crowd with a tray of ice-cream sandwiches. A bunch of builders standing on the first floor of a half-finished block of flats called down to him. He under-armed a couple up to them. There was applause and cheering when they were caught. And then the first vehicles of the race convoy appeared with the now familiar operatic calling of 'Roh-Da-Ni-Ah'. It was carnival time in Zottegem.

The anticipatory clamour built until the PA announced that the riders had entered the final kilometre. Suddenly there was a hush. On his balcony the priest craned so far over to look down the street his rosary beads rattled against the railings. The fat man on the fold-out chair who had been marking up the time gaps on a whiteboard momentarily stopped chewing on his smoked eel. The fans in the full replica kit took time off from admiring their own thighs to look at the course. Then, slowly, a murmur began, the sound of the crowd further down the road responding to the approaching field. The hubbub preceded the peloton by 50 metres, rolling down Bruggenhoek, picking up volume in Désiré Van den Bosschestraat and finally breaking with a roaring crash as the Belgian champion came into view.

Gilbert had held on. He won by 17 seconds from Luke Durbridge, who seemed to be making a habit of coming second behind Belgians. The Italian Simone Consonni was third. The best Flemish finisher was fourth-placed Jasper De Buyst. My old pal from Le Samyn, Guillaume Van Keirsbulck, rattled past in 11th.

In Flemish cycling a crisis is never far away, a cause for national mourning created by a statistic. When Tom Steels won the finish into Zottegem the last time I was here, in 1999, he became the first Fleming to claim a stage in the Driedaagse De Panne–Koksijde since Dirk De

Wolf. Next day, legendary veteran cycling writer Harry Van den Bremt of *Het Nieuwsblad* began his report 'the ban is lifted' and went on to speak of a national sense of relief. De Wolf's victory had come on the Harelbeke–Herzele stage in 1992. From this you may conclude that seven years is a long time in Flemish cycling.

Steels – who came from the Waasland, not far from Kemzeke – won nine stages of the Tour de France and was Belgian road race champion four times. But he's arguably best remembered around the world for the moment of madness in the 1997 Tour that saw him disqualified for hurling his *bidon* at Frenchman Frédéric Moncassin during the sort of bad-tempered sprint finale that Eric Leman might have relished. In Flanders Steels remained a hero, forever surrounded by a clump of female well-wishers (many of them old enough to be his grandmother), juvenile autograph hounds and bulky middle-aged men in reactolite sunglasses and the sort of stunningly bright leisurewear that justified them, who stared at him intently while blowing cigarette smoke in his face. Steels reacted to practically every remark that was made to him with a distracted well-what-can-you-do shrug, his eyes focused on something far away, his massive legs a relief map of bulging veins and clumps of scar tissue.

The second stage of the Driedaagse went back from Zottegem to the seaside resort of Koksijde, passing through Menen along the way. I took a train down to Ypres and hopped in a cab from there to the Kemmelberg, the feature hill of the stage.

The Driedgaagse De Panne–Koksijde is traditionally associated with driving rain and gale-force winds. This week, however, it seemed there was not a cloud in the sky from Antwerp to Lille, from Tongeren to Oostduinkerke. A party of schoolchildren in shorts and t-shirts sat under the shade of the trees of the Kemmelberg licking ice lollies. The heat had clearly affected the minds of several sturdy Flemish matrons who had taken the unprecedented step of removing their stout woollen overcoats several months before the summer equinox.

Usually riders ascending the Kemmelberg fear the slippery, treacherous cobbles. Today, though, the main enemy was the pitiless Belgian sun and the clouds of dust thrown up by the team cars. By the time the riders arrived at the summit their jerseys were unzipped and flapping like the mouths of beached fish.

I caught a ride to Poperinge with a Flemish bloke who had been standing next to me on the Kemmelberg. I had a little wander round the town, which was about all it took. Most of my time was spent studying the statue of Meester Ghybe, leader of the Poperinge Boulder Society, who in the fourteenth century rode a donkey backwards through the town brandishing handfuls of cutlery in protest at the Count of Flanders' decision to make cutbacks in local linen production.

Poperinge had been named 'tastiest town in Flanders' but Flanders still had half-day closing and everything was shut. It was late afternoon and hordes of teenage girls packed into skinny jeans and sequinned tops bustled self-importantly up the pavements waving their arms about and cackling. As the race approached a young woman in front of me started clapping her hands rhythmically and moving up and down on the balls of her feet as if she were pedalling towards Poperinge herself. The old man next to her glanced at me and raised his eyebrows. The helicopters whumped into view. A plane flew overhead trailing a banner advertising a firm of local accountants. An old lady towing a shopping trolley crossed the road on a blind corner and almost sent the implausibly large posse of motorcycle cameramen who ride in front of the race swerving into a bus shelter.

Then the Rodania car, and the race flashed past, the riders coming through under an inflatable arch advertising Plopsaland – the oddly named De Panne theme park – and making a sharp right-hand bend that sent them across the road into the oncoming lane.

If the cobbled hills had been the challenge on the first day, the main obstacle facing the riders on this stage was that other old Flemish staple, the winds, which were particularly horrible after the race left Poperinge and entered the low flat country between Beveren and the sea. A coastal breeze hammering into their faces for mile after mile made progress tough, but a 20-man break got away and built a decent lead, and when they arrived in Koksijde the Norwegian Alexander Kristoff, a former Ronde winner, took the sprint. Edward Theuns, a 25-year-old from Ghent, came second. Gilbert consolidated his hold on the white jersey of race leader.

In De Panne I stayed in a small hotel set back across the road from the beach. It was neat and clean and efficiently run but defiantly low budget. The chosen floor-covering was grey lino. The furnishings were veneered chipboard. When you pulled on a drawer handle the whole cupboard came with it. Surprisingly, I found that two of the teams riding in the race were billeted on the same floor. It was still off-season, and doubles were the equivalent of £40 a night including breakfast. Even that was not cheap enough for the squad budgets. The team leaders got space to themselves but the lowly *domestiques* were squeezed three or four to a room. Fold-out beds and mattresses filled virtually the entire floor. To get to the door in the morning they had to pick their way through a tangle of bobbled pink sheets and fawn blankets.

The *domestiques* went out on their warm-up rides under a dawn sky the colour of a tramp's vest, descended the stairs to the chatter of cycling cleats, came back for sullen breakfasts of pasta at 7.30 a.m., and were on their bikes again before I had finished my first coffee. When you peeked into the rooms in the evening you could see rows of shorts and vests that had been washed in the bathroom basins and were hanging up along the shower rail to dry. Discarded chocolate wrappers, high-energy drinks bottles and racing numbers overflowed from the litterbins.

I went out after breakfast and watched the resort come to life. The beach here stretches from the mouth of the river Ijzer all the way to the French border in an uninterrupted swatch of white sand. At low tide it's so wide you feel you might need to flag a taxi to take you to the water's edge.

Food is important to Belgians, but on holiday no one much wants to cook. A green van came along the esplanade at 9.30 a.m. selling soup to the people who rushed out bearing saucepans at the sound of the ting-tinging triangle suspended above the driver's door. After the soup van had passed, the waiters appeared, arranging the tables on the decking terraces that stretch out on to the beach and chalking up the dishes of the day – tomatoes stuffed with grey shrimps, sole *meunière*, crème caramel – on blackboards that advertise Trappist beer.

The *traiteurs* that line Zeelaan, the main street carrying the tramlines that run to Ostend, do a roaring trade in Galia melons filled with crabmeat, *coquilles Saint-Jacques* and *pommes dauphine*. 'Boiled whelks – buy five get one free!' read the signs in the fishmonger's; the winkles arrived fresh each morning. In the pâtisseries the strawberry tarts come with a choice of frangipane or Chantilly cream, and the raspberry *bavaroises* look like the hats of Ascot ladies. At 10 a.m. the lifeguards arrived on the beach from their headquarters under the art deco clock tower. They wore red just like in *Baywatch*, but this being the North Sea not the Pacific Ocean, they were in red waterproof trousers and anoraks not Speedo swimsuits. The lifeguards wandered the beach in pairs. Each was armed with a flag and a brass hunting horn. They tooted the horn and waved their flags at anyone who swam too far from the shore or took an inflatable shark out to a dangerous depth. The honking of the lifeguards was a chorus that filled the holiday air almost as completely as the stewards' whistles did at a race.

On the pedestrianised esplanade dozens of children whizzed up and down on a variety of rented machines. Go-karts, electric scooters, bicycles and vast eight-seat pedal carriages that all the family could enjoy moved back and forth in a merrily unregulated stream. Sadly it seemed it was too early in the season for the World War Two DUKW amphibious vehicle, painted in jaunty red, white and blue and named *Normandie*, to swing in from the sea and trundle along the beach to pick up passengers.

I walked along the coast until I found the bust of Freddy Maertens in Lombardsijde. It was quite a decent likeness though by no means as arresting as the gigantic fibreglass statue of Cowboy Henk in nearby Middelkerke.

Freddy Maertens grew up in Lombardsijde in the 1960s – his family had a laundry-cum-grocery store there. Like much of his cycling career, Freddy's early childhood was characterised by mishaps – he nearly died after sticking a screwdriver into an electric socket, and almost drove away in the family car after turning the key in the ignition when it was in gear. Like many Flemish pros Freddy had cycling in his blood – his bespectacled cousin René was a pro with Flandria. From an early age he was hurtling about the flat coastal paths, first on a tricycle then on a bike so big he could barely reach the pedals. His father recognised Freddy's talent and drove him on mercilessly. A real martinet from the hard-knocks school of sporting dads, Gilbert Maertens forced his son to follow a brutal training schedule, oversaw his diet and kept careful watch to make sure he did not fall prey to any of the temptations of adolescence, pursuing the latter with such fanaticism the sight of the teenage Freddy flirting with a girl threw him into such a rage he allegedly sawed the lad's bike in half.

Freddy won his first race at 12, burning off boys several years his senior in a 1.5-kilometre time trial in nearby Ramskapelle. He won 65 races in two seasons as a junior and turned pro with Flandria in October 1972. Maertens was an archetypal *flahute* – mighty, powerful, ungainly. He had the big meaty face of John Belushi and his brusqueness marked him out even in the rough and ready world of Flemish cycling. The press nicknamed him 'the Ogre'.

Maertens had a childlike quality that made him likeable to some and infuriating to others. He was gullible, a man adrift in the Byzantine and at times Machiavellian world of 1970s racing. Yet he piled up victories as a pro: 33 in both 1974 and 1975; a barely plausible 54 in 1976 (the only time Merckx's 1971 world record has been matched); and a hardly more credible 53 in 1977. But though he would be world champion twice, win the green jersey three times and take the Vuelta in 1977, the big spring Classics – the measure by which any Flemish cyclist must be judged – eluded him.

Yet Maertens had the skills, including an outlandishly fast sprint – enhanced by slurps of his self-designed cocktail of champagne, fructose and an ampoule of caffeine – that led British journalist Geoffrey Nicholson to describe his riding as 'like lightning outrunning the storm'. He came close to winning the Ronde too. In fact he believed he had. In the 1977 edition the ageing Eddy Merckx attacked early and got away. The Cannibal rode solo over the Koppenberg, the perniciously tight cobbled hill he'd once denounced as being like climbing up a ladder with a bike on your back. He was soon caught by Maertens and Roger De Vlaeminck. The three men had nothing but contempt for each other and, to cap it off, De Vlaeminck seemed to have little respect for the Ronde either, but they rode together for a little while until the Ogre and the Beast got sick of the Cannibal's company and shook him off on the climb up the Taaienberg. By now things had taken an unlikely turn for Maertens. It emerged he had been disqualified for illegally swapping bikes at the bottom of the Koppenberg. He should have pulled over and dropped out but the ineffable Lomme Driessens persuaded him to carry on 'for the publicity'. Maertens dutifully did as he was told, keeping pace with De Vlaeminck all the way. As the finish line at Meerbeke approached, De Vlaeminck, feeling that even disqualification might not see off his rival, allegedly offered Maertens 300,000 Belgian francs (about £6,000) to let him win. The Beast duly took the sprint. Maertens was unplaced. De Vlaeminck announced that he had won the race fair and square, Maertens disputed that and proclaimed himself the moral victor. The debate over who is right still rumbles on. In the Centrum Ronde van Vlaanderen in Oudenaarde every winner has a brick with his name on it. Freddy Maertens has one too.

Maertens was not just a sprinter. He was also a good time triallist and, at least on the flat, he could ride fast off the front like a true *flahute* – for a while he even held the *ruban jaune*.

The idea of awarding a yellow ribbon for record speed in cycling appears to have been copied off the old Atlantic steamship prize. The rules for the prize were strict if a little obscure. The speed had to be achieved in a race or stage of at least 200 kilometres; the time certified independently by two timekeepers using specially calibrated equipment. There also appears to have been an unwritten rule that only speeds in bona fide major races would be counted. There was no use going like the clappers in Britain's Milk Race – nobody cared. The prize was the brainchild of that inveterate inventor of cycling contests, Henri Desgrange. Because of the rules and the variable conditions in every race the *ruban jaune* rarely changed hands. The first rider to hold the yellow ribbon was Gus Danneels, a French-born Belgian, who pounded along at 41.46kph in the 1936 edition of Paris–Tours. It was Danneels' third victory in the race. He also took the bronze medal in the world championships a couple of times. Danneels lost the *ruban* two years later to Italian Jules Rossi, who set his time in the same race. Rik Van Steenbergen wrested the title for the Flemish in incredible style, achieving an average speed of 43.61kph during the 1948 running of Paris–Roubaix. How he did this on the cobbles is a mystery, though his achievement of winning the *ruban jaune* during the Hell of the North was matched by Peter Post in 1964. The Dutchman took the yellow ribbon by clocking 45.13kph. There was some confusion in 1969 when the Milan–Vignola race saw Roger Kindt from Etterbeek, who rode for the Italian Ferretti team, taking the yellow ribbon from Post by racing at

46kph, though he appears to have been disqualified from the race itself over some shenanigans at the doping control, and the race history shows the winner as Attilio Rota. Kindt held the yellow ribbon for six years until Maertens stormed to victory in Paris–Brussels in 1976 at a speed of 46.11kph. After that nobody seemed to bother much for a couple of decades until future Belgian citizen Andrei Tchmil, then still a Ukrainian, took the record thanks to a following wind in the Paris–Tours of 1997. The current holder is Matteo Trentin of Italy (49.64kph in the 2015 Paris–Tours).

Maertens was also a double winner of the Pernod Super Prestige trophy.

Established in 1948 in memory of Henri Desgrange and Emilio Colombo, the editor of *Gazzetta dello Sport* who'd created the Giro d'Italia, the Super Prestige began life as the Desgrange–Colombo Challenge and was awarded to the rider who had accumulated the most points for finishing positions in a series of designated races. As you might expect, in cycling there was always a good deal of arguing over which races should or should not be included (Liège–Bastogne–Liège was not added to the list until 1951, and while the Vuelta didn't feature until 1958, the Tour of Switzerland had been included almost since the start). Whichever races were chosen, the winner got not only a large trophy but also a significant cash prize. The first winner was Briek Schotte (he was also world champion that year). Stan 'the Mathematician' Ockers picked up the trophy in 1955, and in each of the next three years it was won by Fred De Bruyne. Pernod took over sponsorship in 1958 and responded to the continual sniping about the unsuitability or otherwise of the chosen races by making the prize exclusive to French riders. In 1959 they relented slightly and opened the event to all of the peloton, but included only French races. In 1961 they relaxed things further to include most of the major European races. After that things ran more smoothly. Over the years more races were added, the number of points awarded for each race increased, and points were awarded to a wider number of finishing positions. Despite all the carping most people agreed that the winner was generally the best roadman of the season. The first Flemish rider to win the newly formatted drink-sponsored event was Herman Van Springel, from Grobbendonk near Antwerp, in 1968, the year he almost won the Tour de France. Merckx dominated for a long period, but Maertens won in 1976 and 1977. By 1987 there were 33 races in the competition. Now arguments began again because some of the races, such as the Tour de l'Avenir, were aimed at specific groups – in this case young riders – or simply didn't attract a decent enough field. Also, a number of the races overlapped: Paris–Nice and Tirreno–Adriatico, for instance. The bias towards French stage races further irritated some people who wondered what the Midi-Libre was doing on the list, and the allocating of points caused trouble – the seventh-placed finisher in the Tour de France getting as many points as the winner of one of the Monuments. The French government eventually put an end to all the arguing by banning companies that made alcoholic drinks from sponsoring sports events. After that the trophy ceased to exist.

As Maertens' incredible record shows, he was a beast on a bike. He had the talent, for sure, but, by his own account, was constantly outmanoeuvred in the shady deal-making that went on between riders and team management before and during races. In his autobiography, *Fall from Grace*, the words 'I had been stabbed in the back' appear often enough to count as a catchphrase.

Merckx was the main culprit, of course. In the 1973 world championship road race in Barcelona it is claimed he sold out Freddy because Flandria used gears from a new Japanese company, Shimano, while Merckx used those supplied by the Italians Campagnolo. According to Maertens the Italian firm were so fearful of losing sales to Shimano they got Merckx to deliberately sabotage his Belgian teammate's chances of winning, handing victory to the Italian Felice Gimondi instead. Gimondi used Campagnolo gears, naturally.

Maertens was not alone among Flemish riders in detesting the man he referred to sarcastically as 'his highness', but he pushed it further, carrying on a bitter feud that lasted for three decades and included such relentless accusations of sharp practice by his deadly rival that, at times, it seemed he might eventually blame Merckx for masterminding the JFK assassination, the disappearance of Glenn Miller and the sinking of the *Titanic*.

Maertens' paranoia had a bitter tinge but, while there's little doubt that cycling is a sport in which skulduggery has always played a part, his own lack of sense may also have been a contributory factor. Flandria team owner Paul Claeys once denounced him as 'a country bumpkin'. Briek Schotte, then assistant team director at Flandria, was so infuriated by Maertens' lack of nous he complained in an interview that Freddy rode like 'a caveman'. Maertens' view of Schotte was hardly more positive. At times he wondered if he might not have won more with a different man in charge and conspired to have Iron Briek replaced by Lomme Driessens, a man whose autocratic style and irrational obsessions perhaps reminded him of his father (Schotte was outraged by Maertens' duplicity and barely spoke to him for 30 years).

Nor was Maertens impressed by Claeys, a man he said had ripped him off when Flandria collapsed in a wild fiscal mess. The financial meltdown of the Flemish team also pitched Maertens' teammate and friend Marc Demeyer head first into a maelstrom of debt. A double winner of Paris–Roubaix, Demeyer was dead at 31. The cause of death was a heart attack. Some, like disgraced Festina *soigneur* Willy Voet, wondered about the long-term effect of drugs, while others gossiped of despair, suicide and a cover-up by the Roman Catholic Church.

After the glory years of 1976 and 1977 Maertens' riding became increasingly erratic, and his behaviour strained the patience of his employers. In 1979 he won just twice. In 1980 once. He dropped out of races, or forgot to turn up. He bounced from team to team, the contracts getting smaller, the squad names ever less prestigious – from

Boule d'Or–Colnago to Masta–TeVe-Blad–Concorde. In photos his eyes seem to have lost focus, his mouth is lopsided, he appears dazed. Then, in 1981, just when everyone had written him off as a has-been, he unexpectedly won his second world title and third green jersey. The following year he won nothing at all. His last recorded victory came in a *kermis* in Gistel. By then he was riding for a small Flemish team with the unlikely name of Euro-Soap–Crack. He retired for good in 1988.

Freddy had failed drug tests, denied he'd taken drugs, admitted it, then retracted his admission. He had problems with alcohol. His body ballooned until he practically needed his own postcode. In the wake of the Flandria debacle his finances were a hopeless mess. He owed millions of Belgian francs to the tax office. He lost his house, his car and all his furniture. For a while he seems to have fallen in with a Catholic cult who persuaded him he was possessed by evil spirits and, at the suggestion of the improbable Driessens, carried out an exorcism of his apartment. Throughout it all his wife, Carine, who had been introduced to him as a 16-year-old by the ill-fated Jempi Monseré, stood by him. Gradually Flemish cycling rallied to his support. He was given a job at the National Cycling Museum in Roesalare and subsequently at the Centrum Ronde van Vlaanderen in Oudenaarde. If cycling in Flanders was about suffering, then Maertens had suffered more than most. Redemption was surely overdue.

After paying my respects to Freddy Maertens in Lombardsijde I hopped on a tram back to De Panne to catch the conclusion of stage 3a of the Driedaagse. A short stage, covering barely 120 kilometres, it set off from the beach resort then roamed out into the flatlands around Diksmuide and past the Ijzertoren, before looping back into De Panne and making several circuits of the town. In leafy Aloïs Boudrystraat a middle-aged couple sat on striped deckchairs in the shelter provided by an up-and-over garage door. The man had a plate of winkles and radishes resting on the bulge of his stomach. As the racers passed he picked at the winkles with a pin, chewing the meat contemplatively while absent-mindedly dropping the shells into a plastic basin by his chair. In the garden was a rockery. The stones amid the heather and Alpine primulas were entirely encrusted with the shells of edible molluscs. Judging by the speed the man was eating his winkles this display was plainly the work of a lifetime.

The house next door to that of the winkle-picker was a detached brick bungalow with yellow-tinted windows and a studded oak door. Standing on the front step next to a potted azalea was a large garden gnome. The gnome was about a metre high and made of fibreglass. He had rosy cheeks and a cheery, quizzical expression – like John Motson on a frosty FA Cup third-round morning anticipating some jocular banter with Mark Lawrenson.

As the radio brought news that the race was approaching, the owner of the gnome – an old lady with hair the colour and consistency of steel wool, and no-nonsense spectacles framing a face that would dissuade even the most cavalier greengrocer from slipping any squishy tomatoes in with her order – emerged from the house. She picked up the gnome from the doorstep and carried him gently to the garden wall where the two of them stood together watching as the riders swished past in a whirl of primary colours, yells and body odour. After the last had gone by, and the team cars had arrived with a fanfare of klaxons, she plucked the gnome from the wall and carried him back inside.

When the imminent arrival of the peloton was announced for a second time, out popped the lady with the gnome. And when the riders had gone, back into the house they went. When the third circuit began the old lady came through her front door as before, but the gnome was not with her. Perhaps they had had words? Or maybe she thought two glimpses of Jens Keukeleire in an afternoon was enough excitement for the little chap. The shortness of the stage meant it resembled a *kermis* race. There was attack after attack and so many crashes it was hard to keep count. A nine-man break got clear, but was reeled back in a couple of kilometres from the finish, and Gilbert's German teammate Marcel Kittel won the sprint. Edward Theuns was again the best Flemish finisher, coming in fifth.

The final stage was the time trial. In Flanders they like head-to-head mass-start racing – time trialling is kind of a French specialism. The French prize it above all other forms of cycling, relish its purity, technicality and discipline, and have made it the cornerstone of the Tour de France, a race the best time triallists – Anquetil, Merckx, Miguel Indurain – have tended to dominate. The time trials in the Tour are often defining moments. Back in 1968 Herman Van Springel looked set to become the first Fleming to win the yellow jersey since World War Two. He was leading Jan Janssen of the Netherlands by 16 seconds with just one stage to go. Had that final stage been the procession into Paris that traditionally concludes the Tour, then Van Springel would almost certainly have claimed first prize and cemented his place in Flemish cycling lore. But, sadly for the man from Grobbendonk, the organisers had chosen to try something new for the finale of the great race – a 55.2-kilometre time trial around the streets of the capital. In theory a time trial should have suited Van Springel – he'd go on to win the Grand Prix des Nations, the biggest prize in time trialling, twice, while Janssens had no great record in the discipline – but it was the Dutchman who won, completing the course 54 seconds faster than Van Springel to win the Tour by 38 seconds. The next time the race concluded with a time trial was in 1989. Again, it proved costly for the man who was in yellow at the start of the day, Laurent Fignon, who lost out to Greg LeMond by eight seconds.

If the Grand Prix des Nations was the biggest annual prize for time triallists – aside from Van Springel, Flemish winners were Jozef Somers, Maurice Blomme, Ferdy Bracke, Walter Boucquet, Roger Swerts, Freddy Maertens and Johan Bruyneel, who would go on to become notorious as team director of US Postal, Lance Armstrong's team – the ultimate time trial was the world hour record. The first official cycling world hour record was set by (who else?) Henri Desgrange in 1893 when he covered 35.325 kilometres on a bicycle that looked like a medieval torture instrument. Within five years the record had risen by over five kilometres. Over the next 40 years there were 12 successful attempts on the record, but only slightly more than five kilometres was added to the distance. The first Flemish rider to claim the hour record was track rider Oscar Van den Eynde of Mechelen in 1897. Van den Eynde set his record on the track at Vincennes.

The Flemish connection with the race was renewed in 1933 when the French rider Maurice Richard covered 44.77 kilometres on the track at Sint-Truiden in Limburg. The only other Flemish rider to take the record was Ferdy Bracke, of Hamme, who rode 48.093 kilometres in the Olympic velodrome in Rome in 1967.

In De Panne I found a comfortable spot on a grass bank overlooking the finish line and watched the riders coming down the final straight as the clock ticked off their times. I flicked through *Wielerkrant*. Mario Cipollini was bewailing the fact that Italy had no riders worth talking about. 'We have only one man of genuine talent,' said the Lion King, who had won 42 Giro stages during his career despite perpetually looking like he was leaning against the bar in a nightclub. I finally got to see a win for Luke Durbridge, who was having a spring of near misses, but Gilbert did well enough to hold on to overall victory, finishing the race 38 seconds ahead of Austrian Matthias Brändle. Menen-born Maxime Vantomme, who'd won Le Samyn in 2014, was sixth, Theuns seventh.

Philippe Gilbert's commanding performance belatedly catapulted him into a favourite's berth for the Ronde. He was photographed in the back of the team van laden down with bouquets and clutching a cuddly three-foot tall plush bee apparently named Maya – and alongside Kabouter Plop, who is possibly the mayor of Plopsaland. In a gesture guaranteed to endear him to everyone in Belgium, Gilbert gave the flowers to his mother, Anita.

I returned to collect my bag from the hotel. The teams were long gone. The bouquet presented to one of the winners was stuffed into a vase near an out of order lift. 'All over now,' the chap at reception said with a toothy grin. 'Until Sunday!' Outside a young woman walked past pushing a pram with a picture of Tom Boonen attached to the hood.

10

D'YE KEN TOM BOONEN?

Ronde van Vlaanderen, 2 April

It has been said the Flemish love of cycling is so deep as to be a form of lunacy. If that's true, then the heart of the insanity is the Ronde van Vlaanderen. In Flanders this race is the sporting event of the year. It's Wimbledon, the Grand National and the FA Cup final all rolled into one, with a dash of Saint Patrick's Day. It's a festival, a second Christmas.

The pre-race ballyhoo had been cranking up even while the Driedaagse De Panne–Koksijde was going on, and once it had finished the explosion of hype was so great it's a wonder there wasn't a mushroom cloud over Flanders. Greg Van Avermaet had been installed as race favourite with Sagan and Gilbert not far behind. Oliver Naesen was an outside pick. People buzzed with nervous excitement. Would Sep Vanmarcke's rib injury heal? What had gone wrong for Jasper Stuyven? Had fatherhood made Jürgen Roelandts a better rider? Were Quick-Step the greatest Flemish team since Flandria? Could Tom Boonen possibly squeeze another tattoo in somewhere?

On Saturday *Wielerkrant* came with a special Boonen supplement that ran to eight pages, which meant that in total it had over 20 pages devoted to the race. I was so tingling with anticipation my skin could have powered a fridge. I took the train to rural Munkzwalm to walk a bucolic stretch of the course near Sint-Maria-Latem to calm myself down.

Like much of the rolling country to the south of Ghent through which the peloton thrashed during the spring, the area around Munkzwalm was a lovely unspoilt stretch of rural Flanders. Wood anemones were flowering on the banks of the Zwalm, a stream so lazy it is practically comatose. A moorhen paddled busily past a lost black-and-white plastic football. Daffodils, the official flower of the Ronde, bobbed in the westerly breeze. I stopped in at a café in an old watermill. The lady in the café wore a fleece that looked like it might have come free with a bulk order of cattle-lick. She brought out my beer and a small portion of cheese and celery salt to my table in the back yard. 'It is quiet today,' she said. 'But tomorrow . . .' She glanced across the stream, watched a trio of middle-aged mountain-bikers turn down a path that was clearly marked as being for walkers only and tutted noisily. 'These are not real cyclists,' she said.

'They're not real bikes,' I replied.

The café owner laughed, 'Yes. Toys for old men. Twenty-four gears!' she snorted contemptuously. 'They should learn to pedal one first.'

After my glass of sour brown ale I walked on, along a hilly road past fields of expensive-looking horses, piles of gnarly turnips and little white cottages with green shutters. Cyclists on proper bikes who were doing the tourist edition of the Ronde passed by with waves and greetings. Householders were out mowing the lawns and tending to rockeries, getting everything spick and span for the big day. It was like the whole of Flanders was whistling a jaunty tune. Back in Munkzwalm a phalanx of mobile food vans had appeared in the time I'd spent wandering about in the sunshine.

I headed up the road to Herzele to visit the brewery that makes the redoubtable Bierblomme. Bierblomme is a schnapps distilled from Flemish beer and weighs in at a hefty 50 per cent alcohol – which seemed like the kind of thing I'd need if I was going to get a decent night's sleep.

After securing the schnapps I crossed the road to the Torenhof Café, opposite the ruined castle. There was a party of cyclo-tourists rehydrating with the local blonde ale. The café was the local of supporters of Glen Haelterman, a promising junior cyclist from the area.

Hearing me order my drinks in English, one of the cyclo-tourists came over for a chat. He was an avuncular man with silver hair who looked to have been vacuum-packed into his cycling gear. He asked if I was over for the race, who I thought would win, which young riders had caught my attention since the beginning of the season. His questioning reminded me of an incident that occurred 20 years earlier in a bar in Ghent.

Back then on the plane over I had sat next to a conceptual artist from Oudenaarde, who had spent a weekend on Tyneside getting a Celtic design tattooed on his shin. When I mentioned the Ronde, he rolled his eyes. 'People think the Flemish are obsessed with cycling,' he said, 'but obsession is not the right word. It is more like a neurosis.'

Likening a national interest in bicycle racing to mental illness may seem an exaggeration, but anybody who has spent time in Flanders in the week leading up to the Ronde will regard it as a typical Flemish understatement.

After the flight I was sitting in a bar in Ghent eating chicory and chips and trying to make sense of *Het Nieuwsblad*'s coverage of the forthcoming Ronde van Vlaanderen. As my eyes wandered over the pages in the forlorn hope of finding words I knew, the owner of the bar, a kindly middle-aged lady who wore a checked apron and a look of unfathomable disappointment, arrived with a glass of beer I hadn't ordered. 'It is from the Germans,' she said, indicating a thirtysomething couple sitting on a nearby table. When I looked across, the man raised his glass and the woman smiled. I smiled back and, taking this as an invitation, the Germans came over.

Having established that they were not disturbing my peace, they began to ask me about the Ronde. Was Museeuw as strong as everyone said? the man asked. Because, his wife added, there were rumours of a knee injury. What of Andrei Tchmil? And how would the weather affect Fabio Baldato?

The Germans asked their questions and when I answered they listened very attentively, nodding in approval at my obvious wisdom. It was all very flattering, like being the subject of a *South Bank Show* special. In such circumstances it is difficult not to become pompous, and after a while I eased back in my chair and began speaking more slowly, with orotund flourishes, until I began to sound rather as the Yorkshire cricket broadcaster Don Mosey used to when delivering his close of play summary on *Test Match Special*.

Before they left, the German couple asked if they might have their photo taken with me. The bar owner took the snap and the Germans sat on either side of me, putting their arms quickly and bashfully around my shoulders as she called for us to smile. 'Super,' the man said, shaking my hand. 'We will see you at the race on Sunday also, I'm sure?'

After they had gone, the bar owner came over to pick up the empty glasses. 'That is funny,' she said with a dry chuckle. I asked what was funny. 'Those Germans,' the lady said, nodding in the direction of the door. 'You see, they thought you were Edwig Van Hooydonck.'

Van Hooydonck is a Flemish racer who, at that point, had won the Ronde twice. Tall, thin and beaky, with reddish-blond hair, the first time he won the Ronde, in 1989, he wept uncontrollably on the podium and melted the heart of every watching Flemish mother. 'I might have thought you were him too,' the lady in the Ghent café said, 'except, of course, that you don't speak Dutch.'

I asked who she wanted to win the Ronde. 'I don't care,' she said. 'As long as they are Flemish. And if not a Fleming, then someone like a Fleming.' She meant gritty, tough, stoic and down to earth. The sort of man who might travel the world making millions from racing but still take his family holidays at De Panne or Oostduinkerke. 'As Museeuw says,' the bar owner said, pointing at the newspaper, 'you don't have to be Flemish to be a Flandrien.'

It was true enough, of course, and the proof of that was Fiorenzo Magni, who was sometimes called 'the Third Man'. With Fausto Coppi and Gino Bartali he formed the great triumvirate of Italian cyclists whose career spanned the years around World War Two. Magni won the Giro d'Italia three times yet was the least celebrated of the trio, possessing neither the cavalier stylishness of Coppi nor the upright manliness of Bartali. He was pugnacious, bald and ugly (well, by Italian standards anyway). Coppi was compared with a bird in flight. Magni was more like a traction engine. He was all elbows and knees. Coppi gave off the air of a man who, even at the end of a 300-kilometre stage, would smell of expensive cologne. Magni looks like a bloke who would smell of body odour and liniment after he stepped out of a Turkish baths.

There was something else too. Magni had a dubious political record. In the confusion after the Allied invasion of Italy he had ended up wearing a fascist uniform in the puppet government maintained by the Nazis. Magni was tried for his part in the Valibona massacre and, after tense days in court, was eventually acquitted. Despite the court judgement and the testimony in his favour by various Italian cycling personalities, the idea that Magni had been a Blackshirt persisted. There were also doubts about the Italian's tactics. He was said to be literally towed by his teammates in the early stages of races, hanging on to the back of their shorts so he didn't have to pedal. In 1948 he won his first Giro in controversial circumstances, allegedly tugged along by a team car and then pushed up the slopes during a gruelling mountain stage by a long line of fans who had been specially bussed into position. Coppi was so disgusted he quit the race. When Magni crossed the finish line in Milan he was booed. In the press he was denounced as a fascist once again.

In Flanders people were more tolerant of ugliness. They tended to be less judgemental about behaviour during wartime too, and when it came to sharp practice in races, well, many would say the Flemish had invented most of it. What nobody could doubt about Magni – the thing the Flemish would admire in him – was that he was tough, brave and remorseless.

Magni first travelled up to ride in the Ronde in 1948. He came by train with only his bike. He had no mechanic or team support and after a crash was forced to abandon. In 1949 he returned with one of his most faithful lieutenants, Tino Ausenda. The two men checked into a small hotel opposite Ghent station. They got lucky. The hotel was run by a former cyclist. He immediately offered to act as Magni's mechanic and volunteered a friend to hand refreshments to the Tuscan as he pedalled up the Muur. Magni had prepared his bike especially for the Ronde, using wooden rims to better absorb the buffeting on the cobbles and wrapping the handlebars in foam rubber. Ausenda punctured early and withdrew, leaving Magni to battle on alone. He led for most of the race, apparently drawing energy from the cold and the rain, cheered by Flemish fans who recognised grit when they saw it and prized it higher than class, style or political ideology. Magni regarded his victory as vindication, a riposte to those in his homeland who had jeered him.

He was back in 1950. This time he had more of a team around him. Just as well. The weather was even more brutal than the year before. It had snowed and parts of the Flemish Ardennes were covered in drifts. It was too much even for most of the Flemish riders. Dozens abandoned. Magni attacked early and kept on going. By the time he crested the Kapelmuur he was over five minutes in the lead. Schotte counter-attacked in the final stages but even the Iron Man could not close the gap. Magni finished two minutes and 15 seconds ahead of him. Schotte was impressed. Later he said Magni had ridden like an express train: 'Once he set off he did not stop until the finish line.' Not many men out-gutted Iron Briek.

In 1951 Magni was even more dominant, winning the Ronde by five minutes. By now the Flemish had come to recognise him as a force of nature. He was greeted not so much with acclaim as with astonishment and wonder. As he juddered over the cobbles they pointed and yelled, 'It's him! It's him!' as if they had just spotted Santa Claus. At the finish Magni dismounted and vowed never to ride the Ronde again. Even for him four times was enough. In Italy he is known as the Lion of Flanders. In Flanders they are a little more phlegmatic. They call Magni 'the Tuscan Flandrien'.

One thing Magni can be credited with – he was the first man to bring sponsorship into cycling from outside the bicycle industry, in 1951 when he negotiated a major deal with Nivea. And so the Tuscan tough guy ended his pedalling career peddling moisturiser.

My doppelgänger Edwig Van Hooydonck grew up in Antwerp province in a village called Wuustwezel, a name that seems to come from Tolkien. Until he came along, Edwig joked, the best-known man in the village was the bloke who owned the newspaper shop. He biked ten kilometres to school and ten kilometres back again every day and began racing in the Netherlands aged seven. As a junior he accumulated cups in the Merckxian style; looking at them before a race his eyes would bulge with amazement at his achievements. He got his first pro contract with Kwantum straight after winning the under-23 version of the Ronde in 1986. His *directeur sportif* was Dutch tough guy Jan Raas, a man whose name sounds like a Rottweiler growl when pronounced properly. Early on Van Hooydonck lacked the explosive power needed for the sharp inclines of the Flemish Classics and so he trained in the Flemish Ardennes. He'd warm up on the flat then hit the Bosberg five times, hammer over to Geraardsbergen and do five climbs of the Muur. He did that training run three times a week during the winter months. Edwig made more refined adjustments too. He had his Colnago bike frame lengthened by two centimetres to improve his riding position.

Van Hooydonck was no sprinter, winning his races in the classic Flemish style – riding flat out until he was 20 kilometres from the finish and then riding even harder. If Edwig won he won by a big margin. But often his attacking style saw him overwhelmed by riders who preferred to make their move late from the safety of the bunch. It wasn't helped by his natural diffidence. Edwig saw cycling not so much as a battle with other riders as a fight against himself – 'the not giving up, the battling to the bitter end'. Out on his own he would sometimes suffer a kind of existential crisis. Faced with an open road, he needed someone alongside him to reassure him that he was all right, but no friendly rider could keep up with him. A man like Eddy Merckx didn't need anyone. He was a one-man team. But Van Hooydonck was fragile mentally. His right-hand man and nursemaid was Ludo De Keulenaer. They called De Keulenaer 'Old Guard' because he was always complaining that things were better in the past.

When Edwig won the Ronde in 1989 after launching his attack on the penultimate hill, the Bosberg, he was pictured in Flemish cartoons as Napoleon, dominant and conquering all of Europe. He won again in 1991 using the same *modus operandi*, breaking Museeuw and Rolf Sørensen on the cobbled climb he knew so well. The media took to calling him 'Eddy Bosberg' – Eddy in honour of Merckx. Van Hooydonck was later told that if he launched a third successful attack on the hill they would erect a statue of him at the top. He didn't like that. He was brought up to be modest. He'd won bike races from the start, but his parents had treated him the same, win or lose. 'We always drove home from races in a happy mood,' he'd later recall. His father didn't scold him when he lost or praise him when he won. Like Walter Godefroot, the Van Hooydoncks operated by Kipling's creed.

When he won the Ronde in 1991 Edwig wore shorts that were so long they came down to below his knees. The idea was stolen from Eric Vanderaerden, who'd cut off the bottom of his tracksuit pants during a cold stage of the Tour of Valencia. It was the long-shanked Edwig who made them popular, though. Later he'd jokily wonder if he wouldn't be best remembered as the inventor of 'full-length shorts'.

In the 1990s EPO entered cycling big time. One of the first places that they began experimenting with it was Holland. A number of young riders died prematurely as a result. Jan Raas told his team never to get involved with it. Van Hooydonck did as he was told. Soon men he had burned off all through his junior and pro career were motoring past him on the cobbled hills of Flanders. He knew why, though others accused him of being a sore loser, or a wimp for not taking the true victor's path and doping. In the warped morality of pro sport, not being willing to cheat is a sign of somebody who doesn't have enough desire. When Van Hooydonck was 25 he had told interviewers he wanted to carry on racing for another ten years, but he quit when he was 27. There was a lot to admire in Edwig.

* * *

On the Sunday morning of the great race, I stood waiting for the northbound train at Ghent-Dampoort station. The sky was blue and there was a nip in the air. Across the vast bike park a coach horn blared as cyclists cut across the newly installed pedestrian crossing without bothering to wait for the lights to change to green, and the sound of the bell of Sint-Machariuskerk called the faithful to Mass. On the platform a man in a vintage Flandria jersey was pacing anxiously up and down vaping; a cloud of vanilla-scented smoke trailed behind him and evaporated like the peloton chasing Eddy Merckx. A dad was struggling to corral four small boys, their faces bright with excitement and the morning chill, Flemish flags flapping from their backpacks. Other groups of Ronde fans wandered up and down in vintage cycling caps, the colours bleached by rain, hail and sun until the colourful stripes and the team names – Peugeot, Mapei, Festina – were as faded as the paintings on a cave wall. My only cycling cap remained the *Het Nieuwsblad* one I was given in Ghent velodrome. That seemed like years ago, but on careful calculation it had only been five weeks.

This year the Ronde was starting in Antwerp, heading south through the mist-wreathed marshy flats of the Waasland around Sint-Niklaas before hitting the Flemish Ardennes, where it would circle around several times. For the first time in five years the race was also going to be heading up the steep, narrow, cobbled incline of the Muur in Geraardsbergen. Muur means 'wall'. It was here that I'd first watched the Ronde, back in 1993 and 1995: two races that were associated with one man, the cyclocross fanatic from Gistel, Johan Museeuw.

By the end of 1992 Museeuw was tired of Lotto. He moved to Mapei–GB, an Italian team with a Flemish heart. Museeuw rode alongside Carlo Bomans, Ludwig Willems and Peter Pieters. Team manager Patrick Lefevere was also from West Flanders. Museeuw felt at home. His form improved. He put it down to the professionalism of the Italian team, the change in diet. The Belgian riders still ate steaks. In Italy red meat was off the menu. (Others, including Van Hooydonck, say the new 'diet' included more than chicken and pasta. Museeuw has confessed to using EPO during his final season, but strenuously denies taking it during his glory years.)

Museeuw was 3/1 favourite for the 1993 Ronde alongside Italy's Maurizio Fondriest and the now fading Van Hooydonck. He felt ready, mature enough. 'To win the Ronde you have first to understand it. You have to ride it and learn,' Museeuw said.

In those days the Ronde set out from Sint-Niklaas. For the first hour in 1993 the rain poured, yet by the Kruisberg there were still 40 riders in the leading pack. The final thinning occurred on a narrow cobbled stretch shortly after the Eikenberg climb. Van Hooydonck initiated the surge. Only the strongest went with him: Franco Ballerini, Max Sciandri, Frans Maassen, Fondriest, an unknown Italian called Dario Bottaro, and two more Flemings – another old-school iron man, Marc Sergeant, and Museeuw. The group of eight gradually opened up a lead that stretched to two minutes, with an hour of racing left.

Museeuw attacked shortly after the Berendries climb. He and the Dutchman Maassen broke away, taking close to half a minute's lead. Museeuw attempted to shake off Maassen on the Muur at Geraardsbergen, but the Dutchman hung grimly on. Maassen knew he had no answer to Museeuw's power in the sprint, but hoped, as he later said, that 'the pressure of expectation would be too much' for the Flemish favourite.

'People talk about the pressure,' Museeuw commented, 'but you need the pressure. It's what makes you want to go out and do your best. With racing you have to prepare as well as you can. For the Classics you start in October, November. You train and you think about those races. You prepare in your legs and in your head. Then when the race comes you go out confident. The crowd, the expectation, you can't do anything about that. All you can do is prepare yourself.'

And this time Museeuw was prepared. He kept his head. He won the sprint with a minimum of fuss. It wasn't a spectacular victory, but for the Flemish it had one very attractive component – the beaten rider was from the Netherlands. And there is nothing sweeter to the Flemish than defeating the 'arrogant' Dutch.

If 1993 was a performance of consummate professionalism, the following year's race was textbook cock-up. When Museeuw, Andrei

Tchmil, Franco Ballerini and Gianni Bugno swung into the final straight at Meerbeke, Flemish fans anticipated a second successive victory for their man.

However, it was Bugno who hit the front with 400 metres to go. As the Italian jumped away from the left of the group, Museeuw attempted to go with him but was unintentionally baulked by Tchmil. As a consequence the Italian took a five-metre lead. The finish at Meerbeke is slightly uphill and Museeuw's pursuit saw the gap gradually closing. Inch by inch Museeuw clawed his way back. The pair crossed the line side by side, but Bugno got the photo finish by a tyre width. It was one of the most nail-biting climaxes in the Ronde's hundred-year history. But Museeuw's second place was viewed as a failure by many. Mapei–GB team boss Patrick Lefevere, for one, was furious about his rider's tactics, shouting that, 'Museeuw should have won that sprint on one leg.'

Museeuw too was devastated by the outcome. Looking back he blamed himself: 'That was a chance I missed. I had a lot of misfortune that race. I punctured and then I got caught up in a crash on Oude Kwaremont. A bus broke down on the climb and it blocked the route. My brakes got jammed. Because of the bus I had to wait three minutes for a repair. We spent about 60 kilometres chasing down the leaders. I got a small knock from Tchmil just as Bugno made his move. But in a race like the Ronde things always happen. Crashes, punctures. It's the same for every rider. That race I lost because I made a bad decision. I should have gone from 200 metres, not from so far out.'

For the Flemish, every year a local doesn't win the Ronde seems like a decade. The hunger for success mounts exponentially and with it the pressure on the local riders cranks up, and up. In the mid-1990s Belgian cycling had lost ground to other nations – Italy in particular. Up until that point Flanders had produced a string of powerful riders who had dominated the spring Classics. Now – just as it had seemed at the end of the 1960s – the production line appeared to have ground to a halt.

Only Museeuw was left. In despair the local press took to calling him 'the Last of the Flandriens'.

'To win the Ronde,' Museeuw explained, 'you need experience. You can't just turn up and expect victory, no matter who you are. You need to know the race and the course – every hill, every curve, every cobble; how the weather affects things. You don't have to be Flemish to understand this, but you need to know Flanders.'

In 1995 the pressure that Maassen had identified two years earlier was even higher. Museeuw's reaction was to produce a display of such classic attacking riding it even drew murmurs of approval from Eddy Merckx. That day I stood on the top of the Muur. A large and celebratory crowd waved beer glasses in the air and sang a song in Museeuw's honour to the tune of 'Roll out the Barrel' as radios announced his arrival into Geraardsbergen. He got to the base of the steep incline side by side with Italy's Fabio Baldato. They rode up the cobbles together past a vast memorial to the Great War dead and roadside calvaries as if on some torturous pilgrimage. Then, as the pair approached the summit – legs pumping, heads down, bodies hunched – the Belgian dug deep and accelerated. The Italian tried to respond. He gritted his teeth. He grimaced, but his legs had gone to treacle. Museeuw accelerated away from him and over the crest. The crowd went crazy. Klaxons sounded, the veterans in their woollen cycling caps grinned broadly, a group of lads brandishing Flemish flags roared out the anthem: '*Yo-yo Johan/Johan, Johan Museeuw!*' Museeuw did not slacken. His charge continued. By the top of the Bosberg he was 20 seconds clear and rode the rest of the way to Ninove as if it were a time trial. His lead increased almost by the metre. By the finish he was one minute 27 seconds clear. It was a classic Flandrien victory. It cemented Museeuw as a Flemish hero.

The up-and-down course seemed to mirror Museeuw's relationship with the Ronde. After the triumph of 1995 came disappointment in 1996 and 1997 when crashes and mechanical malfunctions thwarted him. Michele Bartoli and Rolf Sørensen kept the race out of Flemish hands on both occasions.

In the 1997 edition Museeuw had finished 13th, the first time he'd been outside the top three in five years. There was talk in the media that his best days were behind him. Not that you'd have known it from the reception he got from the hordes watching at the roadside in 1998. The race started in bright sunshine in Bruges. Hot local favourite once again, Museeuw hid in the Mapei–GB team bus until the last minute. When he finally emerged a huge cheer went up from the crowd. It barely stopped for 250 kilometres.

Museeuw, irritated by chatter that he was past it, channelled his anger superbly, and on the straight, asphalt incline of Tenbossestraat – the section of the race where he'd attacked in 1993 – he powered away from his rivals with such an amazing and unexpected burst of speed he almost crashed into the back of the race director's motorcycle. The field simply could not live with him. By the time he reached the finish in Meerbeke he was 45 seconds ahead of his pursuers and pulling away from them still.

Museeuw hadn't planned to attack on the Tenbosse, but he sensed the moment. The small world of Flemish cycling had also come to his aid. A neighbour in Gistel had ridden the tourist race on the Saturday. He told Museeuw about a tailwind. He said he'd been able to do 50kph on the road from the Bosberg to Meerbeke. Museeuw knew that if an amateur could do 50, he could do 60. He put his head down and seized the moment.

The victory took Museeuw into an elite group of riders who had won the Ronde three times: Magni, of course; Achiel Buysse; and Eric Leman, the fearsome sprinter from Ledegem with victories in 1970, 1972 and 1973 – on the latter occasion taking a three-way sprint with Merckx and Maertens. Nobody has ever won four.

Museeuw did not have long to celebrate. Less than two weeks after his triumph the Last of the Flandriens lay in a Ghent hospital, delirious with morphine as surgeons discussed the case for amputating his left leg. He'd fallen during Paris–Roubaix and, in filthy conditions in the Arenberg, the gash had become infected. The leg was saved, but the process of rehabilitation was long and hard. He was 32. Retirement must have been a temptation. 'I never considered it, not for a moment,' he said later. Museeuw wouldn't have been a Flandrien if he'd thought of quitting because of pain.

The injury, and his brave refusal to succumb, saw Museeuw rise from hero to idol. In 1999 the route of the Ronde was tweaked to take in his home town of Gistel for the first time. A week before, in Zottegem during the Driedaagse De Panne–Koksijde, I watched him emerge from the Mapei–Quick-Step team bus. The Eagles' 'Tequila Sunrise' was blaring from the speakers and, as he descended into a thicket of waving microphones and tape recorders, he seemed more rock god than sportsman.

By now Flemish cycling's production line had started up again. Museeuw had new, younger rivals. Peter Van Petegem had won Omloop Het Volk twice and Tom Steels was one of the world's fastest sprinters. Frank Vandenbroucke was also on the scene.

The 1999 race was on Easter Sunday, the crowds enormous. Half of the population of Flanders seemed to be at the roadside. Most were cheering for Yo-yo Johan. Mapei's preparation had been disrupted during the Driedaagse when police intercepted a package of amphetamines mysteriously sent to the team hotel. But the crowds were not interested in drug scandals, only in seeing their beloved Lion return.

On the platform before the race Roger De Vlaeminck was asked who he thought would win. He picked Van Petegem. The crowd was outraged. The Beast of Eeklo was booed by Flemish cycling fans.

Unpopular though his call may have been, De Vlaeminck got it right. Van Petegem outsprinted Museeuw at Meerbeke after the Flemish pair and Vandenbroucke had broken away on the Muur. After the previous 12 months, second place seemed like a victory of sorts.

Museeuw suffered a further setback in 2000 when he was involved in a motorcycle crash and took a severe blow to the head that left him in a coma. In 2002 he was part of a five-man breakaway but, as the race approached the finish line, he was outmanoeuvred by the Team Mapei pairing of Andrea Tafi and Daniele Nardello. Museeuw came second. Afterwards he sat on the team bus and wept.

'I hadn't expected to get another chance of victory,' he said. 'As well as experience, to win the Ronde you also need to be explosive. Paris–Roubaix is flat. It's a hard race but you can win with stamina and endurance. It's a race for a rider with a big engine. But for the Tour of Flanders, because of the hills, you need a different kind of strength. You need dynamism. When you get past a certain age your muscles don't have it any more. To win the Ronde there is a small window when you have the cunning, the knowledge, but also still that type of power in your legs.'

Museeuw rode his 17th and final Ronde in 2004. Crowds along the route celebrated as if it were a royal procession. He finished 15th and retired from racing two weeks later.

Since then Museeuw's protégé Tom Boonen had won three times, while the Swiss rider Fabian Cancellara took the race in 2010, 2013 and 2014. By 2017 Cancellara, a massively popular figure in Flanders, had retired, but Boonen remained in the hunt for that elusive fourth win. Today was his last try.

'He has a chance of winning a fourth time,' Museeuw said, 'though I think because of his age he's better suited to Paris–Roubaix. There are younger riders coming up on him. It will be difficult.'

The first place I stopped to find out whether Museeuw was right was an early point of the race, Sint-Niklaas. I got off the train and walked up the huge market square that had been the start point for the race during most of Museeuw's glory years. Groups of teenage boy scouts and girl guides in full khaki uniforms including shorts were handing out Flemish flags to crowds milling around the large statues of Saint Nicholas and his helper 'Black Peter' – an increasingly controversial and divisive figure in modern multicultural Flanders. The mass ranks of people waving flags, the uniforms, the cheery patriotism and the uneasy feeling of having stepped back into an earlier and less politically sensitive age put me in mind of the Last Night of the Proms. Though thankfully there was no mass singing.

Sint-Niklaas is, among other things, the global capital of naked women sculptures. There had been dozens of them on my last visit, and since then more and more seem to have been added. In fairness in the statue of God – *Het Woord* – that looms over one corner of the vast square the Almighty appears to have come out wrapped in a sheet having neglected to put any pants on. I had never really considered what God's bottom would look like, but if I had I don't suppose I would have pictured it as being quite so pert and perky as this one.

The race arrived with the traditional rigmarole of motorbikes and cars and the bloke behind me whistling the Rodania tune. A breakaway group had somehow managed to build up a ten-minute lead in the short section from Antwerp, though it was so early in the race that no one much cared, save whichever sponsor had its name on their jerseys.

Back at the station I went into a café and drank a coffee, watching the race on TV. The café had a tiny smoking room with a glass door. It was about the size of a telephone box, and so popular with patrons that going in there must have been like entering a kippering shed. I expected people to come out orange.

The race passed through Zele, a place the commentator referred to as 'Van Avermaetland'. Sagan, who'd been excitedly pointed out to kids as he whizzed through Sint-Niklaas, looked in some discomfort, fiddling about with his saddle as if he'd got a pain in his buttocks.

On the station platform a platoon of cubs were singing a song in English about how when anyone asked them where they were from they would reply, 'We're from Ezele, pretty, pretty Ezele.' Nobody appeared to be asking, but they treated the waiting passengers to 37 choruses just in case.

I leafed through *Wielerkrant* while I waited. Eddy Planckaert said that Oliver Naesen and Yves Lampaert were the only truly Flemish riders left – he was referring, as Museeuw had done, less to their birthplace than their mentality. Just as you didn't have to be Flemish to be a Flandrien, so it was possible to be born in Flanders and *not* be a Flandrien.

I'd hoped to get to Zottegem and see the race pass through the little town before heading to Geraardsbergen, but for some unfathomable reason Belgian railways had decided Ronde Sunday was the ideal time to dig up the line between Ghent and Antwerp, halving the number of trains that were running, so that idea was abandoned.

The singing cubs followed me onto the southbound train along with a gang of adolescent boys dressed as wizards, elves and Yoda, heading for a comic-book convention at Ghent Expo. I asked a boy in a cloak and Robin Hood hat if he was interested in the Ronde. He shrugged. 'Not really. But I guess it would be cool if Van Avermaet won it.' 'Or Boonen,' his friend, who was some sort of anime character in a shiny green bodysuit, added.

In Geraardsbergen there were huge crowds milling about in the main square. The Ronde had grown in popularity since the 1990s. Partly that was because Anglophones had suddenly become interested in bike racing, but mainly it was because the Flemish had started to market the race efficiently and sell corporate hospitality packages. Back in the early 1990s it had still been pretty homespun, with the air of an agricultural show about it. Now it was a massive international event. I followed a group from a cycling club in Carlisle and headed straight up the sloping main street aiming for the Kapelmuur and the place Steve and I had stood to watch Museeuw all those years ago. I went up the footpath through the park and past the war memorial with its golden angel.

There were already such thick crowds lining the narrow pathways along the edges of the cobbled bends it was impossible to make any progress up the hill that way, and stewards and police were preventing anyone from walking up the road itself. In front of me a couple of young women ducked under the rope, crossed the road, slid under the rope on the other side and headed off into the woods. It seemed like a plan, so I did the same, albeit a little less elegantly. As I stomped up the steep slope through the trees, I looked back and saw that I had attracted a group of followers, clearly swayed by my height and general air of command. Soon I was blundering round in the woods at the head of a small party of middle-aged Flemings, all of whom appeared convinced I knew where I was going. I skirted along the edge of a café that was patrolled by suited bouncers with earpieces, dropped down a dramatically slippery muddy bank, grabbing at branches and stumbling over roots, eventually making it to the footpath below without injury. The squeals and grunts of my followers suggested not everyone was so lucky. Turning right and heading up the hill I soon found myself at the base of the Kapelmuur. The slopes were so covered in people it looked like thousands of cycling fans had formed a human pyramid. There were Flemish flags, banners for Van Avermaet and the late Italian cyclist Franco Ballerini, as well as a man who seemed to have travelled from the coast simply to proclaim his devotion to the seaside resort of Knokke-Heist.

The Muur was easily the steepest hill I'd walked up – and the highest too. It's certainly a more daunting climb than the Molenberg or Oude Kwaremont. I weaved through the crowds to the viewing platform behind the chapel, where a man in a yellow cap, beige safari suit and dark sunglasses, with a paramilitary air, was brandishing a giant Flemish flag.

The area around the chapel gave fantastic views in all directions, though some were blocked by a man with a *Het Nieuwsblad* cycling cap worn over the top of his chicken suit who kept bouncing up and down and crowing. The posh hotel on the reverse slope of the hill had set up scaffolding viewing platforms. Smartly dressed guests were being served Aperol spritzes by bow-tied waiters. The café down below me was ticketed entry only. Everyone seemed to be maximising their return from the Ronde.

The Muur was steep, narrow and cut into the side of the hill. Team and publicity vehicles had been banned from coming up it, so the crowd were alerted to the arrival of the race not by the Rodania car but by the appearance of team mechanics and helpers running up the slope with feed bags, *bidons* and spare wheels. Ten minutes later the first helicopter whirred overhead. The Knokke-Heist man started a song, but his attempts to get people to join in were only greeted with laughter.

In the golden days of Van Hooydonck and Museeuw, the Muur had been a key point in the race. This year, however, it was 95 kilometres from the finish and possessed nowhere near the significance it had once enjoyed. Its place of importance had been handed instead to Oude Kwaremont and the Paterberg, which in combination featured twice: 55 kilometres from the finish and then again with around 13 kilometres to go.

I didn't expect to see anything significant happen on the Muur. I was here for sentimental reasons. There was a small moment of magic, though. At the foot of the slope Tom Boonen launched an attack of such ferocious power it cracked the field open. By the time he came into view Tommeke was part of an elite 14-man group that included his Quick-Step teammate Philippe Gilbert, Van Avermaet, Sagan and Oliver Naesen. The Flemish roared at the sight of Tornado Tom leading the bunch, shredding the field. Maybe the dream could come true?

I walked back down into the town, pausing at Olav's *mattentaart* store to buy some sustenance. I was pleased to find the bearded Olav still behind the counter. Two decades ago he'd told me, 'Here in Flanders Monday is a little bit Sunday too,' and I'd smiled about it for months afterwards. Olav's *mattentaart* come in three sizes, the largest about as big as a Basque beret. I'm not sure he makes or sells anything else.

I went into a café on the way back to the station. It was a big, smart place with a horseshoe-shaped bar and a large wall-mounted TV showing the race. There were waitresses running about carrying trays of beer everywhere, but mainly to a group of blokes from West Yorkshire who had occupied a couple of booths directly under the big screen.

I took a seat at the bar with a glass of Brugse Zot. After Boonen's burst the lead group had continued to speed away from the field, then on the first ascent of Oude Kwaremont Gilbert had attacked and broken away on his own. With the rest of the pack too obsessed with Sagan to give immediate chase the Belgian champion had quickly built up a lead of nearly a minute. But he still had over 50 kilometres till he reached the finish line in Oudenaarde. Gilbert had attacked solo in the Driedaagse and got away, but the men chasing him today were of a far higher calibre. It was madness, surely?

In the café all eyes were glued on the race, though the manager kept announcing that he found cycling boring and was going to switch over to the football. A couple finishing their lunch were big Philippe Gilbert fans and the manager was constantly teasing them by shouting, 'Tommeke! Tommeke!' and blowing a whistle as he walked past their table. One of the Yorkshiremen pointed out that Boonen had suffered a series of punctures and mechanical failures and was now well down the field: 'Boonen's had it, he's out. He's no chance.' The manager waved the comments aside. 'You think it's a race. It's not a race. It's a hunt and Tommeke will hunt them down,' he said.

Shortly afterwards Boonen's bike broke down again near the Taaienberg. He got a new one from the team car after a few seconds, rode 100 metres on the replacement, only to have that pack in on him too. The three-times winner stood forlornly by the side of the road waiting to get a third bike, though he must have been tempted to just chuck the one he had into the hedge and run after the race instead. By the time a team car turned up his day was effectively over, though the manager went on chanting his name and blowing his whistle.

Gilbert's mad solo break continued. The chasing pack behind him fell apart and then reconvened as a smaller, tastier group: Sagan, Van Avermaet, Naesen, Dutchman Dylan van Baarle, Belgian-based Frenchman Yoann Offredo and two Italians, Fabio Felline (a sprinter who'd won the points jersey in the 2016 Vuelta) and Gilbert's teammate Matteo Trentin. The kilometres clicked by, hills were ascended and descended. Still Gilbert carried on alone.

As they watched the Walloon's heroic escape people in the bar began shuffling in their seats, feet twitching as if they themselves were pedalling up Steenbeekdries and bumping over the cobbles of the Koppenberg. '*Allez* Gilbert!' the woman sitting behind me yelled, waving a forkful of fillet steak and béarnaise sauce in the air. 'Tommeke! Tommeke!' bawled the manager with less conviction than ever. The bloke sitting beside me at the bar was in his sixties, with the crumpled face of a man who'd spent too long in the sun and too many nights drinking Trappist ale. He was wearing grey slacks, white socks and Italian loafers, and a silvery sports shirt. He occasionally glanced across at me, said something incomprehensible and grinned lopsidedly. He was so drunk the pupils of his eyes were like two Xs.

On the screen a crash did for Sep Vanmarcke and Luke Rowe, but the roars and gasps and chatter that followed had barely died away when the real drama of the day occurred. On the final climb of Oude Kwaremont Sagan attacked brutally. Only Naesen and Van Avermaet could stick with him. As they hit the flat cobbled stretch that followed, Sagan accelerated again, hammering the *pavé*, the two Flemish riders tucked in behind him, hanging on. In the bar the tension and excitement mounted as the Slovak began to wind up, the lead had held steady at around one minute 25 seconds, but suddenly it was down by five seconds . . . seven . . . ten. And then, just as people in the café had begun to rise in their chairs, the chasing trio hit the deck in a tangle of limbs and bike frames.

As Sagan fell, the man next to me howled with jubilation and leapt to his feet with his arms in the air. He'd forgotten he was on a stool, however, and tumbled over almost as dramatically as the world champion, sending loose change spilling everywhere. The roar that greeted the crash was followed by more sober tutting and a post-mortem about what had caused it. At first people blamed a spectator who'd hung his coat over a barrier and which ended up wrapped round the leg of the unfortunate Naesen. But on the third slow-motion replay it became clear that the crash was entirely Sagan's fault. He'd ridden in the gutter to avoid the cobbles and got too close to the barriers, hitting one of the support feet. He'd spun off and taken Naesen and Van Avermaet with him. Van Avermaet bounced up again fast, remounted and set off, but it was clear that neither Sagan nor Naesen would be catching anyone today. There was a smattering of applause for the Slovak in the café, and some muttering that it was all really unlucky for the world champion. The initial elation didn't entirely fade, though. The crash was so unexpected, such an extraordinary twist, it was hard not to view it as somehow magical. Later, people said that, maybe on balance, it had spoiled the race, but the drama of the moment couldn't be so easily downplayed. A few days later I met a couple of Americans in Oudenaarde and when we talked about it their eyes lit up and their voices rose: 'Wow, bike racing! I mean, man, what the hell?'

In the confusion following the crash the fallen man in the café had gathered up his change and disappeared out of the door. Van Avermaet recovered just as quickly but, despite a nasty headwind, Gilbert was away and couldn't be caught. It's the seventh-longest breakaway victory in the history of the Ronde, behind only the solo escapes of the Death Rider of Lichtervelde, Léon Devos, Fiorenzo Magni (twice), Merckx and Germany's Rudi Altig.

After I watched him carry his bike triumphantly across the finish line I walked back to Geraardsbergen station and hopped on the waiting train.

The man who had tumbled from his stool got on shortly after I did and sat opposite me. We began to converse in a mixture of basic English and atrocious French. He told me that he was 67 and the day before had ridden the Ronde sporting event. I asked how long it took. '*Douze* hours,' he said with a grimace. '*Très dur*. My *jambes* is still ache,' he scowled. I now saw his fall from the stool in a different light. Indeed, the fact he could get on the stool at all after 12 hours riding a bike the previous day was frankly a thing of wonder.

'Boonen, ah,' he said with a shrug and a glum expression. 'He *victoire* Paris–Roubaix, then . . . *fini*.'

11

POT BELLIES AND BARBRA STREISAND

Scheldeprijs, 5 April
Kermis Omloop van Zele, 8 April

The days following the Ronde felt like the morning after an outrageous party. There were post-mortems and gossip but all of it seemed slightly hungover and listless. All those weeks spent hopping from one race to another at a rate of roughly one every three days, heading towards the Big Sunday with barely a chance to focus on anything but Rik Van Looy's Ronde racing diet (six jam tarts, three cream-cheese sandwiches, a bar of chocolate and a pear – surprisingly similar to my own) and how many bowls of pasta's worth of energy a rider burned through during the one-day Classic (about 11) and now, suddenly, it was gone – and we had a vast cobble-less desert to get across while facing the horrible reality that we hadn't done any laundry for such a long time that some of our socks could stand up on their own.

I attempted to suppress the feeling of nervous uncertainty (and escape the smell oozing from the wardrobe) by wandering around Flanders looking at cycling monuments. I travelled to Sint-Martens-Lierde to see the bust of Emiel Faignaert. A fair-haired, jug-eared Fleming who looked like a prototype for Johan Museeuw, Faignaert won the Ronde in 1947, the highlight of a career that had been eaten up by World War Two. I went up to the Dutch border to De Klinge to view the square named after the De Loor brothers, Gustaaf and Alfons. The younger of the pair, Staf, had won the first edition of the Vuelta in 1935. He'd won again in 1936, and his elder brother, Fons, had come second. It's the only time in history brothers have finished on the podium of one of the Grand Tours. I went to see the little monument in Ruien that commemorates Eddy Merckx's last victory as a pro in a criterium around Kluisbergen (fittingly, Frans Verbeeck came third), then across Flemish Brabant to Werchter to find the street named after Jef Scherens, one of Flanders' most successful track riders. World professional sprint champion from 1932 to 1937, he'd won the title again in 1947. Had his career not been interrupted by World War Two few doubt he would have won half a dozen more rainbow jerseys. Scherens came to track racing via the *kermis*, his explosive sprint finishes – he was so fast over 30 metres it looked like his bike had been fired from a bazooka – in races like the Omloop van Wetteren convincing his supporters that he would do better to focus on short explosive bursts, ones in which the frenzied effort of pushing a 24x7 or 27x7 gear lasted for just a few seconds.

Small (five feet seven), slight (he weighed a little over ten stone), shy and unassuming, Scherens was nicknamed 'Poeske' (the Flemish word for 'cat', from which we get the English word 'puss-cat'). He found staying in shape easy enough and barely trained, riding just 20 miles on the road three or four times a week, a friend on a motorbike pacing him in short sprints along the way. At his peak he was more or less invincible, many attributing his failure to win every Grand Prix sprint race he appeared in during the 1930s to his all-round niceness and generosity of spirit. Other less charitable observers wondered if he didn't sell a few to line his pockets. Asked about it later the modest Scherens answered opaquely that his occasional losses benefited the sport: 'After all, it wouldn't have done the game much good if I had won everything everywhere, would it?' It was a lesson that Merckx refused to absorb.

All that flitting about passed the time and took the edge off the emptiness, then, finally, on 5 April it was time for another day at the races. The Scheldeprijs is the oldest race on the Flemish cycling calendar. Named after the river that flows through Antwerp, the Scheldeprijs (sometimes called the Grote Scheldeprijs) was first run in 1907. In the early years it started and finished in Antwerp, the last laps around the old velodrome at Zurenborg. The Zurenborg velodrome had been built on the site of a former farm and hosted the world championships in 1894 and 1905. Royal Antwerp FC played their games on the pitch in the centre of it. It was demolished during World War One.

Since those days the start had moved around moderately, shifting to Merksem and Deurne before returning to Antwerp in the mid-1990s. The race finished with three laps around the town of Schoten, which is otherwise best known as the birthplace of Flemish Junior Eurovision Song Contest sensation Thor! (That's his exclamation mark, not mine.)

The Scheldeprijs used to be run on the Wednesday after Paris–Roubaix, a polite easing off after the Hell of the North. Recently, though, it has been shifted to sit in the spot Ghent–Wevelgem had once occupied. It is still the final race of the Flemish Classics season, but now it looks more like a warm-up than a warm-down. Though it has a few cobbled sections and can be hit by the extreme weather that sometimes lashes the other Flemish Classics, it's flat and far less brutal and almost guaranteed to end in a bunch sprint.

The first Scheldeprijs was won by a Frenchman, Maurice Leturgie, who hailed from the old Flemish city of Rijsel – better known to the rest of the world as Lille – and would finish third in the 1912 edition of Paris–Roubaix. After that the Flemish won it fairly consistently, the first truly big-name winner arguably Georges 'Crybaby' Ronsse in 1927. Nearly all the great Flemish riders of the post-war years have won the race – Buysse, Ockers, Van Looy, Schotte, Godefroot, De Vlaeminck, Verbeeck, Maertens, Van Petegem and Boonen. Notably absent from the list were local boy Van Steenbergen, and Museeuw.

One otherwise unheralded rider who'd done well, winning the race three times in the early 1960s, was Petrus Oellibrandt (generally known as Piet) from Beveren in the Waasland. Oellibrandt had single-handedly held the record for the most wins until it was equalled by Manxman Mark Cavendish, but both men were then overhauled by Boonen's German teammate Marcel Kittel, a ferociously fast sprinter who'd finished first in consecutive races from 2012 to 2014 and won again in 2016.

Today's race was departing from Mol in honour of local boy Tom Boonen, whose grandfather was slated to drop the starting flag. It was Boonen's penultimate pro race, his last in Flanders and, unlike those of Eddy Merckx and Freddy Maertens, it had been carefully choreographed so as not to be ignominious.

I took the train up to Antwerp-Zuid, bought a flat white from a Melbourne-style coffee bar at the station and then hopped on the connection out into the Kempen, west of Antwerp. On the way to Lier we passed through lush meadows filled with big smoky-grey-and-white beef cattle, the famous Belgian Blues, a breed that has a unique genetic property – it does not have the natural inhibitor on muscle growth that is common to almost every mammal. Too much muscle is unconducive to survival, which is why the muscle-inhibiting gene exists. Thanks to selective breeding the Belgian Blues don't have that gene, which means they are able to develop the enormous muscular bodies of some kind of hulking superhero from a comic. Muscle is meat, so clearly this works in favour of beef farmers. And if you wonder what that might have to do with cycling, then you need to think about the future of doping a little more clearly.

On a lighter and altogether less sinister note, cattle have already had a part to play in Flemish cycling history. During the Ronde of 1925 Gustaaf Van Slembrouck, a handsome, smiling man from Ostend, was speeding along a narrow cinder path apparently on his way to victory when a dairy cow, startled by the sound of his tyres, reversed into him and knocked him into a ditch. A similar fate befell Jules Van Hevel, a heroic fellow from Koekelare who'd been wounded by mortar fire in World War One and recovered to win the Ronde and Paris–Roubaix. Van Hevel might have added the rainbow jersey to his *palmarès* too, but for some oxtail. In Hungary in 1928 he and Georges Ronsse were in a two-man breakaway that had burned off the opposition before, 100 kilometres from the finish, they passed a couple of harnessed oxen that were grazing by the side of the road. Ronsse passed them without incident but, according to legend, as Van Hevel came alongside one of the oxen swished its tail. The tail caught Van Hevel's brake handle and sent him spinning to the ground, his leg so badly hurt he could barely finish. Ronsse won the race, a feat he would repeat the following year. Neither of the cattle seems to have been harmed.

Out by Kessel the train rattled past the ruins of a massive World War One fortress that formed the centrepiece of a UCI cyclocross race. The fortress had been part of Belgium's defensive line, but, like the great World War Two fortifications to the west at Eben-Emael, it proved no match for the Germans, who battered it with artillery fire and then overran it.

228

At Nijlen an enormous turkey surveyed the train with beady-eyed aggression, its tail feathers opening and closing as if to deter the driver from attack.

There were Arab horses in paddocks, and copses of elegant deciduous trees. Floodlit dressage arenas and all-weather tennis courts. It was wealthy country. The Dutch own lots of property around here, avoiding the higher taxes in their own country by living in Belgium and commuting to work across the border, but there are plenty of rich Flemings too.

Mol is a prosperous-looking place filled with cafés, restaurants and clothes shops selling high-end Italian brands. Boonen was born in the town and brought up in nearby Balen. He was a Flemish idol of a different order from Briek Schotte. His life was lived in the public domain. For several years his wife, Lore, had a daily column in *Het Laatste Nieuws*. In the columns her total and utter admiration for her husband shone through to such a degree she made Nancy Reagan look like Lorena Bobbitt.

Not that life was perfect. Boonen tested positive twice for cocaine and admitted publicly to having problems with alcohol. Lore miscarried a child then later gave birth to twins. It was revealed that she had a heart problem and had to follow the latter stages of races with a pillow in front of her face so she didn't get too excited. In 2005 the Boonens moved to Monaco for tax reasons and then, in 2016, got slapped with a two million euro bill by the Belgian inland revenue because Tom spent so much time in Flanders he still counted as a resident. In a Belgian TV interview he confessed to drinking until he blacked out, saying, 'I'm not a murderer, but that's the way people see me.' His body is covered in life-affirming tattoos.

Boonen's tax difficulties stemmed from an old problem afflicting sports stars – that of putting faith in experts who turn out to be idiots (though, of course, if he'd just paid his tax like a normal person there would have been no problem). In Belgium, where tax-fiddling was once described to me by a Flemish hotel-owner as 'our most popular national pastime', Boonen drew less flak than he might have in Britain. Why did the Belgians feel this way? I suspect it was a legacy of being an occupied nation, controlled from Spain, Austria, France and the Netherlands and then by a government that imposed a foreign language on Flanders. Cheating the government wasn't cheating yourself – it was cheating outsiders. The Flemish tend to look down on the Dutch as law-abiding bum-kissers. The Netherlands had run its own affairs for four centuries. The laws the Dutch obeyed were ones they themselves had made.

Boonen was big-hearted and generous to his teammates, revelling in their successes almost as much as he did his own (he had punched the air in delight when Stijn Devolder won the Ronde). His record was comparable with any of the great Flemish riders of the past – indeed it was better than almost any of them. He'd won the Ronde three times, Paris–Roubaix four times, the E3 on five occasions. He'd won six stages of the Tour de France and carried off the green points jersey in 2007. He'd been world champion in 2005, Belgian champion twice, won Ghent–Wevelgem three times, Kuurne–Brussels–Kuurne three times and won today's race, the Scheldeprijs, twice.

It seemed to me that compared to men like Schotte there was more glamour in Boonen's life but less romance – which is a reflection of our times, and also mirrors the way Flanders had changed in the last three decades of the twentieth century. During that period, shrewd investments by the now more autonomous regional Flemish government in everything from the massive expansion of the seaport at Zeebrugge to the Antwerp fashion industry, an increasingly well-educated population and the fact the region had never been a place of traditional heavy industry and was therefore more able to adapt to new technologies than the steel and coalmining regions of Wallonia, saw Flanders experience massive economic growth. From being proverbially poor, the region was suddenly as rich as the pralines that lined the shelves of the chocolatiers of Bruges.

The change was clear in Ghent. Thirty years ago the city was charming but rundown, the great Flemish baroque buildings begrimed with dirt, the river Leie choked and emitting the dank odour of a thousand blocked drains. Nowadays Ghent is a place transformed, sparkling and fragrant. Everyone from England who visited me went away impressed, often even a little awestruck. 'Wow, some money here, isn't there?' they said as we passed Michelin-starred restaurants that were booked up for months in advance, the lights twinkling on the nearby canals, laughter rippling out from the cocktail bars. It was true. If it had been independent of poor, post-industrial Wallonia, Flanders would, per capita, be the wealthiest state in the EU. The Flemish no longer aspire to perhaps one day owning a washing machine or getting away for a week at the seaside in the quirkily upmarket Edwardian resort of De Haan (modelled after Liverpool's Sefton village). Flanders, the land of the muddy, turnip-snagging peasant, was now wealthy and draped in threads from Dries Van Noten and Raf Simons.

Not everyone thought this was a good thing, though. One of the differences between Protestantism and Roman Catholicism concerns the redemptive benefits of penance. Catholics believe that suffering earns credit with God, that the endurance of torment helps gain entry to heaven. Protestants don't. Cycling, more than any other sport, was designed to inflict pain on competitors. The organisers of the Grand Tours and the one-day Classics set out to make things as hard as possible – the more brutal the course, the more glowing the legend; the greater the suffering, the more glistering the glory. Perhaps that is why up until the last few decades nearly all the most successful cyclists have come from Catholic countries. And Flanders is one of the most devoutly Catholic regions of Europe – for most of the twentieth century close to 90 per cent of its inhabitants were baptised Catholic, a higher percentage of the population than anywhere else in Europe with the possible exception of the Republic of Ireland. At least part of the Flandrien myth was based on a general fear of the corrupting power of wealth, of the

Franciscan benefits of honest poverty. At times it seemed the raffishly dressed and distinctly portly newspaperman Karel Van Wijnendaele was rather too eager to promote a world view in which children with full stomachs grew up ill-disciplined and unable to steel themselves to struggle. Briek Schotte himself, when he was team manager at Flandria, would protest that paying riders too much would make them uncompetitive and lazy.

As the years rolled on some felt that *Sportwereld*'s championing of those who emerged from poverty and hardship had become less a celebration of the doughty peasant underdog than propaganda for the social status quo. Ironically, the very Flemish virtues Van Wijnendaele had begun his newspaper to celebrate – intelligence, craftsmanship, artistry, shrewdness, prudence – had brought about the end of the tough, almost feudal world from which the cyclists he loved had sprung. Boonen was a swashbuckling hero for the new Flanders and in truth his sins and his redemptions were little different from those of Van Steenbergen, Maertens and a peloton of others who had gone before.

I walked from Mol station into the town centre. It was midweek but it seemed most people in the town had taken the day off to wave goodbye to the great man. There were banners thanking Tornado Tom, displays in shop windows devoted to his career, children with his name painted across their faces – and a general sense of both celebration and mourning. On a street corner among café tables full of middle-aged couples drinking Irish coffee, a woman in her sixties wrapped in a Tom Boonen flag, a Quick-Step hat tugged down over a wisteria-coloured perm, yelled, 'Look! Look! A Quick-Step team car! Look! Look!' – frantically pointing it out to a child in a pushchair who was barely old enough to recognise the word 'biccy'.

When Boonen emerged from the Quick-Step bus he was followed to the sign-in podium by popping flashbulbs and TV cameras and the sort of applause that might greet the Pope – worshipful adulation.

I watched the race pass on its ceremonial lap and then walked out to where I thought it might be going next, past several tattoo parlours, a shop selling Russian speciality foods and a snooker hall called the Buckingham, which suggested that in one corner at least the 1980s British comedy drama *Minder* had a faithful following. When I got to the junction where the road crossed the railway tracks I found stewards and police, but no fans.

I walked back into the centre of the town and bumped into the Slovak family I'd first seen in the Kuipke before the start of the Omloop. The son was still dressed in full national cycling kit and his mum and dad were armed with Sagan banners. Earlier, fans had crowded round Sagan's team bus and eagerly photographed him when he appeared. 'He looks like a gypsy,' I heard an estuarine voice behind me say.

I took up a position on some benches opposite the town hall and tourist information centre. There was a giant inflatable cyclist opposite – the *Het Nieuwsblad* version. He had bandy legs and was punching the air in a victory celebration. From certain angles it looked like he was having a fist fight with the steeple of Sint-Peter en Pauwelkerk. A man who was promoting some hipsterish Edwardian-looking electric bike got the Slovak family to pose with his bicycle next to the big inflatable cyclist. The Slovaks waved their flags, the *Het Nieuwsblad* giant swayed in the wind. It was another boring day in Belgium.

The crowd that had dispersed earlier reappeared an hour later when the race again passed through the town centre. The breakaway group got polite applause, but the sight of the Quick-Step riders produced excited yells and whoops. 'Boonen! Tommeke! Hey!' a middle-aged woman in leopard-skin leggings who'd come scuttling out of a hairdresser's minutes before squawked, waving her arms in the air.

And then he was gone.

A man appeared in a van, got out and began to deflate the *Het Nieuwsblad* cyclist. As I walked back towards the station I realised I had heard the Rodania car for the last time and I was filled with wistful sadness. I passed the chip vans, the doughnut carts and the beer stalls, thinking of the three chubby old men in full cycling gear who'd parked themselves in front of the Bahrain team bus and been asked for autographs by a couple of possibly sarcastic children. And the old guy in the greying jersey who'd appeared on the road seconds after the peloton to cheering and calls of, 'Look! It's Boonen's granddad!'

I took a train to Lier, a pretty walled town with a celebrated chiming clock. By the time the race left Mol for the last time a seven-man breakaway led by the Dutch Roompot team had already built up a considerable lead, and they kept on extending it. When I eventually found a convenient TV in one of the best bars of the trip they were still over three minutes in front, though the lead had been nibbled down from five.

I ordered stew and chips, and beer from a local brewery called Vicaris that scored highly in the CAMRA guide. I watched the race. The break group's lead dwindled further as I ate. In eight kilometres the chasers wiped off another minute, and by the time they entered the first of the three 15-kilometre laps of Schoten that concluded the race the seven riders were just 59 seconds in front.

I smiled at the barman and he brought me another beer and took my empty plate away. The break was finally caught with 19 kilometres to go, and the race came to its inevitable finale. Boonen had once had a devastating sprint but that had long gone. He did his bit for his team, though, helping Kittel through to the front then easing off and watching the German hammer to the finish ahead of Elia Viviani and Nacer Bouhanni.

The barman watched, put down the glass he was polishing, and shrugged, 'You want another one?' The beer I'd been drinking was 9.5 per cent. 'If I have another one you'll have to carry me to the train,' I told him. The barman looked out of the window. 'It's only 100 metres,' he said.

Saturday came and there was a race to go to, a *kermis* in Zele, slap in the heart of what the Flemish media might have called the Kingdom of Van Avermaetia. The *kermis* came at the end of what had been a week-long celebration of the Ronde that had also involved running races for adults and children, carnival floats and a full-blown travelling funfair. The town hosts another race in October, also associated with a fair, the GP Zele. The GP Zele is a much bigger deal than today's race and since its inception in 1955 has been won by some of the biggest names in Flemish cycling, Verbeeck, Godefroot, Van Petegem and Boonen among them. Still, today's Omloop had also attracted a decent field, including younger riders from Lotto–Soudal and Tarteletto–Isorex, a trio of Norwegian under-23 riders and Joeri Stallaert.

I arrived when the riders were just starting to assemble around the Café De Lantaarn in Kloosterstraat, and so I went off to find some lunch among waltzers and merry-go-rounds spray-painted in garish shades of puce and lavender and covered with airbrushed images of what looked like Beyoncé. A few families with small children wandered about, the kids arguing that since all the rides that were currently open were rubbish this didn't actually count as going to a fair at all. At the only food stall that was open I ordered a small *frites*, and the man behind the counter repeated 'small?' as if he couldn't quite believe it. I'm not sure why he was doubtful. In Flanders 'medium' will feed a family of four, while 'large' will satisfy an entire football team including the subs, the coaching staff and the bloke who packs the kitbags.

The Kermisloop van Zele covers 138 kilometres and offers prize money of 810 euros, with a pot of money for the intermediate sprints totalling 315 euros. For a long while these sorts of races, particularly the ones that traditionally fell in the four weeks after the Tour de France, had been the way many pro riders had made their money. British rider Vin Denson, who'd made his home in Ghent and opened a café there, reckoned that on the appearance fees and prizes he picked up in a month of Flemish *kermis* races he and his family could live for a year. The money that was floating about in cycling in those days was colossal compared to other European sports. Riders like Tommy Simpson earned far more than a top-flight professional footballer in England. Eddy Merckx was picking up around £200,000 a season in the early 1970s at a time when First Division stars such as George Best and Bobby Charlton were lucky to get a tenth of that. Factor in the cash that came – often stuffed in a pillowcase and tax free – from the world of the *kermis* races and it's easy to see how men like Rik Van Looy could afford their distinctly regal lifestyles.

After my chips I wandered off to the start line. It was a warm day and people had set up their chairs and cool boxes along the pavements. Young women sat out on balconies, faces tilted to the sun. Stewards in high-vis gilets advertising a local fashion store slapped their paddles on their thighs and fiddled eagerly with their whistles. A couple walked past with four Chihuahuas on leads. I have never seen as many Chihuahuas as I did in Flanders – it's hard to comprehend the Flemish passion for them. Every time one appears, men, women and children begin simpering with joy. There were times when I felt tempted to go into a pet shop, buy a gerbil, put a tartan coat and a pink sparkly collar on it and take it for a walk, just to be part of the experience.

There was quite a cluster around the start. A middle-aged blonde with a deep tan who dressed in red cycling kit was taking photos of the assembled field. She'd been at the Omloop van Wetteren and in Kemzeke too. There were a few other faces I recognised – big-boned elderly men in padded coats. We nodded at one another like non-League football fans, bound together by shared joy and shame.

The race got under way. There were yells as the riders passed and members of the peloton bellowed instructions and warnings to one another. It was a tricky course with cobbles, sections of road made from tessellated bricks, speed bumps and wide storm drains that looked purpose built to send a rider toppling. The peloton sped along the road, splitting as it went around a war memorial opposite the Café TGV with its sign featuring a buxom woman in a jumpsuit sitting astride a high-speed train – public transport meets Whitesnake – and Easter decorations in the windows.

The commentator kept a steady stream of blather going over the PA, a common feature of bike racing of which the best that can be said is that it's often better than the music. He seemed to be name-checking sponsors and at one point delivered a long prepared speech that sounded like he was telling us about an unmissable bulk deal on Lynx African body spray (though even after seven weeks my knowledge of Dutch was still so sketchy it could have been that he was actually outlining his personal take on the miracle of transubstantiation).

Towards the end of each lap the race came past an arts centre and then took a hairpin bend between a lingerie shop and a cantor's office and into the narrow Kloosterstraat where mothers, wives and girlfriends were operating the feeding station, passing out *bidons* to the riders opposite the Sari pizza and kebab restaurant. With a couple of laps to go a small group had broken away. Next to the finishing straight a woman in her late twenties, who looked like Victoria Beckham, stood on the barrier, ran her fingers repeatedly through her hair and muttered, 'Oh my God . . . Oh my God . . .' The bunch were still ahead when the last lap commenced. There was no bell, just a bloke holding up his fingers to indicate how many laps remained – which must be tricky to see when you're stuck in a mass of 70 riders. The commentator was in fine voice, reeling off the times and the names of riders, speaking in Dutch, French and English.

As the peloton disappeared past the war memorial for the final time the PA started playing Duck Sauce's 'Barbra Streisand' and everyone around me began dancing and pumping their arms in the air like they were doing the 'Let's All Have a Disco' chant that was popular on football terraces in England in the 1990s. Victoria Beckham was probably just joining in to ease her nerves, but by the time the race came into view again whoever she had been rooting for had evidently disappeared into the bunch with the rest of the breakaway and she slumped her shoulders and wandered back towards the main car park.

After three hours in the saddle the race came down to a mass sprint in a street that was no more than eight yards across. One wiggle and there'd have been carnage. Joran Mertens, one of the under-23s, crossed the line first, Laurent Pieters of Tarteletto-Isorex was second, Gianni Marchand third and Jelle Camps – the lad who'd won the junior cyclocross event in Oostmalle – fourth. The old chap from Kemzeke's favourite, Joeri Stallaert, was 13th.

I walked back along the road past the riders now reunited with their families. Near the station an elderly steward was taking off his armband and stowing his red paddle and whistle in the saddlebag of an old bicycle. He looked up at me, nodded in greeting, then mounted his bike and pedalled off down the street.

12

STAYING SMALL

Paris–Roubaix, 9 April

A decade ago I travelled up to the Cairngorms to write an article about shinty. It was December and so cold even the air had turned blue. Shinty is a swashbuckling sport, an Errol Flynn version of hockey. The ball was blasted about and the curved sticks cleaved the heavy atmosphere like claymores. 'Do a lot of people get injured playing this?' I said to the bundle of clothes standing next to me. 'Not at all, not at all,' the man inside them replied, in a Highland accent that wasn't so much lilting as capering o'er hill and dale. 'For yourself, now, it would be dangerous, naturally. But these lads have played since they left the cradle. They can anticipate the flight of the ball and the movement of the sticks as surely as—' At which point our conversation was interrupted by the dull thunk of wood on skull and cries of, 'Doctor, doctor!' from the pitch.

After the wounded player had been sent off to hospital in Inverness, the gash above his eye flapping like a second mouth, I said to the man, 'So that doesn't happen very often, then?' 'Oh no,' he replied cheerily, 'very rarely. Hardly ever more than once a game.'

Just as when the dentist tells you that 'this won't hurt a bit' you know to brace yourself, so it is with sport. The more violent and dangerous it is, the more people talk up its safety. The opposite holds true. Football, for instance, is constantly marred by horrific and shameful brawls, brutal fracas and mass fights from which, mysteriously, everyone emerges without a nick or a scratch. Generally, the more a sport struts and sneers and pronounces its machismo, the less tough it really is. There are exceptions, however. One of them was taking place this second Sunday of April. Paris–Roubaix really does live up to its billing as 'the Hell of the North'. The course runs through the killing grounds of Arras and the Somme, across sections of tooth-loosening cobbles and muddy tracks, and traditionally through a lumpy squall of horizontal rain.

When Johan Museeuw fell on the sharp cobbles, he almost lost a leg to gangrene. Even the 1981 winner, Bernard Hinault, who had fallen seven times on his way to victory (one crash caused by a small black dog named Gruson), denounced the race with the memorable words 'Paris–Roubaix is bullshit' and refused to ride in it. The Breton was a man of legendary belligerence who boasted that the only reason he attended school was because he was guaranteed a fist fight, and who spent his spare time between Tour de France victories blowing up badger setts with dynamite, so if he thought the Hell of the North was too infernal to contemplate you'd have to think there was something in it.

Steve and I had only got to Paris–Roubaix once, in 1995. Our method of following races in those days was the same simple one I had been following in Flanders. We picked an interesting section of the course and sat in a bar watching on TV until the field approached, went out, watched the race pass then went back to the bar. We watched most of Paris–Roubaix in a bar on the outskirts of Lille. It was one of those northern French street-corner boozers with florid 1970s wallpaper, a poster of Vanessa Paradis and a view through the back into the owner's sitting room where, in obeisance to some ancient law, there always seemed to be a canary in a cage and an old lady dozing in an armchair in front of a dubbed rerun of *Columbo*. The customers had the kind of mashed-up, booze-and-black-tobacco mushes that made Serge Gainsbourg look like Reese Witherspoon.

We had watched races in bars in Belgium, Spain and Italy, accompanied by shouts and laughter. The Hell of the North was different. People regarded the screen mordantly, like alcoholics staring at the first drink of the day. On the TV in the bar in Lille the peloton entered the cobbled stretch of road known as the Arenberg Trench. Dust clouds filled the air, spectators lined the route so thickly the riders seemed in danger of being crushed. A cyclist broke away. Nobody asked who it was. Leading seemed immaterial. Just surviving was a victory.

As the race neared Hem we got up to go out and watch it pass. The man who had sat silently beside us for the previous three hours drinking brandy, chain-smoking and farting so diabolically that in the Middle Ages they'd have called the Inquisition, introduced himself as Pascal and offered us a lift in his 2CV. It was a memorable journey, during which I found it hard to decide whether we were more likely to die in a collision with a lamp post or a mephitic fireball of ignited methane.

Pascal abandoned the car on a bridge over the E15 motorway. While we waited he whipped a copy of *L'Équipe* out of his back pocket, held it in front of his groin in respect for public decency, and urinated mightily into the gutter. As we watched the foaming yellow stream flow past, Steve remarked, mildly, 'You can say what you like about the French, but they certainly understand the art of life.' L'Enfer du Nord, indeed.

I might have been tempted to repeat that experience for nostalgia's sake, or at least to travel to Carrefour de l'Arbre where the Belgian fans congregated in their thousands and you could still occasionally hear the 'Yo-yo Johan' song echoing across the flat stubbly fields. But it was my last weekend in Flanders and I was reluctant to leave it for a foreign country, even though Lille had once been the Flemish capital and there was still a Dutch-speaking minority sprinkled on the southern side of the border. And so instead I went to Eeklo, home town of Roger De Vlaeminck, to watch the Hell of the North in a bar.

Back in the 1970s De Vlaeminck had won the race four times, earning himself the nickname 'Monsieur Paris–Roubaix', which he probably liked better than the Beast of Eeklo or the Gypsy (his family had a business selling clothing door to door).

Although the course of Paris–Roubaix, which finishes slap on the Belgian border, never leaves France, the race has all the ingredients – cobbles, crosswinds, filthy weather – that Flanders holds dear. For that reason, to Flemish riders, victory in the Roubaix velodrome is second in prestige only to crossing the finish line first in the Ronde, and they have dominated the Hell of the North almost as completely. Since the race was first run, in 1896, Flemish riders have won it more times than those from anywhere else. The only riders to have won L'Enfer four times were both Flemish: Tom Boonen and De Vlaeminck. Of the seven riders who've been triple winners, a trio – Gaston Rebry, Rik Van Looy and Johan Museeuw – were from Flanders. Ten riders have done the 'cobbled Classic double' of the Ronde and Paris–Roubaix. Eight of them were Flemish (the other two, Heiri Suter and Fabian Cancellara, were Swiss, incidentally).

The record number of finishes in the Hell of the North (16) is held jointly by Dutchman Servais Knaven and Raymond Impanis, from Kampenhout in Flemish Brabant. Kampenhout is in the same municipality as Berg, and since Impanis's father had a bread shop, the rider was nicknamed 'the Baker from Berg'. Knaven was as tough as a tortoise sandwich and won Paris–Roubaix in slithery rain in 2001, but his record didn't quite match that of the Baker. Impanis won Paris–Roubaix and the Ronde in the same year, 1954, that he won Paris–Nice. Since he also finished in the top ten in the Hell of the North nine times and won the Flèche Wallonne in a snowstorm in 1957 it's fair to say that the cold weather suited him.

Not that it was cold today. Quite the opposite. Eeklo was so hot the tarmac was melting, and even a passing Labrador looked like he might have to pause and wipe sweat from his brow.

Eeklo is one of those places that runs on for miles without ever seeming to start. Apart from a vast church, which is said to have the second highest spire in Belgium, there is not much to the centre, no market filled with bars, or anything much in the way of shops. The wide main street seemed designed to get motorists through the place as fast as possible.

I wandered off to find the park, through estates of neat white detached houses with fir trees in the front gardens and large dogs barking behind wire-mesh fences. I passed a boy scouts' centre and a strolling couple in slogan t-shirts, hers saying 'Boom Boom – All Over You!' And his reading 'Not My Problem'. Well, it avoided the trouble of conversation, I suppose.

In the park there was a sports area offering an interesting assortment of activities: a hammer-throwing circle, a couple of courts for a Belgian game that's played with wooden blocks and seems to mix *pétanque* with skittles, and a fenced-off area among a grove of blossoming cherry trees containing a narrow metal tower that I instantly recognised from my visit to the Ghent City Museum as an arena for vertical archery, or popinjay, as it is known in Britain. Popinjay was invented in Scotland. The idea of the sport is to simulate the hunting of birds. Competitors fire up at the targets, which look a bit like some kind of exotic pigeons (there are four smaller ones and a large one, which I feel ought to be called the poppycock, but isn't), and attempt to knock them off their 'perches'. I had watched various YouTube clips of competitions and it was plain that, particularly during matches between Belgium and the Netherlands (the two undisputed kings of popinjay), things could get pretty tense. In one youth international a Belgian competitor's heavily set mum ran on to congratulate the lad after a brilliant shot and collided with him at such velocity she hammered him to the ground. The poor lad never fully recovered from this dizzying blow and finished third. Quite why this odd Scottish sport should have caught hold in Belgium is a mystery. But then Belgians have embraced other singular sports, and it is worth remembering that the nation still holds the Olympic titles for both the equestrian long jump and live pigeon shooting.

In order to observe the pole-archery arena, and because I was thirsty, I took a table at the bar next to it. The day was so sunny that when the waiter brought me my beer and an epic portion of cheese he also offered me a parasol.

When I had cooled down a bit I went inside to watch the race. Philippe Gilbert had elected not to ride, which placed even more focus on Greg Van Avermaet and Tom Boonen. Boonen was part of a large breakaway group, and for a while as he powered along over the cobbles it looked like he just might have enough left to pull off a minor miracle. Then, with 30 kilometres left, the group split again, and as half a dozen riders (including Van Avermaet, Jasper Stuyven and Jürgen Roelandts from Asse) surged away Tornado Tom found his afterburners had run out of fuel. It was a similar and familiar story for Peter Sagan. As he attempted to go with the break his tyre punctured and he was left stranded by the side of the road. The barman lifted his chin. 'It must be the Curse of the Rainbow Jersey,' he said, with a dry laugh that suggested he didn't believe in such nonsense except as a topic for jokes.

The breakaway had now arrived at the cobbles of Carrefour de l'Arbre, where the Belgians roared Van Avermaet on. He pummelled his way over the cobbles at such a speed only Boonen's Czech teammate Zdeněk Štybar and Sebastian Langeveld of the Netherlands could stay with him.

It looked like being a three-way sprint finish, but then Jasper Stuyven produced an almost superhuman effort and bridged the gap to the trio just as they were coming into the velodrome. Without pausing he swept by them and into the lead. I'd been a bit sceptical about Stuyven, but watching him now, thinking of the Kortrijk pensioner bouncing up and down in her seat as she watched him, I pointed at the screen and yelled him on. Sadly the chase had burned the youngster out and Van Avermaet roared past him to win from Štybar and Langeveld. It was his first victory in one of the Monuments. He was nearly 32. At the start of the season the head-to-head with Peter Sagan that the Flemish press had talked up had looked like a total mismatch. And so it had proved, but in completely the opposite way to the one I'd imagined. Van Avermaet had hammered the Slovak like he was a carpet tack.

After watching Van Avermaet's victory lap I went out to find Eeklo's monument to another Flemish winner of Paris–Roubaix, Noël Foré. I was sure the memorial was somewhere near the bar, but couldn't see it, so I asked an old man who was coming up the pavement if he knew where it was. Despite the burning heat the old man wore a beige flat cap and a beige blouson zipped to the throat. Grey wool slacks and shoes with Velcro fastenings completed his outfit. His hair was white – the only bit of it that was showing was sharply squared off several inches above his jacket collar. He said he had just been watching the race with a friend and now he was heading to his daughter's for dinner. 'I'm going right past it, I'll show you,' he said.

We walked along chatting about Van Avermaet's win and Sagan's disasters. 'Of course everyone wanted Boonen, but cycling is not a fairy story,' he said. His English was impeccable, with a clipped edge. I asked where he'd learned it. 'The army,' he said. 'I was with NATO, in Mons.'

I asked him if that was back in the days when all the orders in the Belgian forces were still barked out in French. 'Hah,' the man said. It wasn't really a laugh, more the sort of gruff and forceful sigh that was typical of Flanders. When most people sigh it is a sign of regret or wistfulness. The Flemish sigh may contain those things too, but generally it seems more scornful than anything else, as if whatever bad thing has just happened was entirely to be expected and the sigher is indifferent to it. 'Hah,' the old man said again. 'Yes, the sergeant would shout, "*Peloton à droite!*" and then under his breath in Dutch, "And that goes for the Flemish bastards too."'

He said that Noël Foré had been a good rider and a decent bloke. 'You used to see him about the place. Even when he'd won the Ronde in 1963 he didn't take on any airs.'

I asked him if there was a statue or monument to Eeklo's other famous cyclist, De Vlaeminck.

'Hah,' he said again. 'Well, you know De Vlaeminck was a great rider, but . . .' He paused for a moment and thought about his reply. On the other side of the street a very fat man in a leisure suit sauntered past dragging a drinks fridge mounted on a shopping trolley.

The Flemish have a knack for finding a pithy comment in English that as somebody who has struggled to master even the basics of a foreign language I constantly find astounding. Once in a bar in Antwerp the man sitting next to me had been explaining a poem Flemish schoolchildren were made to learn. The poem listed virtues: 'The next one, I don't know what it is in English. It means to be careful with your money.' 'Thrifty?' I suggested. A bearded bloke who was also sitting at the bar held up his hand. 'No,' he said. 'Not thrifty, prudent. Thrifty is the way a Dutchman translates it.' The Dutch had a reputation for tight-fistedness. 'The waiter knew they were a Netherlands family,' the Flemish joked, 'because they ordered one Coca-Cola and four straws.'

The old man showed a similar gift for scathing wit. 'De Vlaeminck,' he said. 'Well, let me tell you – you would not want him to sit down next to you on the bus.'

We were outside the municipal swimming pool now. 'Here it is,' the old man said, gesturing to a metal plaque. 'I think it's quite good. And, you know, it's not too big.'

He said goodbye and continued on up the street to his daughter's house. I imagined him sitting down to a big plate of shrimp vol-au-vent and chips.

As he'd said, the tribute to Foré wasn't very big. Indeed, it was so understated a person might walk past it every day without really noticing. Foré's monument is outside the baths, close to a crazy golf course. It's a nice enough tribute, the two Os in his name rendered as bike wheels. Foré was actually born in Adegem, but he lived most of his life in Eeklo. Photos of him in his verdant Groene Leeuw team jersey show a jug-eared rumple-faced man with a vague resemblance to William H. Macy. In 1963 Foré had won Kuurne–Brussels–Kuurne, the E3 and the Ronde, but it was his performance in a rain- and sleet-swept Paris–Roubaix in 1959 that caught the imagination of the Flemish public. The Hell of the North was at its most fearsome that year – only 75 riders finished the race. Foré was part of a seven-man break that got away close to Amiens. Behind them were scenes of carnage on the wet cobbles as riders crashed, and a large bunch was flattened by a skidding motorcycle. The break contained Rik Van Looy, Fred De Bruyne and Frenchman Roger Rivière, holder of the world hour record, but it was the less celebrated Flemish trio of Foré, Gilbert Desmet from Roeselare and Marcel Janssens of Edegem who rode off the front to crack open a lead of just under a minute over the Emperor and his companions. In the Roubaix velodrome Foré took the sprint by two bike lengths, his teeth flashing white in his mud-blackened face, his left arm flapping in celebration. Despite the conditions it was at that time the third fastest edition of the race ever run, Foré averaging a barely credible 42.76kph.

I sat down beside the statue to make some notes and thought about the old man's comment. Not being too big was a Flemish thing. Briek Schotte had wanted his statue 'no more than lifesize' and not on a pedestal. They liked sporting heroes who retained a sense of proportion, who didn't let success go to their heads. After the 1998 World Cup I was staying in Limburg and more than once people pointed out to me the captain of the Belgian team, Marc Wilmots, driving a tractor on his parents' farm. It was impossible to imagine an England international footballer doing that. Unless, of course, the tractor had been made by Lamborghini and had a Louis Vuitton interior. In Limburg they loved Wilmots because he was an extraordinary footballer, but an ordinary man.

This focus on remaining humble might be one of the reasons Flemish riders have struggled to win the Tour de France in the post-war era. Few non-cycling fans can name the winner of a particular year's Paris–Roubaix or Liège–Bastogne–Liège, but every sports fan knows who's finished first in the Tour. Winning the yellow jersey makes you a star, a celebrity, all over the world. And who but a show-off would want that?

There's another thing too. No matter how well they disguise it, all great sports people have a solid core of arrogance. They win, partly at least, because they feel they deserve it. Arrogance is necessary in the Tour because a winner needs to dominate day after day after day. Some, such as 'Maître' Jacques Anquetil, and to some extent Eddy Merckx, did this by displaying a lofty hauteur that made their rivals feel small and feeble. Others, like Bernard Hinault and Lance Armstrong, bullied them with an implicit threat of violence. All of the great Tour winners have had a degree of loftiness about them, a sense of entitlement. When Anquetil announced he would not be riding in the 1965 Tour de France, journalists asked who he wanted to win in his absence. To everyone's surprise Anquetil answered with the name of his arch-rival, Raymond Poulidor.

'Really, Pou-Pou?'

'Well, of course. After all, I have beaten him so often his victory would only enhance my reputation.'

That is how a Tour winner talks. A tribute to him can never be too big, only not big enough.

In the post-war years Herman Van Springel came agonisingly close to taking the top prize, and Michel Pollentier might have done so had he not been, ahem, 'controversially' expelled, while the only Fleming to actually bring home the yellow jersey seemed to do so more or less against his better judgement.

Lucien Van Impe was that most singular of creatures: the Flemish mountain specialist. He was born in Mere, close to the river Dender in East Flanders, in 1946. True to tradition, three uncles were professional riders. Van Impe's curly dark hair gave him a buccaneering appearance, but he was just five feet six inches tall and had the physique of a flat-race jockey. In many ways he was the anti-*flahute*: tiny, waif-like. In Flemish cycling he was a butterfly among bumblebees. Many great climbers seem to dance on the pedals as lightly as a pond skater across the surface of a stream, but Van Impe attacked them in the Flemish style, hammering away like he was battering the climb into submission.

Despite his diminutive stature Van Impe was a decent time triallist – the hours of pounding along flat Flemish roads had taught him how to race against the clock. And on an undulating course he could be brilliant. In the 1975 Tour de France he beat Eddy Merckx in a time trial by over a minute.

Van Impe started his first Tour de France in 1969, just two days after signing his debut pro contract. He finished 12th. In the next five years on the Tour he'd finish third twice, as well as placing fourth and fifth. The polka dot jersey had been introduced for the 1975 race and Van

Impe was the first man to wear it. He said later that the jersey was so stupid-looking that when he put it on for the first time all the other riders laughed at him.

In *The Great Bike Race*, his masterful book on the 1975 tour, Geoffrey Nicholson was disparaging about Van Impe, saying that, like Flandria's Dutchman Joop Zoetemelk, he ended the race with no suntan because he had spent every day riding in Merckx's immense shadow. In 1976 Merckx, his incredible powers already failing partly as a result of a fan punching him in the kidneys on the ascent of the Puy de Dôme in 1975, was injured and could not start. That was a psychological boost for everybody, not least the spectators who had got a little weary of watching the Cannibal stuffing his face. Van Impe had just come under the control of one of cycling's greatest coaches, Cyrille Guimard. The Frenchman drove Van Impe hard, at one point even threatening to run him off the road in a team car if he didn't put in more effort. Van Impe responded by setting such a blistering pace to the finish that the time limit (ten per cent slower than the winner's) would have eliminated nearly half the field and had to be relaxed.

As a consequence of his mad dash Van Impe had effectively won the Tour by the end of the second week.

Van Impe was easy-going and relaxed. He annoyed other riders by whistling cheerily as he rode. If he seemed immune to pressure, that was probably because he didn't really care too much about winning. Van Impe never saw himself as a top rider, just as a top climber. No matter how many races he won he never felt like a winner, not in his heart.

Perhaps the thing that really sums Van Impe up is this: he was King of the Mountains six times and he could easily have won a seventh title. He refrained from doing so because that would have meant breaking the record set by his idol and mentor, Federico Bahamontes. The Spaniard, known as the Eagle of Toledo, was a man so at ease in the high peaks it was said he once paused on an Alpine summit during a Tour stage to admire the view and eat an ice cream. Van Impe didn't think himself worthy of taking such a great man's record away.

And that is why people in Flanders like Van Impe so much. He is an everyday bloke who did an amazing thing. Back then, if it seemed astonishing to them, it seemed almost as incredible to him. There is something heartening and endearing about that.

I got up from Noël Foré's monument, patted it and walked back to Eeklo station. Eeklo is the end of the line, and the train back to Ghent was waiting.

But there was a little bit of time before it left and I began my journey home – enough to say something about Wim Vansevenant.

Peter Van Petegem was highly popular in Flanders. A big, swarthy, amiable man with a reputation as a joker, he'd entertain fans during races by taking his hands off the bars, leaning back in the saddle, tilting his face to the sky and pretending to be sunbathing. Van Petegem's right-hand man was his friend Wim Vansevenant. The Diksmuide-born rider helped Van Petegem win the Ronde in 1999 and 2003.

Despite his part in those victories Vansevenant is best known to the cycling world for something else entirely. In 2008 he became the first rider in history to finish last in the Tour de France three times. He managed to take the Lanterne Rouge in consecutive years too. The fame that came with that was an embarrassment to a hardworking and decent pro, but he shrugged it off with a show of good humour.

These days Wim Vansevenant works on a farm not far from the birthplace of Karel Van Wijnendaele. Spring mornings, you can see him on his tractor drilling beets in the thick, dark West Flanders soil. The races and the riders come and go, season follows season, memories of elation and ignominy ebb, but the land remains, steadfastly indifferent in the crackling wind, beneath the low Flemish sky.

ACKNOWLEDGEMENTS

I would like to thank my friend Steve Marshall for introducing me to professional cycling and accompanying me on many fine trips to watch races; Ben Clissitt, Adam Sills and Ian Prior at *The Guardian* for letting me write about them and Lionel Birnie and Richard Moore of the Cycling Podcast for encouraging me to waffle on about Flanders.

The editorial team at Bloomsbury – Charlotte, Ian and Zoë – have done a fantastic job untangling my prose and I am greatly indebted to them and to Jasmine Parker for the maps and Eliza Southwood for the cover illustration – both are far better than I deserve.

Thanks to Francis de Laveleye of Editions Jacques Brel for permission to quote from the great man's lyrics.

I have read too many books about cycling to keep track. The following titles have lodged in my brain: *A Peiper's Tale* by Allan Peiper with Chris Sidwells, *Continental Cycle Racing* by Noel Henderson, *Cycling in the Sixties* by David Saunders, *In Pursuit of Stardom* by Tony Hewson, *Brian Robinson: Pioneer* by Graeme Fife, *World Champions I Have Known* by Rene de Latour, *The Full Cycle* by Vin Denson and *For the Love of the Cobbles* by Chris Fontecchio.

A number of books provided insight into the history of Flanders, notably Jan-Albert Goris' *Strangers Should Not Whisper*, *The Coburgs of Belgium* by Theo Aronson and Hugo Claus's monumental and brilliant novel *The Sorrow of Belgium*. Tim Webb and Joe Stange's *CAMRA Good Beer Guide to Belgium* ensured I was never thirsty, if sometimes dizzy.

Without exception the Flemings I met on my travels were, as ever, friendly, courteous and showed a kindness to an often bedraggled

Englishman that went far beyond good manners. In particular I would like to thank Kristof and Eva who looked after me in Ghent, the staff at the Krook library, the Wielermuseum in Roeselare, the Centrum Ronde van Vlaanderen and especially the Wielermuseum de Gistelse Flandriens. I was also well entertained by the excellent bar and waiting crews at Bidon Coffee & Bicycle, Gruut, Trappistenhuis, Aba-Jour and, of course, the Trollekelder.

And finally, and most of all, I would like to thank Deryn for giving me the best possible reason to come home.

INDEX

Picture credits

Plates 1, 2, 4, 8, 13, 17, 18, 20, 21, 22, 24, 28, 30, 33 © Getty; plates 3, 5, 6, 7, 19, 23, 31, 32 © Offside; plates 9, 10, 12, 14, 15, 16, 25, 29 © Harry Pearson; plate 11 © Deryn Chadderton; plates 26, 27 © Albert Plans Feixas.